For Marvin,
who has taught me
more about many of
these issues than
he may suspect —
With thanks for
your friendship —

Bill
Sept 1989

Prospects for Faculty in the Arts and Sciences

Prospects for Faculty in the Arts and Sciences

A STUDY OF FACTORS AFFECTING DEMAND AND SUPPLY, 1987 TO 2012

William G. Bowen and Julie Ann Sosa

PRINCETON UNIVERSITY PRESS
PRINCETON, NEW JERSEY

Published by Princeton University Press, 41 William Street,
Princeton, New Jersey 08540
In the United Kingdom: Princeton University Press, Oxford

Library of Congress Cataloging-in-Publication Data

Bowen, William G.
Prospects for faculty in the arts and sciences : a study of
factors affecting demand and supply, 1987 to 2012 / William G. Bowen
and Julie Ann Sosa.
p. cm.
Bibliography: p.
ISBN-0-691-04259-4
1. College teachers—United States—Supply and demand. 2. Science
and the arts—Study and teaching (Higher)—United States. I. Sosa,
Julie Ann, 1966- . II. Title.
LB2335.3.B66 1989
331.12'3137812'0973—dc20 89-34930 CIP

This book has been composed in Palatino

Clothbound editions of Princeton University Press books
are printed on acid-free paper, and binding materials are
chosen for strength and durability. Paperbacks, although satisfactory
for personal collections, are not usually suitable for library rebinding.

Printed in the United States of America by Princeton University Press, Princeton,
New Jersey

Contents

List of Illustrations

Tables

Figures

Preface

THE AUTHORS of this book first met when one was a university president and the other was chairman of the student newspaper. Odd as it may seem, we were friends even then, not mortal enemies.

As we concluded our respective terms in office, we decided (in May 1988) to embark on what we believed at that time would be a modest effort to examine the outlook for faculty staffing. The topic was important to the Andrew W. Mellon Foundation because it has had a long-standing interest in graduate education and faculty development. College and university presidents had been urging the Foundation to undertake new initiatives in these areas, and it was evident that there was no adequate base of information on which to build a well-conceived program.

The initial plan was to use the summer of 1988 to conduct a literature review that would bring up-to-date the analysis contained in an earlier study prepared by one of us (William G. Bowen, "Graduate Education in the Arts and Sciences," *Report of the President*, 1981). It quickly became apparent, however, that what was needed was not so much a review of the literature as a large-scale effort to assemble, link, and analyze many sources of data in new ways. Conversations at the National Research Council (NRC) in Washington, D.C. persuaded us that a number of difficulties with the 1981 study (and with other studies) could be overcome by careful specification of the variables involved in developing projections of supply and demand within specific academic fields and particular sectors of higher education.

Thus, we set out to construct an apparatus that could be used to generate projections incorporating various assumptions about factors such as age distributions of faculties, retirement rates, population trends, enrollment patterns, duration of graduate study, degrees conferred, and faculty/student ratios. The issues were intriguing, and we decided to undertake a vastly more complex project than the "modest effort" anticipated originally. By the end of the summer, we appreciated the larger implications of the research and realized that we were, in fact, writing a book.

The logistics of the project became—and remained—highly complicated. An undergraduate working at the Foundation's office in Princeton, Sarah Turner, organized the computerized tabulations that were so essential. Other students, faculty colleagues, friends, and family members assumed duties of many kinds, including providing transportation for people and data between New York, Princeton, and Avalon, New Jersey.

In the fall, one of us (JAS) moved to England to pursue her graduate studies while the other (WGB) was responsible for the administration of the Foundation. Still, data collection, analysis, and writing proceeded apace—notwithstanding the perils of trans-Atlantic communication between New York and Oxford (now regarded for the first time by us as a developing country with characteristics all its own). To be fair, we imposed what may well have been inordinate demands on all concerned. We did this because of our conviction that the study needed to be finished and published so that it might contribute in a timely way to discussion of issues important to higher education.

In December, we were both back in New York when a serious problem arose. By this time much of the manuscript had been drafted, but we were still unable to explain satisfactorily results pertaining to fields of study grouped under the rubric "other humanities." Various cross-checks led us to question the underlying data, and we then discovered that a programming mistake had contaminated the data—with horrendous consequences. While the resulting errors proved to be small, they had worked their way into many of our most important calculations and a large portion of the text.

Thanks to the efforts of people at the NRC, the dedication of another undergraduate at Princeton, Mark Slavonia, and the indulgence of our families at Christmas, the relevant tabulations and calculations were redone and redrafting proceeded. When we stopped grumbling, we were able to see that the results were now clearer, more consistent, and stronger than before. We learned an obvious lesson: to be sure to ask if results (especially peculiar ones) really make sense when examined from all perspectives. This experience reminded us of a Maine story illustrating the need to have "the full facts before negotiating an opinion." The classic example is given by John Gould in *The Fastest Hound Dog in the State of Maine:*

> " 'Is that a white horse?'
>
> 'Seems to be from this side.' "

From that (low) point on, the project stayed on course, thanks to the cooperation of several organizations and the efforts of a great many people, whose help we would like to acknowledge.

The Andrew W. Mellon Foundation provided the resources that have permitted this project to be carried out. In addition—and more important—our colleagues in the New York and Princeton offices have been ever-present sources of encouragement. They have provided advice and assistance; beyond that, they have understood and respected the demands that the study has made on our time. We are very grateful.

As always, Neil Rudenstine, executive vice president of the Foundation, has been a particularly valuable source of advice from the inception of the project; he read several drafts of the manuscript and alerted us to issues and implications that otherwise would have gone unnoticed. Carolyn Makinson, whose field is demography, accepted responsibility for defining the conceptual basis of our work with age distributions and exit probabilities; in addition, she played a pivotal role in creating the spreadsheet models that integrated the elements of the projections of demand. Among other staff members, special mention should be made of Margaret McKenna, Jan Maier, Kamla Motihar, Kellum Smith, James Morris, and Kate Ryan.

Sarah Turner not only worked directly with important data sets during the summer of 1988, but also continued to assist during the school year while simultaneously writing an ambitious senior thesis. Laura Lazarus entered the project at a later stage, and provided indispensable research assistance—working cheerfully amidst the chaos of our reference materials in New York. These two friends of ours worked extraordinary hours and were vital to the completion of the book.

The NRC provided both the raw data and special tabulations that constitute much of the foundation of the study. Alan Fechter saw the importance of what we were trying to do, and he and his colleagues Mary Belisle, Susan Coyle, Prudence Brown, and Delores Thurgood assured that the necessary data were compiled under tight time constraints. The Association of American Universities (principally through the efforts of John Vaughn) collected data on federal support of graduate education.

Albert Rees and Sharon Smith, who are directing the Project on Faculty Retirement, provided preliminary results from their own study and also commented on other aspects of our research. Derek Bok, president of Harvard University, took time from a busy schedule to read the manuscript and offer helpful advice. Robert Durkee, vice president for public affairs at Princeton University, made important contributions to the discussion of questions of policy in Chapter Nine. Allen Sanderson, associate provost at the University of Chicago, offered useful comments on parts of the study in its early stages.

The Campaign for Oxford provided logistical assistance that was vital to communicating across the Atlantic. Lindsay Hossack was especially kind and helpful. The NCR corporation also facilitated our work at several remote locations, and we want to thank George Kappel for his extra efforts on our behalf. A less likely contributor to the project, Island Mortgages of Avalon, N.J., rendered assistance in an only slightly less remote location.

The figures in the book were prepared by Diane Van Houten, and readers will see why we are so pleased with her work. The Princeton University Press adopted a very compressed schedule for publication so that the book could be available in September 1989. We are especially grateful to Sherry Wert, who skillfully copyedited the manuscript under great time pressures.

Mrs. Bowen, David, and Karen joined two members of the "extended family," Kevin Guthrie and Seth Shepetin, in making calculations and providing other forms of assistance whenever needed. More generally, we wish to say a deeply felt word of thanks to Dr. and Mrs. Sosa, as well as to the Bowen family, for accepting so stoically our absences at holidays and (it must have seemed) all other times. We hope they know how much we appreciate their unflagging affection and support.

While we have benefited from help provided graciously by many people, responsibility for errors that remain is ours alone. The alphabetical listing of our names is but the smallest sign of what has been a warm and mutually rewarding partnership.

WGB and JAS
New York, New York
April 1989

Prospects for Faculty in the Arts and Sciences

CHAPTER ONE

Introduction

AMERICAN HIGHER EDUCATION has experienced periods of rapid expansion and retrenchment since World War II, with swings that have been sharp and at times destabilizing. The war itself had major consequences: returning G.I.'s swelled enrollments, and there was a new appreciation of the power of scientific research. After a brief hiatus in the early 1950s, the launching of Sputnik in 1957 stimulated another strong wave of interest in higher education. Then, in the 1960s, the baby boom combined with rising enrollment rates to create one of the greatest expansions ever seen. Shortages of faculty were widely proclaimed, faculty salaries increased markedly, and there was talk of a "golden age" for academics. Both students and graduate schools responded enthusiastically to the heightened demand for faculty, and the number of doctorates awarded increased more than threefold between 1958 and 1970.

An unintended result was the creation of a substantial excess supply of potential faculty members in the 1970s, when higher education entered what came to be called a "new depression." The number of doctorates awarded subsequently declined almost as rapidly as it had risen, creating a roller-coaster pattern in many fields of graduate study. In recent years, improved economic conditions have permitted at least a modest recovery in the financial circumstances of faculty members, but there has not yet been any significant change in the number of new doctorates awarded annually.

We are now in an unsettled period for higher education, and even short-term prospects for faculty members are far from clear. The current climate of thinking is illustrated by a recent article entitled "Uncertainty is Rampant as Colleges Begin to Brace for Faculty Shortage[s]. . . ."[1] The title is apt, both in indicating a growing concern about faculty staffing problems and in acknowledging the extent to which people are unclear about what lies ahead and what steps should be taken to ward off possible dangers. At the same time, it is widely agreed that the future shape of higher education will be affected profoundly by decisions that are made—and not made—over the next few years.

When the presidents of a number of colleges and universities were

[1] Mooney 1989, A-14ff.

asked by the Andrew W. Mellon Foundation in the spring of 1988 to identify pressing problems facing higher education, they were nearly unanimous in expressing deeply felt worries about their ability to recruit outstanding faculty in future years. Yet these presidents were also quick to acknowledge that most of their expressions of concern were based on either knowledge of local conditions or anecdotal information.

At present there simply is no body of evidence and analysis that would allow a comprehensive assessment of the outlook for faculty staffing. That reality—the need for a framework shaped by reasonably "hard" data—has been a primary motivation for our research.[2]

The purpose of this study, then, is to develop a systematic analysis of the factors affecting prospects for faculty in the arts and sciences over the next twenty-five years. We hope to provide both a clearer sense of whether the "boom" and "bust" pattern of faculty staffing is likely to repeat itself and an improved understanding of how to avoid such disruptive and inefficient cycles.

We are well aware that this particular study is a highly quantitative analysis of issues with personal, political, and social dimensions that reach far beyond projections of numbers of students and faculty members. At stake is the quality of teaching and research, by which we mean the ability of faculty members to encourage active engagement with the kinds of learning and scholarship that enable colleges and universities to be the source of new ideas as well as effective communicators of what is already known. Also at stake is the ability of higher education to continue to be an avenue of opportunity for individuals from diverse backgrounds.

The continuing capacity of our colleges and universities to serve such large purposes depends on the willingness of society at large, and especially institutions of higher education, to address some very direct questions. What incentives should be provided to encourage

[2] There is, however, a considerable body of literature on which to build. A pioneering study of the labor market for individuals with advanced training in the sciences was made by Richard B. Freeman (1971), who also did much important work thereafter. Perhaps the most seminal study of the outlook for academics was Allan Cartter's 1976 analysis, which predicted a growing excess supply of Ph.D.'s. Cartter's book was part of a series of research projects in the late 1970s prepared for the Carnegie Commission on Higher Education that culminated in a number of widely read publications that continue to be relevant (including *Three Thousand Futures* [1980]; Radner and Miller 1975; and Gordon 1974). In 1986, Howard R. Bowen and Jack H. Schuster published a comprehensive review of the status and outlook for academics. Even more recently, David W. Breneman and Ted I.K. Youn (1988) have compiled a book of essays that contains an excellent bibliography as well as two summary articles by the editors.

aspiring academics? What should universities do to strengthen their graduate programs? What is the right role for the federal government in this area, given the widespread agreement that a highly educated populace constitutes one of this country's major sources of comparative advantage?

There is, we believe, a broadly based willingness to think hard about such questions. The acrimonious nature of much of the recent debate over educational philosophy and curricula (the role of the "great books," for instance), and over levels of tuition and the cost of higher education, has masked the degree to which people on all sides of these issues are committed to the educational enterprise itself. A widely shared dedication to higher education is special to this country, even if it sometimes appears to be taken for granted.

General Approach

While this study adopts the usual convention of analyzing factors that affect the demand for and the supply of faculty, it differs from its predecessors in significant respects. One distinguishing characteristic is that we have made determined efforts to look separately at major fields of study and at principal sectors of higher education. Prospects for the sciences, for example, may differ from prospects for the humanities. Liberal arts colleges may need to see their future in terms other than those which are most relevant to the large universities.

This approach can be thought of as "disaggregation," but it is better understood as "aggregation" in that we build results for the arts and sciences as a whole from data for particular fields and sectors of higher education. This emphasis has made our research more complicated than it would have been otherwise, but we think that the resulting increase in the precision of the results, and the attendant ability to compare changes across fields of study and sectors of higher education, justify the effort.[3]

In designing our research, we sought to construct a "machine" that could be used to generate a variety of projections of supply and de-

[3] Bowen and Schuster (1986, p. 195) recognized that projections based on subclassifications such as academic discipline and type of institution would have been valuable, but they doubted their feasibility. Our ability to work at this level of detail is due in large part to the cooperation of various providers of data, especially staff members at the National Research Council. Appendix A contains a discussion of the principal sources of data used in this study and definitions of the academic fields and sectors of higher education referred to below.

mand. This involved identifying clearly both the relevant "parts" and the ways in which they interact. We have tried equally hard to be sure that each part is congruent with all the others (covering the same universe of faculty members, fields, institutions, time periods, and so on). This permits ready substitution of alternative assumptions and makes it possible to test the sensitivity of results to such substitutions. As a consequence, we are able to learn that some components of the machine, such as student/faculty ratios, are powerful in determining outcomes. Other factors, such as retirement patterns, can be seen to be relatively unimportant quantitatively, even though they may be very important for other reasons.

While we make use of supply and demand terminology, we wish to emphasize that this is in no sense an econometric analysis. Throughout most of the pages that follow, we use the terms "demand" and "supply" in the crude sense of the expected number of positions to be filled and the expected number of candidates for vacant positions—assuming specified salaries, terms of employment, and other labor market conditions. In short, we are concerned primarily with *shifts* in demand and supply functions over time, not with the shapes of demand and supply curves seen as functions of salaries and other conditions of employment at points in time. Although we discuss adjustment mechanisms, including both demand-side and supply-side responses to changing labor market conditions, "price" variables as such do not play a major role in our effort to project longer-term trends.

We also wish to emphasize that the projections of labor market conditions presented in this book are designed primarily to quantify the consequences of adopting various assumptions about the future. Properly understood, they can serve several worthwhile ends. They provide an "early warning system" that may allow us to anticipate emerging problems in time to take some sensible corrective actions. In addition, they can help inform both the career choices of individuals and discussions of policy within academic institutions and governmental bodies. In short, they can assist in testing out the implications of various courses of action. But such projections should never be thought of as predictions of what will actually happen or as instructions as to what should happen.

One of the most perceptive commentaries on the value of the kinds of projections we have tried to develop was written in the mid-1970s by Allan Cartter in a little-known article that preceded his major study. In reflecting on some of his earlier efforts to study the supply and demand relationships for teachers, Cartter observed (1974, pp. 282–83):

One should draw a careful distinction between projections and predictions; the former may illustrate the consequences of current trends and thus serve to alter the course of events. In a meaningful sense, successful projections may be those that turn out to be poor predictions of actual events. My projections of 1964 and 1965 that the academic labor market would reverse itself in 1969 and 1970 and become a surplus labor market could be called unsuccessful in the sense that few persons took them seriously, thus permitting them to become accurate predictions.

Any set of projections that uses fixed coefficients is suspect because the coefficients themselves are likely to change in response to variations in labor market conditions.[4] Ideally, we would use a more sophisticated mode of analysis that included well-specified behavioral relationships and that took account of feedback mechanisms and the recursive nature of some of the implicit labor market equations. Perhaps subsequent studies will incorporate improved techniques of this kind. In the interim, we have tried to indicate the general nature and significance of such relationships and interactions, especially when we integrate different kinds of assumptions (about enrollment patterns and student/faculty ratios, for example) and when we discuss adjustment mechanisms.

We agree with Cartter that there is a place for studies that rely on projections as well as for studies that are more behavioral in their approach. In at least a limited sense, this study represents an effort to take some advantage of both ways of thinking. We have made heavy use of the kinds of simplifying assumptions that facilitate longer-term projections; and we have also sought (especially in the last part of the book) to recognize the ways in which the responses of individuals and institutions, and the workings of markets, will affect what actually transpires. In adopting this dual approach, we are aware that, as Isaiah Berlin once wrote (1978) in an entirely different context, "the middle ground is a notoriously exposed, dangerous, and ungrateful position."

In pursuing this general approach, we have chosen, first, to define "faculty" quite carefully. We limited our universe to those in the professorial ranks plus instructors and lecturers (excluding "adjunct faculty"). We also elected to focus on full-time faculty. Failure to

[4] This is a principal reason why traditional efforts to make manpower projections and to engage in manpower planning have an undistinguished history—and are generally as out of fashion as is the word "manpower" itself. Individuals, institutions, and labor markets are too adaptable to permit mechanistic extrapolations of past relationships to define the future with any precision. For a good discussion of the hazards of common forecasting techniques, and an evaluation of a number of earlier efforts, see Freeman and Breneman 1974.

distinguish full-time faculty from part-time faculty would have made it more difficult to come to clear conclusions—pertaining, for instance, to changes in age distribution—that otherwise might be masked by the shifting weights of full-time versus part-time faculty. Our universe of faculty also has been limited to those holding doctorates. This decision, driven in part by the nature of one of our primary sources of data (the biennial Survey of Doctoral Recipients), is consistent with our general desire to look closely at the core group of full-time faculty.

In addition, our study focuses almost entirely on faculty members in the arts and sciences. The decision to exclude faculty members in engineering, agricultural sciences, medical sciences, education and other professional fields in no way reflects on the importance of these subjects. Their circumstances are often quite different from the circumstances confronting the arts and sciences, and simply combining all schools and disciplines seemed to us to entail the serious risk of confusing the analysis. Also, the centrality of the arts and sciences to all of higher education justifies, we believe, some concentration of attention on these disciplines.

Within the arts and sciences, we have paid separate attention to eight broad fields: (1) mathematics; (2) physics and astronomy; (3) chemistry; (4) earth, environmental, and marine sciences (hereafter referred to as "earth sciences"); (5) biological sciences; (6) psychology; (7) social sciences; and (8) humanities. In addition, some of the subsequent analysis includes a breakdown of the humanities into four components: (a) history; (b) English and American languages and literatures; (c) foreign languages and literatures; and (d) other humanities. We have also found it useful in parts of the analysis to work with three "clusters" of fields: (1) mathematics and physical sciences; (2) biological sciences and psychology; and (3) humanities and social sciences.

We have also devoted a great deal of attention to distinguishing among sectors of higher education. Specifically, we have used the institutional classification system of the Carnegie Foundation for the Advancement of Teaching, but we have elected to combine some of the categories and to concentrate on five principal sectors, which we have defined as follows: (1) Research I; (2) Other Research and Doctorate; (3) Comprehensive I; (4) Liberal Arts I; and (5) Other Four-Year. (See Appendix A for a full discussion of the ways in which we have combined types of institutions.) In general, it was not possible to provide separate breakdowns for public and private institutions. However, we do comment briefly (especially in Chapters Six and Eight) on some of the major differences associated with the public/private classification.

Over at least the last two decades, there has been strong concern about the composition of faculties classified by gender and race. Extremely important questions of educational and social policy grow directly from studies of the participation of women and of minority groups in higher education. However, these questions—important as they are—are not the subject of this study. To have included cross-tabulations by gender and by race would have produced an overwhelming mass of statistics concerning subjects that deserve separate and intensive analysis.

The period covered by this study extends from the present through 2012. We recognize that a twenty-five-year time-span is very long, and we certainly do not believe that anyone can foresee many of the most important changes that are sure to occur between now and 2012. But some of the major demographic factors affecting higher education do cast long shadows, and it seems desirable to look as far ahead as possible. It is also the case that many of the policy questions that must be considered require a long time horizon, since changes can often be introduced only slowly, and long response lags need to be taken into account. This is true, for example, of changes in the distribution of faculty by field and in the number of recipients of doctorates.

We are all too aware that we have had to make what can generously be called "bold" assumptions at various points in the analysis. In a number of instances other assumptions might well have been made, and we therefore have tried throughout to explain quite precisely what has been assumed, to provide derivations of important factors used in adjusting data and making projections, and to indicate how sensitive our results are to the particular assumptions chosen. In these ways, we have tried to avoid claiming too much, and we have also tried to make it possible for others to substitute their own assumptions for ours. At times this approach may make for somewhat heavy going, but it has seemed the only responsible way to proceed.

Another of our objectives has been to identify and highlight opportunities for further research. Some of the trends we describe are parts of larger changes in society that are worthy of more comment than is appropriate here. The broad framework that we have sought to provide may also stimulate case studies and other efforts to probe particular patterns of institutional behavior that we did not investigate.

Organization

There is considerably more to be said about the demand side of the labor market equation than about the supply side, and that is where we begin our analysis. It has become customary to divide the demand for faculty members into a *replacement* component and an *enrollment-driven* component. This is, however, a somewhat arbitrary distinction. Decisions made by institutions concerning the creation or elimination of faculty positions are often affected by the interplay of anticipated retirements (or departures for other reasons) and increases or decreases in enrollments.

While the number of faculty positions assigned to an academic department depends on enrollment, other factors are involved as well: the perceived "critical mass" required if a department is to function effectively; the faculty time to be devoted to research and to other functions, such as governance and outreach activities; opportunistic considerations (the sudden availability of an outstanding candidate for appointment); and the financial resources that are available. All of these considerations are reflected in the student/faculty ratio.

Recognition of the complexity of the process of estimating the number of future faculty positions cannot immobilize us, however. The task, as in any research of this kind, is to make simplifying assumptions and, at the same time, to remain aware of what considerations have been set aside. The well-known aphorism attributed to Einstein is relevant: "Everything should be made as simple as possible, but not more so." That kind of balance, hard as it is to achieve, has been our goal.

We begin, in Chapter Two, with an examination of the replacement demand for present faculty. The starting point of this part of the analysis is some revealing data on the age distributions of faculty members, classified by field of study and sector of higher education, made available to us for both 1977 and 1987 in the form of special tabulations. After we analyze some of the dramatic changes in age distribution that have occurred over the last decade, we begin to develop estimates of replacement demand by five-year intervals from 1987 through 2012. This involves careful specification of "exit" probabilities: the likelihood that a faculty member will leave the academic profession altogether (not simply move from one institution to another). Exits occur for three reasons: (1) decisions to work in different settings, which we call "quits"; (2) retirements; or (3) deaths.

Chapter Three is the first of a group of three chapters concerned with other factors affecting demand. The focus in this chapter is on developing projections of aggregate enrollment. These projections, which are so critical to the rest of the analysis, are based on "macro" assumptions about trends in population by age group and age-weighted enrollment rates. We also take account of differences between full-time and part-time enrollment and discuss the implications of the changing ethnic/racial mix of the population.

Then, in Chapter Four, considerable attention is devoted to the extraordinary movement of students in recent years from study of the arts and sciences to pursuit of professional and job-related degrees. We also show, for example, the extent to which the Liberal Arts I institutions have resisted this trend, as compared with other sectors. Needless to say, future patterns of enrollment will have a great deal to do with the outlook for academic employment, and this chapter includes projections of enrollment based on alternative assumptions about the degree of student interest in the arts and sciences.

Student/faculty ratios are introduced in Chapter Five. This proved to be one of the most important parts of the study, since changes in student/faculty ratios capture the extent to which trends in enrollment are translated into faculty positions. These ratios have a powerful effect on the economics of academic institutions as well as on staffing patterns. Separate projections are made for different fields of study and different sectors. Also, alternative models are presented in order to direct attention to the significance of key assumptions about trends in the arts-and-sciences share of enrollments and changing student/faculty ratios.

In Chapter Six, we consider the factors affecting the supply of holders of doctorates in the arts and sciences. Extensive use is made of the Survey of Earned Doctorates. This includes very interesting information on the percentage of doctorate recipients, by field, who are citizens of other countries, and allows us to study in some detail trends over the last thirty years in the numbers of doctorates earned in various fields by United States residents and by non-residents. In this chapter we also take into account differences among fields—and over time—in the non-academic employment of new doctorates. Finally, we consider the available evidence concerning trends in the quality of graduate students.

We bring together the demand and supply aspects of the analysis in Chapter Seven. This permits a detailed examination of the possibility that there will be "shortages" of prospective faculty members in various fields at different times. Once again, we take special care to highlight alternative sets of assumptions in an effort to bound the field of realistic projections.

In Chapter Eight, we discuss the adjustment process. We comment on the role of salaries in equilibrating academic labor markets and then consider the effects of labor market conditions on demand-side adjustments (including student/faculty ratios and the quality of faculty appointments) and on supply-side adjustments (quit rates, retirement rates, the flow of new students into Ph.D. programs, and the duration of graduate study).

The study concludes, in Chapter Nine, with a brief discussion of the implications of our analysis for public policy, as well as for initiatives that might be taken by academic institutions.

Principal Themes

In thinking about education, many of us are autobiographical. We tend to make judgments about the future on the basis of our own experiences and the experiences of friends, which makes it difficult to anticipate changes in circumstances. This is a particularly serious problem in planning for higher education because of the exceptionally long lead time involved in moving from recognition of a problem to effective action.

Our analysis leads us to believe that the next decades will be different in important respects from both the postwar period of expansion and the more recent period of sluggish labor markets for academics in most fields. No new baby boom is anticipated; nor do we expect significant increases in enrollment rates. The rapid expansion of the 1960s, which had such profound effects on American higher education, will not be replicated.

Population changes will produce some increases (as well as some decreases) in enrollments. However, any significant increases in enrollment *rates* would seem to us to require major changes in public policy and in the quality of elementary and secondary education. Such changes could be stimulated by the growing complexity of the economy and an attendant increase in the demand for better-educated employees, but it is far from certain that this will occur.

The fluctuations in enrollment that can be projected will, nonetheless, have important effects. Enrollment-driven changes in the number of new positions will have greater influence on period-to-period *variations* in demand for faculty than will other factors—such as the number of retirements.

Contrary to what is often said, the replacement component of demand will not, we believe, fluctuate appreciably over the next twenty-five years. We foresee no cataclysmic bunching of exits from academia; instead, our analysis suggests a relatively smooth (but steady) pattern of departures. Replacement demand will, however, be the dominant determinant of the *level* of demand for faculty. Overall, we estimate that perhaps 90 percent of all openings will be attributable to vacancies. In this respect, the years ahead will be dramatically different from the 1960s.

Our enrollment projections depend heavily on assumptions about student interests, and another theme of this study is the importance of the flight from the arts and sciences that has been so pronounced in recent years. We were surprised—and concerned—to learn that between 1971 and 1985 the arts-and-sciences share of degrees conferred fell from 40 percent to 25 percent. In 1985, less than 5 percent of all degrees were awarded in the humanities. This level is *so* low that any further decline is unlikely; indeed, some evidence suggests that there is already a very modest recovery of interest in the humanities underway.

The increasing concentration of arts-and-sciences enrollments in certain sectors of higher education is a related concern. The research universities and the selective liberal arts institutions have become responsible for larger and larger fractions of the teaching in these fields, and especially in the humanities and social sciences. At the same time, the general trend toward pre-professional and job-related courses of study has been especially pronounced in other sectors. The resulting bifurcation of functions within higher education has implications that reach beyond faculty staffing.

The fall-off in student interest in the arts and sciences between 1977 and 1987 was not matched by a comparable decrease in faculty positions. As a result, student/faculty ratios actually declined, and this development buffered what otherwise would have been a precipitous drop in the number of faculty members teaching in the arts and sciences. In projecting the number of faculty positions, we have assumed that these key ratios are likely either to remain constant or to decline much more modestly. We have also made projections that allow for the possibility that student/faculty ratios could rise if there were to be a significant recovery in arts-and-sciences enrollments.

Labor market conditions in the 1970s made it difficult for young people in many areas of the arts and sciences to find suitable academic employment, and the drop in the number of new Ph.D.'s was more pronounced than people such as Cartter had assumed. At the same time, a larger number of the Ph.D.'s that were awarded went to nonresidents, and a larger fraction of all recipients of Ph.D.'s chose to pursue non-academic careers. The consequent decline in the pool of candidates for academic appointment—especially when we take account of qualitative considerations—is another source of considerable concern.

When we combine projections of supply with projections of demand, we find no compelling reason to expect major changes in academic labor markets within the next few years. But we do project some significant increase in demand relative to supply as early as

1992–97—and then far more dramatic changes beginning in 1997–2002. All of our models project demand to exceed supply by *substantial* amounts from that point on. A surprising conclusion is that the projected imbalances are particularly severe for the humanities and social sciences. For at least a decade, beginning in 1997, three of our four models imply that there will be only seven candidates for every ten positions in these fields.

As always, adjustments of various kinds will take place, correcting some of the potential imbalances. In general, however, we do not believe that adjustments on the demand side of the equation will be very large. The supply of new doctorates is likely to be much more responsive to improved labor market conditions. We expect supply-side adjustments to take two principal forms: larger numbers of candidates for doctorates in the arts and sciences and (we hope) some shortening of the average time spent obtaining a degree.

Another potential supply-side adjustment, retirement, is the subject of a great deal of discussion these days; we have concluded, however, that even extreme changes in retirement patterns would have little effect on projected supply/demand ratios. Retirement decisions are, of course, very important to individuals and institutions, but primarily for other reasons.

Policy decisions are potentially at least as important as any of the market-driven forms of adjustment. Universities can strengthen their graduate programs while simultaneously reducing the time that it takes a student to earn a doctorate. A particularly strong case can be made for beginning now to establish the incentives that will attract a larger number of excellent candidates to graduate study and then to academic careers. Although both private and public support is needed, we believe that the federal government must take a leadership role in providing the amounts and forms of student aid that will be required.

CHAPTER TWO

Age Distributions and Exits from Academia

DURING MOST of the postwar period, rising enrollments were the primary force creating openings for new faculty members. Today, however, higher education is not expanding at a rapid rate; nor, as we will show in the next few chapters, is there reason to expect a sudden upsurge in enrollments any time soon. Replacement demand—vacancies created by individuals leaving the profession—will be the dominant determinant of the number of job openings in academia for the foreseeable future.

A number of warnings have been heard recently concerning a possible "bunching" of retirements. For instance, President Michael Sovern of Columbia University has observed that "at Columbia, nearly half of the tenured professors in the arts and sciences will retire in the 1990s. Colleges and universities all over the country are facing a massive wave of retirements" (1989, p. 24). While our findings do not support this generalization, we agree that the underlying question is important. Prospective graduate students, as well as faculty and administrators responsible for staffing departments and overseeing Ph.D. programs, need to have a realistic sense of both the likely number of "exits" from academia and when they are expected to occur.

The time-path of exits, and therefore of replacement demand, also affects future age distributions of faculties. Several case studies have concluded that many universities will have an increasingly large proportion of older faculty members before the turn of the century, especially if mandatory retirement is prohibited.[1] Age distributions have direct consequences for teaching, as well as for scholarship and for the academic leadership of departments and programs. The access that students have to faculty of various ages and perspectives undoubtedly influences their classroom experiences. More generally, the vitality of departments often depends on maintaining an age structure that permits an orderly infusion of new people and a reasonably stable sense of departmental direction.

[1] See, for example, Lozier and Dooris 1987; and COFHE 1987. (Lozier and Dooris are now conducting a new survey under the auspices of Teachers Insurance Annuity Association-College Retirement Equities Fund [TIAA-CREF].) See also Rosse 1987.

Age Distributions of Faculties

None of these questions can be addressed without knowing the current age distributions of faculties, preferably classified by both field of study and sector of higher education. Historically, there has been a dearth of such information.[2]

There is available, however, a rich source of raw data that can be used to construct detailed age profiles: the Survey of Doctorate Recipients (SDR). Conducted biennially by the National Research Council, the SDR is a longitudinal survey that reports demographic and employment characteristics of Ph.D.'s who have received their doctorates in the United States during the last forty-two years (with particularly good data from 1977 on, as explained in Appendix A).

Special tabulations based on the SDR data show that the age distribution of the arts-and-sciences faculty in 1977 was skewed dramatically to the younger age groups (principally 30–34 and 35–39). This was a direct result of the massive hiring in the 1960s that accompanied what was surely one of the most extraordinary expansions of higher education in the nation's history. (See Fig. 3.6, in the next chapter, for a graphic depiction of the sharp increases in enrollment during these years.) The faculty has aged significantly since then, and Figure 2.1 allows a direct comparison of the age profiles in 1977 and 1987.

The most pronounced shifts since 1977 have occurred at the two ends of the age distribution. To cite only two comparisons: the percentage of all arts-and-sciences faculty under age 40 in the five sectors fell precipitously, from 42 to 22 percent, while the percentage over 49 went up by more than one-third, from 27 to 39 percent. This basic demographic message is striking in its clarity.

Differences among Sectors

The age distributions are reasonably consistent across the five major sectors of higher education (see Table 2.1 for the 1987 distributions). There are, however, some significant variations that will have major consequences for future staffing in particular sectors.

[2] Bowen and Schuster appear to have made no use of any explicit age distribution in projecting demand for faculty; rather, they used an omnibus assumption about average annual attrition of faculty of all ages for all reasons (see Bowen and Schuster 1986, ch. 10 and app. C and D). Carol P. Herring and Allen R. Sanderson, in their Technical Appendix to William G. Bowen's 1981 *Report of the President* (p. 9), used estimates contained in a 1978 American Council on Education study that provided a single aggregate age distribution for all of academia.

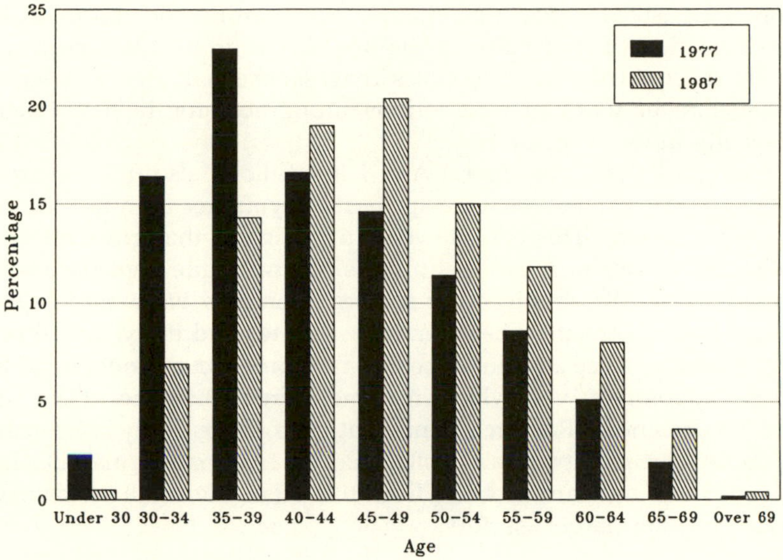

FIGURE 2.1
Faculty Age Distribution, 1977 and 1987
Source: SDR tabulations for five sectors only.

The faculties at Other Four-Year institutions were measurably older than faculties in the other sectors (with only 17.5 percent of their faculty members under 40 in 1987 and 42.5 percent over 49). Comprehensive I institutions also had less than 18 percent of their faculty members under 40, but their percentage in the over-49 age category was equal to the norm for all five sectors (38.9 percent).

The striking characteristic of the Comprehensive I institutions is the relatively large number of their faculty in the 40–49 age range (43.2 percent versus 39.4 percent for all five sectors). In contrast to the

TABLE 2.1
Faculty Age Distribution, by Sector, 1987

Sector	*Under 40 (%)*	*40–49 (%)*	*Over 49 (%)*
Research I	24.2	36.6	39.3
Other Research/Doctorate	22.4	38.8	38.7
Comprehensive I	17.9	43.2	38.9
Liberal Arts I	29.3	37.2	33.4
Other Four-Year	17.5	40.0	42.5
Five-Sector Total	21.7	39.4	38.9

Sources and Notes: SDR tabulations. Detail may not add to total because of rounding.

Comprehensive I institutions, the Research I group had an unusually small fraction of its faculty in the 40–49 age group (36.6 percent). While these particular differences may seem small, we will see in Chapter Seven that they have serious implications for the recruitment of faculty in these sectors.

Age distributions in Liberal Arts I institutions also differed from the norm. Their faculties were appreciably younger than faculties in the other sectors. This is somewhat surprising in that growth in enrollments at Liberal Arts I institutions has not quite kept pace with growth in enrollments in other sectors. Normally we would expect to find some correlation between growth rates and the youthfulness of the faculty, since additional positions are most commonly filled by young appointees; yet, while enrollments rose 3.6 percent overall, and 7.5 percent for Research I universities, they rose only 2.7 percent in these selective liberal arts colleges. The explanation may be that there is more outward mobility from this relatively small sector than from the other (larger) sectors.

Differences among Fields of Study

Age distributions differ more across fields of study than across sectors. The same broad pattern of age distribution presented above by sector (percentage under 40, percentage 40–49, percentage over 49) is presented by field of study for 1987 in Table 2.2. Then, in Figures 2.2 and 2.3, changes between 1977 and 1987 in the percentages of faculty at the two ends of the age distribution are highlighted.

Mathematics is a particularly noteworthy case because of the large percentage of faculty under the age of 40 in both 1977 and 1987. In 1977, over half of all faculty members with doctorates in mathematics were under 40 years of age. Many of these faculty members then moved through the age groups, and by 1987 the percentage under 40 had fallen to 28.5 percent. Over this same ten-year period, the percentage of mathematics faculty who were over 49 rose from 18 percent (in 1977) to just over 31 percent.

A group of four fields—social sciences, earth sciences, biological sciences, and psychology—had similar age profiles in 1987. All four had above-average fractions of faculty members under 40 years of age in 1987 with correspondingly lower-than-average fractions of faculty members in the over-49 category.

Physics/astronomy and the humanities deserve special mention. In 1987, both had small fractions of their faculty members under 40: 17.6 percent in physics/astronomy and 16.4 percent in the humanities. At the other end of the age distribution, physics/astronomy had by far

TABLE 2.2
Faculty Age Distribution, by Field of Study, 1987

Field of Study	*Under 40 (%)*	*40–49 (%)*	*Over 49 (%)*
Humanities	16.4	39.8	43.8
Social Sciences	25.2	40.3	34.5
Humanities/Social Sciences	20.3	40.0	39.7
Mathematics	28.5	40.2	31.3
Physics/Astronomy	17.6	34.1	48.3
Chemistry	19.3	38.9	41.8
Earth Sciences	26.2	35.5	38.3
Mathematics/Physical Sciences	22.9	37.7	39.4
Biological Sciences	22.6	41.1	36.3
Psychology	25.0	38.0	37.0
Biological Sciences/Psychology	23.6	39.8	36.6
All Arts/Sciences	21.7	39.4	38.9

Sources and Notes: All figures are based on SDR tabulations and are for five sectors only. Detail may not add to total because of rounding.

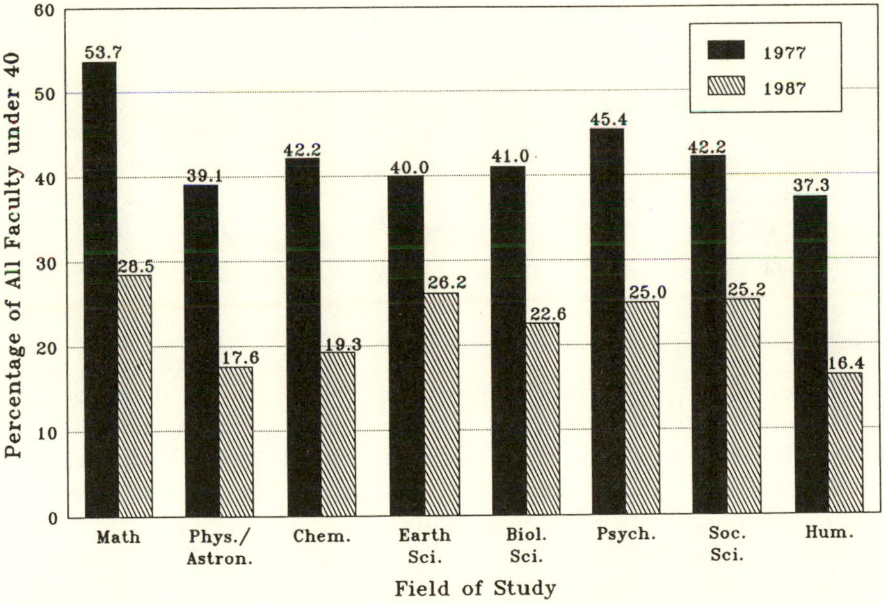

FIGURE 2.2
Faculty Age Distribution, Percentage under 40, by Field of Study, 1977 and 1987
Source: SDR tabulations for five sectors only.

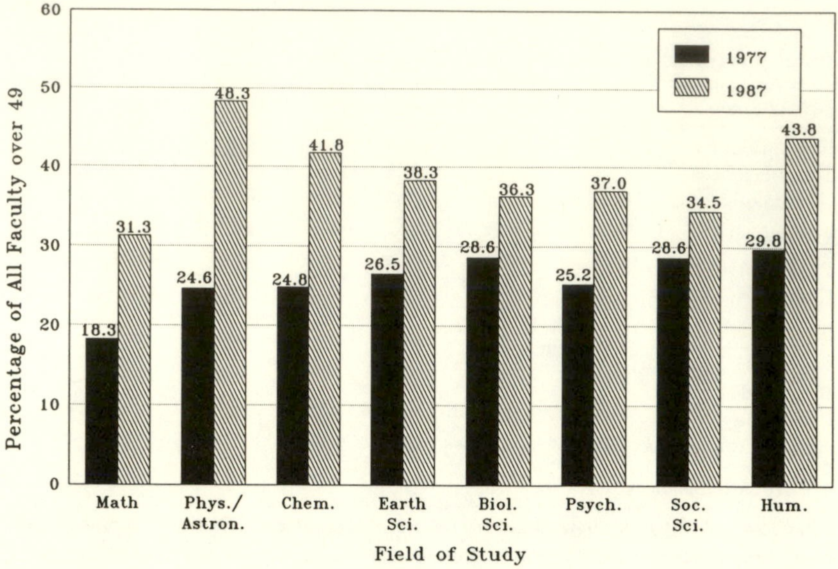

FIGURE 2.3
Faculty Age Distribution, Percentage over 49, by Field of Study, 1977 and 1987

Source: SDR tabulations for five sectors only.

the largest fraction of its faculty in the over-49 age group (48.3 percent). The humanities had 43.8 percent of its faculty in this age range overall, with history (at 49.6 percent) and English and American languages and literatures (at 45.1 percent) having the most extreme age distributions. Planning for retirements is especially needed in these fields.

ESTIMATING EXIT PROBABILITIES

Detailed data on age distributions are a prerequisite of developing credible estimates of vacancies, but they are by no means sufficient. The other key ingredient is a set of what we call "exit probabilities."

In brief, exit probabilities are the odds that the typical faculty member in a particular five-year age group will *not* be present in the next five-year age group five years later. As indicated earlier, faculty members who do not continue, and whose departures create vacancies, may exit from academia by one of three routes: (1) voluntary or involuntary decisions to seek other kinds of employment—"quits," in our terminology; (2) retirement; or (3) death.

Overall exit probabilities for each age group are derived from the joint probabilities of quitting, retiring, and dying. The method used to obtain estimates of these probabilities, and to move age cohorts of faculty through time, proved to be quite complex. It is described in detail in Appendix B. Here we state our principal assumptions so that readers will be aware of the underpinnings of an important part of this study. We want to emphasize that there is no magic formula guaranteed to yield "right" estimates of exit probabilities, and that the results are no better than the assumptions upon which they rest.

The quantitative findings of this part of our analysis are summarized at the end of this section. The reader who is interested primarily in these results, and not in how they were obtained, may turn directly to Figure 2.4 and the associated discussion.

"Quit" Rates

"Quit" rates are particularly difficult to estimate, in part because the rates that are important for our purposes are for higher education as a whole, not for individual institutions. That is, we want to know the probability that a faculty member will leave academia altogether, not the probability that the faculty member will move from one college or university to another. For this reason, attrition rates obtained through case studies of experience at individual institutions are of little value.[3]

The quit rates needed for our purposes represent "net" flows out of academia, reflecting the balance between faculty members leaving higher education and faculty members returning to higher education from other employment sectors. All of the quit rates presented below should be interpreted in this way, not simply as one-way movements ("gross" flows) out of higher education.

Because of the complications and uncertainties, we decided that it would be best to test out alternative quit-rate assumptions so that we could see how sensitive our results were to them. Initially, we employed two sets of assumptions: a high-quit set and a standard-quit set.

[3] There is a further complication. Some individuals who are full-time faculty members move to research positions or to administrative posts, and it is difficult to measure these flows. However, data from the National Science Foundation and the National Research Council permit rough estimates of these shifts for doctorates in various fields. Amongst all doctoral scientists in four-year colleges and universities, the percentage of those whose primary work activity is teaching decreased from 59% in 1975 to 51% in 1985. Of all doctorates in the social sciences employed in four-year institutions, 71% were teaching in 1975; ten years later, 70% were teaching. Even rougher calculations for humanities doctorates also show little change in the comparable percentage of faculty engaged in teaching during this period (roughly 80%).

Under the high-quit assumptions, 1 percent of all tenured faculty members and 10 percent of all non-tenured faculty members are assumed to leave academia each year. It is surely the case that tenured faculty, secure in their positions and having occupied them for some time, are appreciably less likely to quit than non-tenured faculty, many of whom are bound to be disappointed by their tenure reviews, discouraged by the actual job opportunities available to them, worried in many cases about their finances, and less certain in any event about their calling.

We then obtained a "blended" quit rate for each age group by weighting these two sets of quitting probabilities according to the ratios of tenured to non-tenured faculty in each age group. These age-specific quit rates—expressed as a percent per annum—were used to construct a "quitting life table" from which five-year "survival" probabilities were derived for each age group.

The standard-quit assumptions were constructed in an analogous fashion, except that we divided each of the five-year high-quit probabilities by two. This may be thought of as roughly equivalent to assuming that 0.5 percent of tenured faculty and 5.0 percent of non-tenured faculty leave academia each year (remembering that these are *net* flows).

We believe that the standard-quit assumptions are more realistic, and these are the rates that we use in the main part of the analysis that follows. These quit rates also have the advantage of not exaggerating the demand for faculty that will be generated by our overall exit probabilities.

In the spring of 1989, the National Research Council published longitudinal data on humanities doctorates that reinforce strongly our decision to rely primarily on the standard-quit rates. Although the universe covered by these data differs in significant respects from our universe of faculty, we were able to convert the NRC data into rates that could be compared directly with ours. When expressed as an average annual quit rate for faculty of all ages (using the 1987 age distribution), our standard-quit assumptions yield a rate of 1.8 percent. The corresponding net quit rate derived from the NRC's data is amazingly close: 1.85 percent.[4]

[4] See Appendix B for a detailed explanation of how these rates were derived. The range of the high-quit and standard-quit assumptions also seems generally consistent with past estimates made by other authors. Roy Radner and Charlotte V. Kuh (1978, p. 13) examined this question in essentially the same terms used here and argued for an annual quit rate of between 0.5% and 1.0% for tenured faculty and a rate of between 4.0% and 13.0% for non-tenured faculty. The overall exit probabilities developed here

While we rely mainly on the standard-quit rates in this study, we also show the differences in results when the high-quit rates are substituted. In Chapter Eight, we discuss further the sensitivity of our findings to other quit-rate assumptions, including the possibility that tighter labor market conditions will lead to quit rates even lower than the standard-quit rates.

Retirement Rates

Institutional case studies are more useful in estimating retirement rates, and we have relied heavily on an Association of American Universities (AAU) survey of recent experience at 12 public universities, conducted by G. Gregory Lozier and Michael Dooris of Pennsylvania State University. This study has the important advantage of providing a distribution of retirements by age groups. We also referred to a Consortium on Financing Higher Education (COFHE) survey of experience at 36 mostly private colleges and universities, which provides a useful check on the wider applicability of the results obtained by Lozier and Dooris. However, the COFHE study itself does not show distributions of retirements by age groups.[5]

Unfortunately, institutional studies of this kind do not allow us to measure return flows from retirement back to academic appointments. Nor do they distinguish individuals who retire from academia altogether from individuals who retire from one institution only to accept appointment at another institution. Also, all of these institutional studies are based on experience under present federal and state legislation. We have not made any allowance for the likelihood that mandatory retirement will be illegal under federal law in 1994, by virtue of amendments to the Age Discrimination in Employment Act, though we do examine in Chapter Eight the implications of possible reductions in retirement rates.[6]

---

are also close to the estimates used by Bowen and Schuster (1986, pp. 294–95), who in turn cite several other studies.

5 See Lozier and Dooris 1987, Table 3; and COFHE 1987, Table 4, p. 13.

6 We are also following closely the work of others who are studying in detail the likely effects of this possible change in the law. Albert Rees and Sharon Smith, working in the Industrial Relations Section of Princeton University, are concentrating on behavioral aspects of retirement decisions, and their work should illuminate many questions concerning the effects of both legislation and incentives on the timing of retirement decisions and on which faculty are most affected by pension plans and other financial considerations. Professors Alan Gustman at Dartmouth College and Thomas Steinmeier at Texas Tech University are also working on the effects of financial variables on retirement decisions.

Mortality Rates

We used TIAA-CREF data to estimate mortality rates. Starting with separate age-specific survival probabilities for men and women, we arrived at an overall survival probability for each age group by weighting the separate gender-specific probabilities by the relative numbers of men and women in our universe of faculty within each age group. We then constructed another life table, from which we estimated, for each five-year age group, the relevant five-year survival ratio.

Overall Exit Probabilities

Overall exit probabilities for each five-year age group were derived from the joint probabilities of surviving all three hazards (quitting, retiring, and dying) over a five-year period. This is equivalent to regarding the probabilities as mutually exclusive since, from the point of view of exits from academia, an individual who leaves the system for any reason is no longer exposed to the risk of exiting by any other means. Simply summing the separate probabilities would, therefore, have caused us to overestimate the total number of exits. The results of this entire estimating process—using the standard-quit rates—are summarized in Figure 2.4.[7]

The relative importance of quits, retirements, and deaths is seen to change markedly as we move from one age group to another, with quits dominating the exits in the younger age cohorts and death and retirement becoming much more important in the older age cohorts. The pronounced J-shaped curvature of the graph relating exit probabilities to age illustrates the desirability of using age-specific exit probabilities rather than relying on estimates of attrition rates that are independent of age group.

The estimated overall five-year exit probability starts out at 16.9 percent in the under-35 age groups, where the majority of faculty members are non-tenured and, therefore, more likely to quit. The exit probabilities then fall rather steadily until a trough is reached at the 8.0 percent level in the 45–49 age cohort. A steep ascent follows, as mortality and (especially) retirement begin to play significant roles.

[7] Consistent with what has just been said, the quit, retirement, and death components of the overall exit probability shown on Fig. 2.4 have been adjusted to take account of the multiplicative character of the process of arriving at an overall exit probability. This procedure recognizes that each component operates simultaneously with the other two components, rather than requiring, for instance, that quits occur first within any given age interval, retirements next, and deaths last.

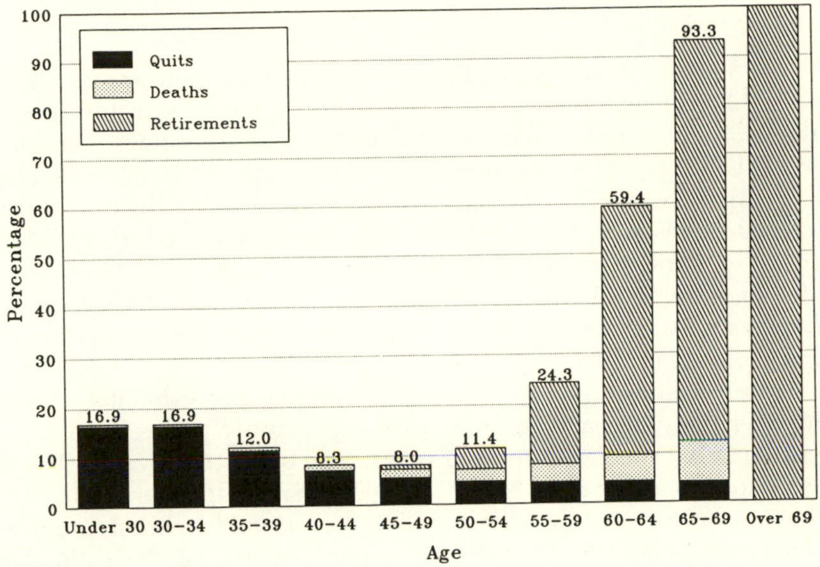

FIGURE 2.4
Five-Year Exit Probabilities (Quits, Retirements, Deaths), by Age Group

Source: See Appendix B.

Note: The standard-quit rates are used here. We also made the simplifying assumption that everyone who reaches age 70 retires within the next five years.

Overall exit probabilities are estimated to be just under 60 percent in the 60–64 age group, 93.3 percent in the 65–69 age group, and (we assume) 100 percent for the over-69 group.

Initial Estimates of Replacement Demand

If we assume provisionally that replacements occur on a one-for-one basis, estimates of the number of present faculty who need to be replaced at the end of each five-year period can be obtained by multiplying age-specific exit probabilities by the number of present faculty members in each age group at the start of the period and then summing across age groups. These calculations yield both an estimate of the total number of present faculty members who will have left the profession by the end of the period under review and a new age profile of continuing faculty members as they enter the next time period. This estimating process is then repeated for each successive five-year period.

Overall Estimates

In the five sectors of higher education on which we concentrate, there were 139,350 faculty members in the arts and sciences at the start of the 1987–92 period. Using the standard-quit assumptions, we estimate that 26,863 of these "starters" will have quit, retired, or died by the end of the first five-year period (see Table 2.3). By the end of the second five-year period (1992–97), we estimate that another 23,876 of these starters will be gone. Estimates for later periods are also shown in Table 2.3, along with the cumulative totals. After twenty-five years, we estimate that 116,984 of the present faculty will have quit, retired, or died.

If we substitute the high-quit assumptions, the estimates of the number that will have gone increase significantly in the initial five-year period (from 26,863 to 36,127), but then begin to converge. These assumptions imply that 124,278 of the original complement of faculty will be gone by 2012. Similar comparisons, period by period, are presented in Table 2.3. As indicated earlier, we regard the estimates generated by the standard-quit assumptions as more realistic. The vacancies projected by using the high-quit assumptions are best interpreted as an upper bound.

An examination of the sensitivity of the projections to alternative quit-rate assumptions should not be allowed to obscure one absolutely central finding: *the flow of present faculty members out of higher education will be remarkably steady over the next twenty to twenty-five years.* In spite of the dramatic changes in age distribution between 1977 and 1987,

TABLE 2.3
Estimated Exits from the Present Faculty, Standard-Quit and High-Quit Assumptions, 1987–2012

	1987–92	*1992–97*	*1997–2002*	*2002–07*	*2007–12*
Standard-Quit Assumptions:					
Exits by Interval	26,863	23,876	23,405	23,065	19,775
Cumulative Exits		50,739	74,144	97,209	116,984
High-Quit Assumptions:					
Exits by Interval	36,127	27,494	23,722	20,878	16,057
Cumulative Exits		63,621	87,343	108,221	124,278

Sources and Notes: Estimates are for all faculty in the arts and sciences in five sectors only. The total base population of faculty is 139,350.

See text and Appendix B for explanations of assumptions and procedures used in making estimates.

Detail will not add to total because of rounding and a small number of "no reports."

and contrary to widespread belief, we have found no evidence to support claims that there will be anything like a cataclysmic bunching of exits.

Expressing these results (using the standard-quit assumptions) in percentage terms, we estimate that 19.3 percent of the present faculty will be gone by the end of the first five-year interval (by 1992), another 17.1 percent by 1997, another 16.8 percent by 2002, yet another 16.6 percent by 2007, and a final 14.2 percent by 2012—leaving 16.1 percent still employed. Nor are the period-to-period variations in estimated exits more pronounced under the assumptions of the high-quit model—with the exception of the results for the first two periods, which are dominated by exits of young non-tenured faculty.

We suspect that one reason the pattern of projected exits shown here is so much steadier than what most people seem to have expected is that we are concerned with exits that result from quits (and deaths) as well as with exits that result from retirements. The age distribution that existed in 1987—while assuredly quite different from the age distribution in 1977—was also in some sense more "normal" (with a smaller fraction of faculty concentrated in the very young age categories), and this may be another part of the explanation for the surprisingly smooth character of the pattern of exits.[8]

Differences by Sector and Field of Study

The pattern of projected exits is generally consistent across sectors. There are, however, two notable variations that could prove to be significant. The Research I universities can expect to lose a relatively high percentage of their present faculty in 1987–92 (21.0 percent) and a relatively small number in 1997–2002 (15.9 percent). The Comprehensive I institutions face very different prospects, with 18.0 percent of present faculty expected to leave in 1987–92 and nearly as many (17.8 percent) expected to leave in 1997–2002. We defer a full discussion of the consequences for faculty recruitment until Chapter Seven,

[8] Since there has been so much discussion of the possible bunching of retirements, we also made separate calculations directed specifically to this question. We find that 11.0% of all faculty present in 1987 should be expected to retire by 1992; 11.4% between 1992 and 1997; 12.7% between 1997 and 2002; 13.8% between 2002 and 2007; and 12.6% between 2007 and 2012. Thus, even when we look at retirements alone, the results reveal a steady pattern over the next twenty-five years. The peak is in the 2002–07 period (not in 1997–2002), and the percentage retiring then is not all that different from the percentages retiring in the other periods.

when replacement demand is combined with estimates of net new positions.

Projected vacancies by field of study are summarized in Table 2.4. While there are obvious differences, one general conclusion is that exits are expected to occur relatively smoothly across time periods in all fields. There is no significant bunching of exits in any field.

Humanities is the largest field in absolute size, and it loses the most faculty in every time period—starting with 7,791 vacancies anticipated during 1987–92. Physics/Astronomy, however, is expected to experience the largest relative loss of faculty during the first five-year period, and this pattern persists. In twenty years, 76 percent of all current faculty members in this field will have left academia. The sharpest contrast is the social sciences, which will have lost 67 percent of its current faculty by 2007.[9]

TABLE 2.4
Estimated Exits from the Present Faculty, by Field of Study and Period, Standard-Quit Assumptions, 1987–2012

Field of Study	*Starting Faculty*	*Estimated Exits*				
		1987–92	*1992–97*	*1997–2002*	*2002–07*	*2007–12*
Humanities	39,895	7,791	7,214	7,237	6,866	5,475
Social Sciences	30,696	6,032	4,932	4,732	5,031	4,546
Hum./Soc. Sci.	70,591	13,823	12,146	11,969	11,897	10,021
Mathematics	11,052	1,902	1,757	1,774	1,854	1,623
Physics/Astronomy	7,819	1,696	1,457	1,456	1,347	912
Chemistry	10,361	2,035	1,879	1,862	1,729	1,376
Earth Sciences	5,144	989	910	833	762	703
Math/Phys. Sci.	34,376	6,622	6,003	5,925	5,692	4,614
Biological Sciences	19,837	3,645	3,298	3,227	3,250	3,009
Psychology	14,546	2,775	2,429	2,285	2,225	2,131
Biol. Sci./Psych.	34,383	6,420	5,727	5,512	5,475	5,140
Five-Sector Total	139,350	26,863	23,876	23,405	23,065	19,775

Sources and Notes: See text. Estimates are for faculty in five sectors only. Detail may not add to total because of rounding.

[9] Physicists are well aware of the serious problems posed by their age distribution. Professor William Walters of the University of Wisconsin-Milwaukee, who chairs a committee of the American Association of Physics Teachers, has pointed out (in personal correspondence) that the need for replacements is aggravated by the fact that physics regularly experiences "out-migration"—faculty leaving physics for other fields—without a corresponding "in-migration." The American Institute of Physics and the American Physical Society have also drawn attention to the particular circumstances of the field.

New Entrants

As an overall measure of replacement demand, the analysis up to this point is defective in one major respect: it makes no allowance for new entrants. As vacancies occur, new appointments will be made. Over time, these "new entrants" will be affected by the same exit probabilities as the present faculty. Some of them, in turn, will need to be replaced by still more new entrants.

Although new entrants are important, their numbers can be estimated only after we have first studied what is likely to happen to the total number of faculty positions by field of study and by sector. Plainly, contractions of fields and of sectors can occur, and in such situations it may not be appropriate to replace all of the present faculty members who have left. Alternatively, expansion of fields and sectors will dictate that new entrants exceed the number of vacancies created by the departure of present members of the faculty. After we have examined the factors that determine the overall number of faculty positions, we will return in Chapter Seven to a further examination of replacement demand, including replacements of new entrants.

CHAPTER THREE

Population Trends and Enrollment Projections

PROSPECTS for faculty members in the arts and sciences are inevitably affected by the overall scale of the educational enterprise. There have been periods—the boom years of the 1960s are a good example—when changes in scale were so overwhelming as to dominate staffing decisions. We do not foresee such periods in the near future, but that hardly means that trends in population and enrollment can be ignored. Such trends define the context within which all other factors affecting faculty staffing must be considered.

While this chapter is concerned primarily with aggregate enrollment, it is, of course, the size and composition of the underlying population base that determine the pool of potential students. Thus, we begin with an examination of population trends.

POPULATION TRENDS AND ENROLLMENT RATES

Education at all levels has been affected powerfully by changes over time in the demographic profile. Births climbed sharply following World War II, rising from 2.9 million in 1944–45 to approximately 4.3 million per year in the mid-1950s. This high plateau lasted through 1960–61. Annual births then fell to a low of just over 3.1 million in 1973–74 before rising again—but not to the previous level (see Fig. 3.1).

The postwar "baby-boom" birth cohorts reached college age between the mid-1960s and the early 1980s, and they were of course a primary cause of the unprecedented growth in enrollments that occurred then. By 1990, this baby-boom generation will be in the 25–34 and 35–44 age groups. Trends in the sizes of the 18–24, 25–34, and 35–59 age groups are shown in Figure 3.2, which presents projections through 2012.

The implications of these population trends for faculty staffing depend on how many individuals in each age group attend college, and on whether they attend on a full-time or part-time basis. Age-specific

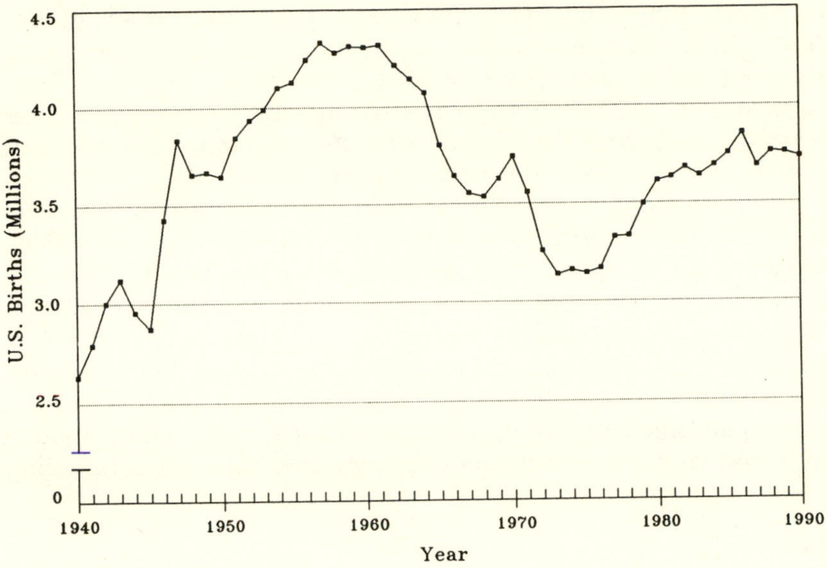

FIGURE 3.1
U.S. Births, 1940–90
Source: National Center for Education Statistics 1988, Table A1, p. 117.

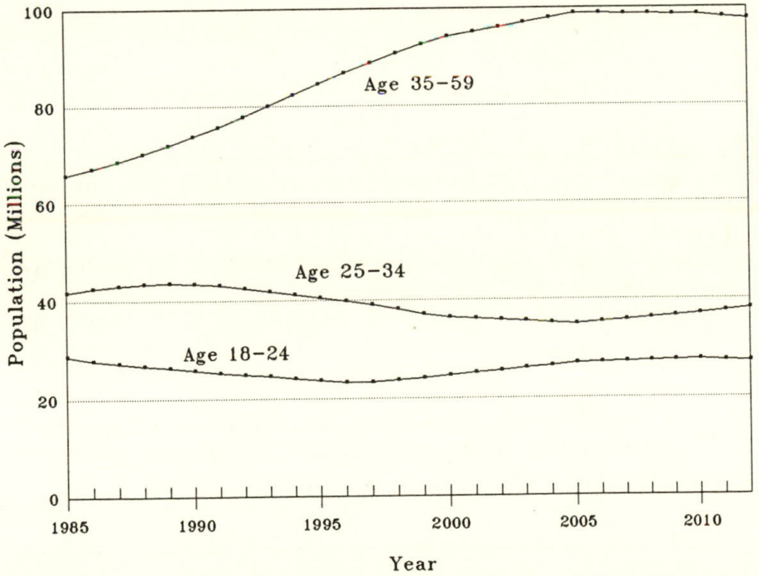

FIGURE 3.2
Population Projections, by Age Group, 1985–2012
Source: Office of Population Research, Princeton University.

enrollment rates—defined as the percentages of various age groups that attend an institution of higher education—are very important in making projections of the future demand for faculty members. These rates for 1980 and 1985 are summarized in Table 3.1, which presents separate calculations for full-time students, part-time students, total enrollment, and full-time equivalent (FTE) enrollment.[1]

The age-specific enrollment rates tell a most interesting story. As we would expect, enrollment rates for full-time students are much higher in the 18–21 and 22–24 age groups (the traditional college-age population) than in other age groups. Combining full-time enrollment with part-time enrollment, we obtain an FTE enrollment rate of 28.9 percent for the 18–21 age group in 1985. The FTE enrollment rate for the 22–24 age group was 11.2 percent.

The part-time enrollment rates are of course much higher relative to the full-time rates for the older age groups, but it is worth noting

TABLE 3.1
Age-Specific Enrollment Rates, 1985 and (1980)

	Enrollment Rates			
Age Group	*Full-Time Enrollment (%)*	*Part-Time Enrollment (%)*	*Total Enrollment (%)*	*FTE Enrollment[a] (%)*
16–17[b]	2.8 (2.6)	0.4 (0.4)	3.3 (2.9)	2.9 (2.7)
18–21	27.4 (26.4)	4.4 (3.9)	31.8 (30.4)	28.9 (27.8)
22–24	9.4 (9.2)	5.4 (6.4)	14.8 (15.5)	11.2 (11.3)
25–29	3.2 (3.1)	5.8 (6.4)	8.9 (9.5)	5.1 (5.2)
30–34	1.6 (1.5)	4.8 (5.5)	6.3 (7.0)	3.1 (3.3)
35–59	0.5 (0.3)	2.3 (2.0)	2.9 (2.4)	1.3 (1.0)

Sources and Notes: The population bases were provided by the Office of Population Research at Princeton University, and they represent the total population, including armed forces overseas and those in institutions.

The enrollment data are fall enrollments at all institutions of higher education, and they were obtained from the *Digest of Education Statistics 1987*, Table 103.

The enrollment rates are all percentages of the relevant age-group populations. The 1985 rates are presented first, with the corresponding rates for 1980 following in ( ).

[a]FTE enrollments were calculated by assuming that three part-time students are equivalent to one full-time student.

[b]In the case of the 16–17 age group, it was necessary to divide the enrollments for the 14–17 age group (which is the grouping used in the *Digest of Education Statistics*) by the population aged 16–17.

---

[1] As explained earlier, we follow the usual convention and treat three part-time students as equivalent to one full-time student for the calculation of FTE enrollments.

that the absolute value of the part-time rate is not as high for any of the older age groups as it is for the traditional college-age population. While the older age groups contribute far larger numbers of students—especially part-time students—than was formerly the case, it is important not to understate the role that is still played by the 18–24 age group in determining enrollments.

We have included the 1980 age-specific enrollment rates on Table 3.1 so that enrollment rates in 1980 and 1985 can be compared. The basic patterns have remained very much the same. The single most important change is the upward creep in the full-time enrollment rate for the 18–21 age group: from 26.4 percent in 1980 to 27.4 percent in 1985. The part-time rate also increased modestly for this same age group, and the result is an overall increase in the FTE rate of this group from 27.8 percent in 1980 to 28.9 percent in 1985.

There also have been small increases in enrollment rates for older persons, resulting in an increase in the FTE rate for the 35–59 age group from 1.0 percent to 1.3 percent. Finally, we should note the absence of continuing increases in the part-time enrollment rates of the 22–24, 25–29, and 30–34 age groups. Part-time enrollment rates actually declined slightly between 1980 and 1985 for all three of these age groups.

Enrollment Projections

Projections of enrollment in future years are no more reliable than the underlying assumptions concerning population trends and enrollment rates. Since the population groups under study have been born already, we can have considerable confidence in the accuracy of the population projections. Enrollment rates are trickier than population projections, however, since they can change for any number of reasons related to social, economic, and political developments.

For the purposes of this analysis, we have adopted the simple assumption that the age-specific enrollment rates that prevailed in 1985 will prevail for the next twenty-five years. Plainly, this will not, in fact, happen. But it is extremely hard to anticipate with confidence even the direction of change, quite apart from the magnitude. Moreover, there are reasons to believe that the 1985 rates may not be that far off as indicators of what lies ahead.

If we look at years prior to 1980, we find indications that some of the most important age-specific enrollment rates have been reasonably steady over time. For example, the FTE enrollment rates for the 18–21 and 22–24 age groups have stayed at about 28 percent and 11 percent, respectively, since 1973. Similarly, the FTE rates for the 25–29 and 30–34 age groups have hovered around 5 percent and 3 percent, respectively.[2]

The only steady increase has been in the 35–59 age group, where the FTE rate has climbed from 0.4 percent in 1968 to 0.6 percent in 1973, to 0.8 percent in 1978, to 1.0 percent in 1980, to 1.3 percent in 1985. These statistics alone would certainly justify projecting at least some continuing increase in the FTE rate for older persons. However, there is one offsetting consideration: the increase in part-time enrollment among older age groups has been concentrated among women, and there are reasons to believe that the upward trend in enrollment rates for women is largely over.

So long as women in the 18–24 age group enrolled in college at lower rates than men, there was an identifiable pool of potential women students in the over-24 age groups to be tapped. By the early 1980s, however, there was no longer any difference in college-going rates for women and men.[3] It is entirely possible that the modest decline in part-time enrollment rates between 1980 and 1985 for the 25–39 age groups noted above is the first-stage effect of the tendency for more and more women to enroll as full-time and part-time students at the same ages and in the same proportions as men—thereby diminishing the pool of potential part-time students at later ages. It would seem risky, therefore, to count on a continuing rise in enrollment rates within the 35–59 age group in the coming decades. The cohorts of women who had higher enrollment rates when they were younger will be moving into these age groups.

It is hard to know what trend in enrollment rates to expect within the traditional college-going population (18–24). The increasing complexity of the economy, with more emphasis placed on knowledge-based skills, could cause larger numbers of families to conclude that a college education is necessary for a high school student to find a suitable job. The economic "return" to college education could rise for that reason. Consideration must also be given, however, to the problems of public education—which could limit the realistic academic aspirations of many students—and to the possibility that more

[2] See Herring and Sanderson 1981, Table A2, p. 8. Other references to enrollment rates in 1968 and 1973 are from this source.

[3] In 1963, 38% of all students (full-time and part-time) were women. This percentage rose every year for the next 18 years until it was 51.7% in 1981. It has hovered around the 52% level since then (51.5% in 1982, 51.7% in 1983, 52.1% in 1984, and 52.5% in 1985). See *Digest of Education Statistics* 1988, Table 117, p. 142.

interest in vocational education will be the main consequence of changes in job requirements.

Shifts in the ethnic and racial mix of the population could also affect enrollment within the 18–24 age group. As is well known, the black and Hispanic populations have lower college-going rates (21.9 percent and 17.6 percent respectively in 1986) than the white population (28.3 percent).[4] And blacks and Hispanics are expected to comprise increasingly large proportions of the 18–24 age group over at least the next twenty years (see Fig. 3.3).

We believe that it is very much in the nation's interest that the black and Hispanic rates reach the level of the white rates. Whereas in the early 1980s these differences became greater, there is now some evidence to suggest that the gap may be narrowing again (especially for the black population). Although these recent figures are encouraging, there is no firm basis for concluding that a new trend has been established. Moreover, differences in enrollment rates are almost certain to persist for a considerable period under any circumstances.[5]

One other piece of evidence supports the decision to use the 1985 age-specific rates to project enrollments. Applying the age-specific rates for 1985 to the population data for 1986 yields estimates of the full-time, part-time, and total enrollments in 1986 that are close to the actual figures reported in the official Department of Education surveys of academic institutions. The differences are about 1 percent for both full-time and FTE enrollments. Given the errors of estimation that are inevitable in any procedure of this kind, it is reassuring to see that,

[4] We obtained 1986 data from the U.S. Department of Education. See also National Center for Education Statistics (NCES) 1986, Table 2.15, p. 126. It should be noted that these categories are not strictly comparable because the Hispanic population includes both whites and blacks.

[5] Two graduate students at the John F. Kennedy School of Government at Harvard University, Melissa Roderick and Thomas Kane, have examined data from the *Current Population Survey* and found that between 1985 and 1987 the percentage of black 18- and 19-year-olds enrolled in college increased from 9.1% to 11.1% (based on use of a three-year moving average). They also report that the number of black high school students taking the Scholastic Aptitude Test has increased markedly the last few years, which suggests that the black enrollment rate may continue to rise as these students enter college. It should be noted, however, that more complete data from institutional surveys (IPEDS, which currently are available only through 1986) thus far fail to show any gain in enrollment for blacks relative to whites—in spite of trends in the sizes of the respective populations, which themselves should lead to higher enrollment shares for blacks. (See *Digest of Education Statistics* 1988, Table 146, p. 170. The Hispanic share of enrollment in four-year institutions of higher education did rise form 2.0% to 2.2% between 1984 and 1986, but presumably as a result of a relatively rapid increase in population.) When comparable data are available for 1988, we may have a better sense of emerging trends.

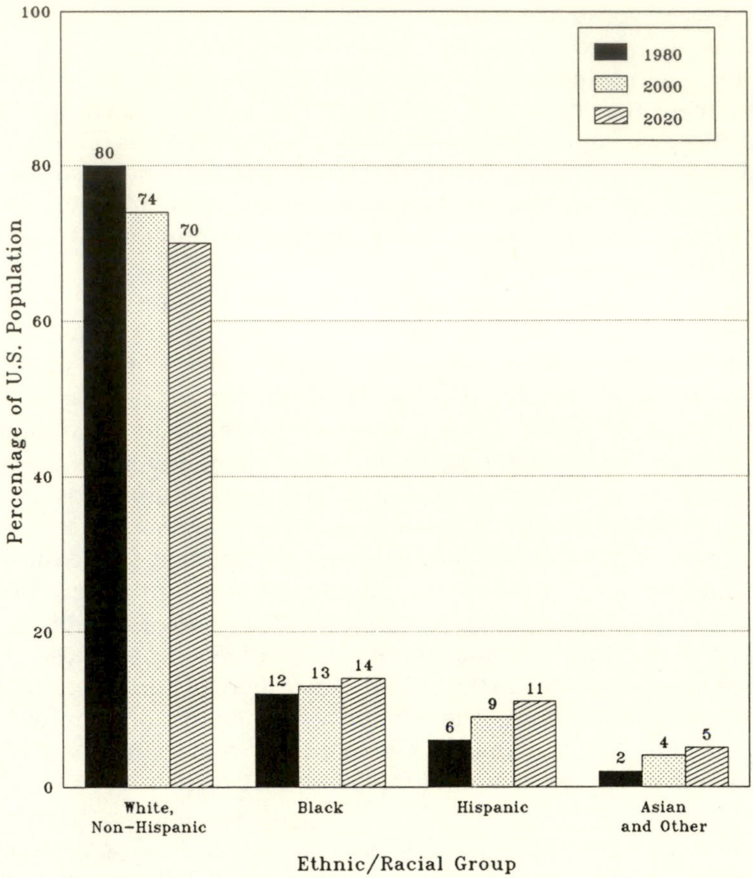

FIGURE 3.3
Projected Changes in the Ethnic/Racial Composition of the U.S. Population
Source: Davis, Haub, and Willette 1983.

at least in the short run, multiplying the 1985 age-specific enrollment rates by the relevant age populations produces enrollment figures that correspond generally with the observed data.[6]

We now bring together the projections of population trends and of age-specific enrollment rates to obtain projections of enrollment. The

[6] No one could claim, however, that constant age-specific enrollment rates are the only reasonable assumption. The most plausible variant would seem to be to assume some continuing upward creep in the rate for the 18–21 age group. A case can be made, based on historical data, for assuming that the enrollment rate for this group will increase about 2.5% over each of the five-year periods with which we are concerned in this study. (Between 1967 and 1986, the total enrollment rate for the 18–24 age group rose from 25.5% to 27.9% [see Bureau of the Census 1988, p. 85]. For present purposes,

major components of projected enrollment are summarized in Figure 3.4. It shows the year-by-year projections of full-time, part-time, total, and FTE enrollments from 1985 through 2012.

Part-time enrollment is projected to be remarkably constant over this entire period, as decreases in the contributions of one age group are offset by increases in the contributions of other age groups. On the other hand, full-time enrollment is expected to decline for about a decade, with the trough occurring in 1996. Total enrollment and

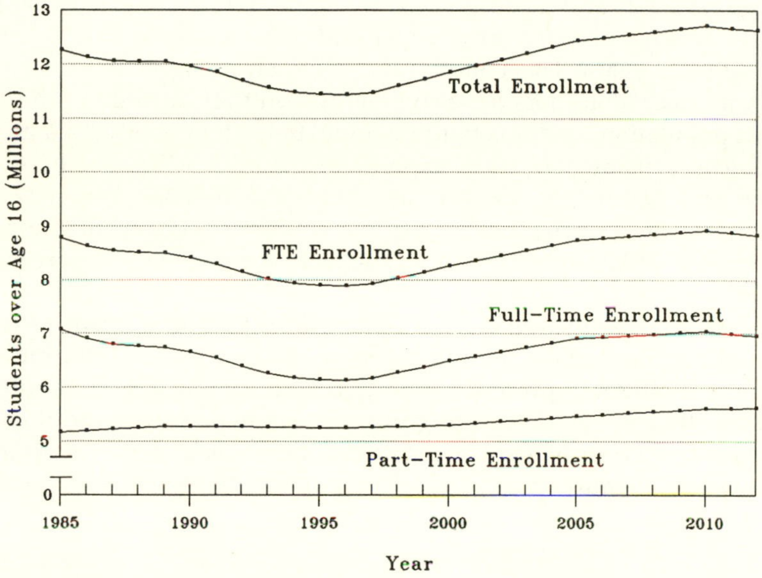

FIGURE 3.4
Projected Enrollment, by Attendance Status, 1985–2012
Source: See text.

---

we assume no significant difference between this rate of increase and the rate of increase in the FTE enrollment rate for the 18–21 age group.)

This assumption implies increasing the projected age-specific FTE enrollment rate for the 18–21 age group from 28.9% in 1987 to 29.6% in 1992, 30.3% in 1997, 31.1% in 2002, 31.9% in 2007, and 32.7% in 2012. We do not present alternative projections of enrollment incorporating these higher enrollment rates, but we have calculated the rough effects of the higher enrollment rates on our projections of demand for faculty. They make less difference than one might suppose, increasing demand by about 2% in 1987–92; this percentage then rises gradually until it reaches about 6% in 2007–2012. (These percentages do not allow for the need to replace some fraction of the number of additional faculty members hired in response to larger enrollments; taking account of this interaction between components of demand would increase these percentages by less than half a percentage point.) See Chapter Seven for a full discussion of projections of supply and demand.

FTE enrollment follow the same course. In 1996, FTE enrollment is projected to be 905,000 less than in 1985—a drop of just over 10 percent. A steady recovery in enrollment should then begin, with the 1985 level of FTE enrollment (8,788,000) regained in about 2007 and a new peak of 8,876,000 reached in 2010. Table 3.2 summarizes these results at five-year intervals.

Before we compare these overall projections with those made by others, we should look briefly at the projected composition of enrollment by age group. If we divide the population into two groups, those under 25 and those over 24, we can examine projected changes in the relative numbers of younger and older students over the next twenty-five years. This comparison is shown in Figure 3.5.

A number of authors have commented on the "ageing" of the student population, and this figure demonstrates that the over-24 group will gain considerably at the expense of the under-25 group between now and about 1996, when the trend will reverse. Whereas the younger age group accounts for just under 60 percent of the total student population in 1985, it will account for just over 51 percent in 1996.

However, the picture is quite different for FTE enrollments. When we take account of the radically different proportions of full-time and part-time students present at the two ends of our age distribution, we see that the younger age group always makes up more than 65 percent of FTE enrollment. Thus, while there will be some continuing movement toward an older student population for another decade,

Table 3.2
Projected Enrollment, by Attendance Status, 1987–2012 (in Thousands)

Year	*Full-Time Enrollment*	*Part-Time Enrollment*	*Total Enrollment*	*FTE Enrollment*
1987	6,806	5,220	12,059	8,543
1992	6,391	5,265	11,698	8,145
1997	6,167	5,253	11,477	7,923
2002	6,654	5,364	12,086	8,452
2007	6,957	5,517	12,544	8,808
2012	6,953	5,616	12,636	8,835

Sources and Notes: See Table 3.1 for sources.

Enrollment projections are the product of population projections by age group and 1985 age-specific enrollment rates.

Full-time and part-time enrollment will not add to total enrollment because of rounding. (Separate age-specific enrollment rates were used for each category of enrollment, including total enrollment.)

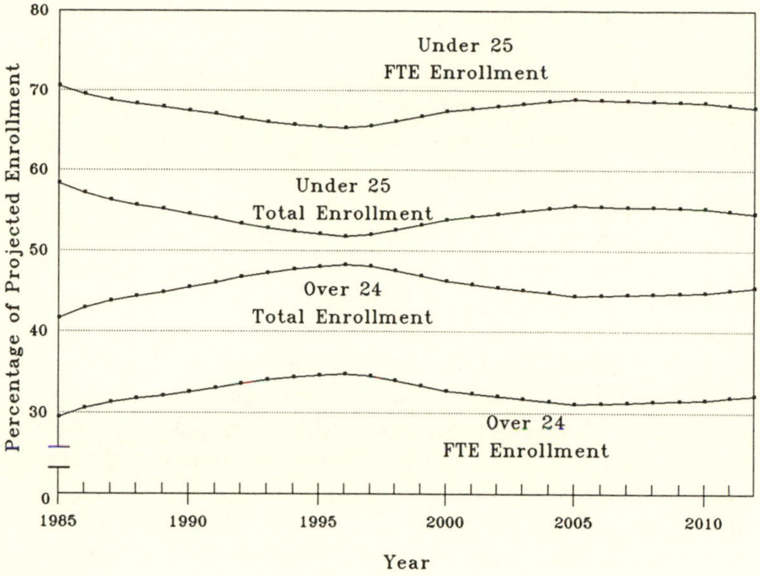

FIGURE 3.5
Projected Enrollment Shares, by Age Group, 1985–2012
Source: See text.

the change will not be nearly as drastic as it would appear to be if we looked only at the commonly cited figures for total enrollment.

There also has been interest in how the ratio of part-time to full-time students is likely to change in the future. We were able to examine trends in this ratio because our projections are based on age-specific enrollment rates that were calculated separately for part-time and full-time students. Part-time students are estimated to be 43.3 percent of all students in 1987, 45.0 percent in 1992, 45.8 percent in 1997, 44.4 percent in 2002, 44.0 percent in 2007, and 44.4 percent in 2012. In short, after a modest increase between 1985 and 1997, the percentage of part-time students falls back to about the 1987 level and remains there for the duration of the period under study.

Comparisons with Other Projections

Comparing these projections with those made by others is a tedious process, in part because every maker of projections defines the problem in a slightly different way. There is nothing to be gained by subjecting the reader to a litany of the complications that are involved in making these comparisons, but a brief summary of conclusions is in order.

We have made careful comparisons of our projections with those reported in studies by: (1) the National Center for Education Statistics (NCES); (2) Bowen and Schuster; and (3) William Bowen in 1980.[7] In the main, the results are remarkably similar. When one study projects a fall-off in enrollments, all project a fall-off, and so on.

The most precise comparisons are possible for the 1985–90 period, and all four sets of projections under review show declines in full-time enrollment in the range of just over 2 percent to 4.5 percent. The only consistent difference deserving mention is that the NCES systematically projects larger numbers of part-time students.[8]

Brief comments may also be made concerning the two other sets of projections. The Bowen-Schuster study presents only total enrollment data, and therefore does not allow comparisons of projections disaggregated according to attendance status. Still, the figures that these authors present for total enrollment in the 16–34 age range are similar to the corresponding numbers in other studies. For example, they project a decline of 556,000 between 1985 and 1990 in total enrollment for the 16–34 population, and we project a decline of 527,000. The Bowen-Schuster projections are quite different from our numbers in only one year (2005–06), and we do not know what accounts for the surprisingly large increase in enrollment that they show over the corresponding five-year interval.

The last eight years also have revealed shortcomings in the projections made by William Bowen in 1980. His study underestimates enrollment in 1985, primarily because of a failure to anticipate the increase that occurred in the full-time enrollment rate within the 18–21 age group. However, the post-1985 increments in enrollment reported in that earlier study (calculated after adjusting the 1985 base) are very close to the corresponding increments projected here.

The striking general similarity of the available projections is of course no guarantee that any of them is "right." At the same time, there is comfort in knowing that several independent investigators have come to similar conclusions.[9]

[7] See NCES 1982; Bowen and Schuster 1986; and Bowen 1981.

[8] See NCES 1982, Table 8A, p. 36. For the purposes of these comparisons, we have used the "intermediate alternate projections" prepared by the NCES. It is possible that the higher projections of part-time enrollment presented in this study stem from the fact that they were made somewhat earlier than our projections, and therefore were less able to take account of the declines in the part-time enrollment rates that have occurred recently.

[9] We are aware of only one paper that reports quite different figures: an essay by

Interpreting the Projections

Without doubt, the most salient single characteristic of this picture of projected enrollments graphed against time is its overall flatness. There is no marked, continuing trend in enrollments, either up or down.

To be sure, the enrollment trough in 1996–97 is important, and we do not mean to downplay it. When projected decreases in enrollment between 1985 and 1996–97 are translated into projected changes in faculty positions in Chapter Five, the significance of this trough will be evident. Nonetheless, the swings in enrollment anticipated during the 1985–97 period are modest compared to earlier swings. When we compare projections for the next twenty-five years with the postwar experience in this country, it is the persistent lack of growth in projected enrollments that leaves the dominant impression.

Perhaps the easiest way to appreciate the magnitude of this pronounced change in circumstances for higher education is to plot the path of enrollments between 1963 and 1985 on the same chart as the path of projected enrollments from 1985 through 2010. This has been done on Figure 3.6.

As this figure shows, the contrast between the earlier and later periods could hardly be more marked. Between 1963 and 1985, total enrollment rose from 4,766,000 to 12,262,000—an increase of nearly 7.5 million. By 2012, total enrollment is projected to rise from its 1985 level by only 374,000 students—with a significant decline in enrollment sandwiched between the 1985 and 2012 enrollment figures.

This is why we said at the beginning of Chapter Two that, for the foreseeable future, replacement demand will be a more important determinant of the number of faculty positions to be filled than demand generated by increases in enrollment. In other words, we see

---

Philip Kaufman (1986). Kaufman cites U.S. Census data purporting to show an enrollment rate of 37.1% for the 18–21 age group in 1985. This figure is inconsistent with other official data published by the Office of Education. The *Digest of Education Statistics* (1987, Table 103), presents total enrollment data for the 18–21 age group that differ by 10% from the enrollment data presented by Kaufman, and that imply an enrollment rate for this age group of 31.8%. A representative of the Office of Education who was asked about this problem had no explanation for the major discrepancy. The *Digest* figures are much more congruent with other data than are the figures cited by Kaufman. Kaufman appears to have relied on U.S. Census survey data that were not constrained by the more complete data for overall enrollment collected through HEGIS/IPEDS and used to construct the enrollment tables presented in the *Digest*.

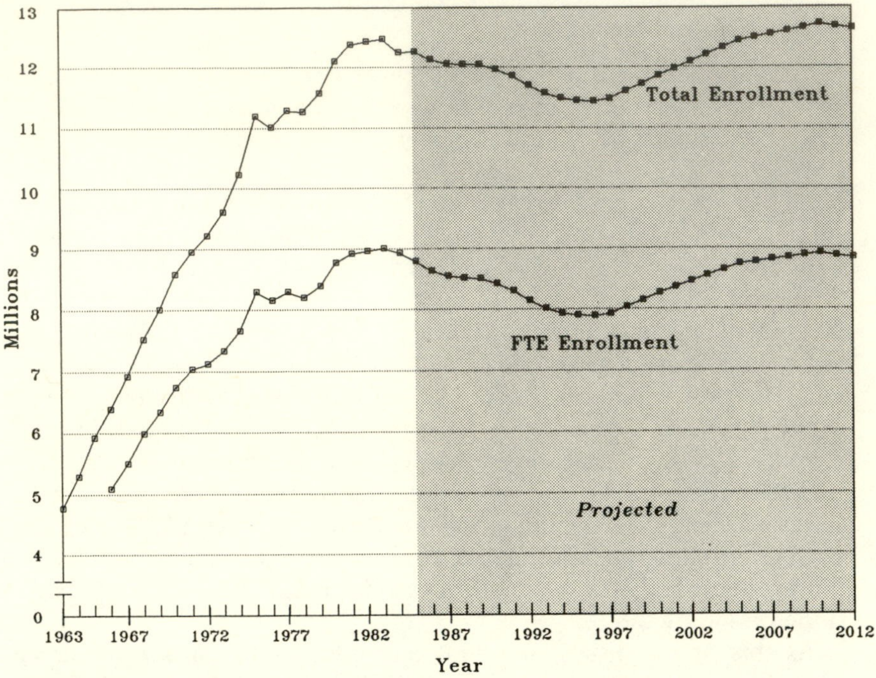

FIGURE 3.6
Enrollment Trends and Projections, 1963–2012
Source: See text.

no basis for anticipating an increase in the overall number of faculty positions over the next quarter of a century that would be anything like the increase that occurred in the postwar period.

CHAPTER FOUR

Enrollment by Sector and Field of Study: Trends and Projections

WHILE THE PROJECTIONS of aggregate enrollment developed in the last chapter are essential to understanding the outlook for faculty in the arts and sciences, they are by no means sufficient. As we shall see in this chapter, trends in enrollment in the arts and sciences (as best they can be inferred) do not always move in parallel with trends in aggregate enrollment. In the last decade, in particular, there has been a dramatic decline in the arts-and-sciences share of all degrees conferred, and shifting student interests must be taken into account when projecting the demand for faculty. It is also necessary to examine trends in enrollment by sector of higher education, but we shall see that there has been much more stability in enrollment by sector than by field.

We begin with the sectors and then turn to the more complex question of what has been happening to the various fields of study. The analysis of recent trends is revealing in many respects, but its principal role is to prepare the way for the projections of enrollment classified by both field and sector that conclude the chapter.

ENROLLMENT BY SECTOR

Not surprisingly, the absolute sizes of the major sectors of higher education, measured by enrollments, vary considerably—as do the relative numbers of full-time and part-time students in each. A simple taxonomy for 1986 is presented in Figure 4.1.[1]

The Two-Year institutions enrolled nearly 4.5 million students in 1986, but nearly 3 million of those students were part-time. Comprehensive I is the next largest sector, with a total enrollment of nearly 3 million and an FTE enrollment of about 2.2 million. The Research I sector, with an FTE enrollment of about 1.4 million, clearly exerts

[1] The sectors are defined according to the Carnegie Classification with some of the sectors combined for present purposes. See Appendix A and Appendix Table D.1 for a fuller explanation. Enrollments in the particular sectors shown here do not equal total enrollment in all institutions of higher education because "Specialized" and "Other" institutions are excluded; together, these two sectors enrolled about 5% of all FTE students in 1986.

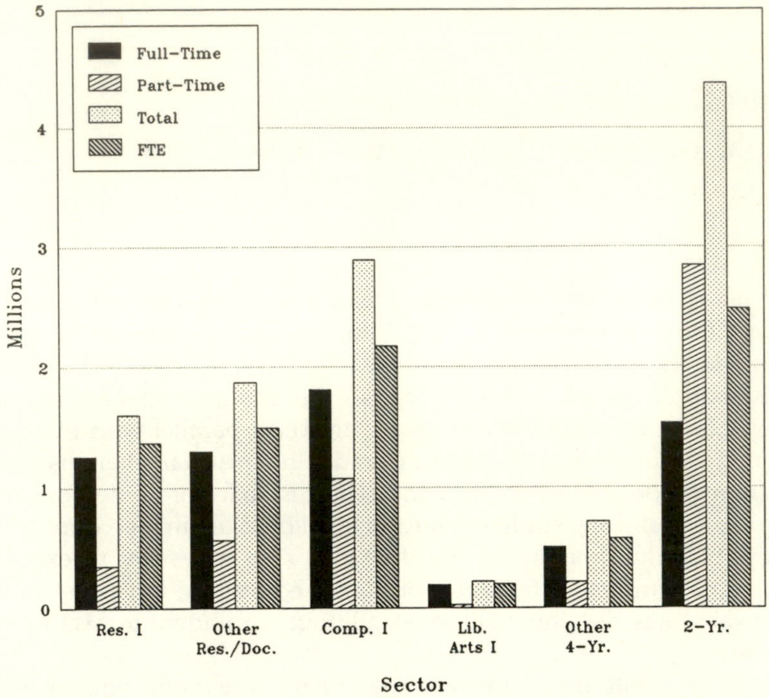

FIGURE 4.1
Enrollment by Sector, 1986
Source: Appendix Table D.1.

an influence on higher education—particularly at the graduate and professional levels—that is disproportionate to its size. Similarly, the Liberal Arts I institutions play a greater role in determining the tone and content of undergraduate education than their FTE enrollment of less than half a million would suggest.

Our ability to project enrollments depends on understanding if particular sectors are gaining or losing students relative to other sectors. As can be seen from Figure 4.2, the percentage shares of enrollment were in fact remarkably constant between 1976 and 1986.

Research I universities consistently account for 15 to 16 percent of all FTE enrollments; the enrollments of the Other Research/Doctorate universities have been equally consistent at a slightly higher level (about 17 percent of all FTE enrollments). Since 1976, Comprehensive I institutions have maintained almost precisely a one-quarter share of all FTE enrollments. Their share is exceeded only by that of the Two-Year sector, where the percentage of FTE enrollments has fluctuated between 28 and 31 percent over this period. The Liberal Arts I institutions have been more successful in retaining their small but

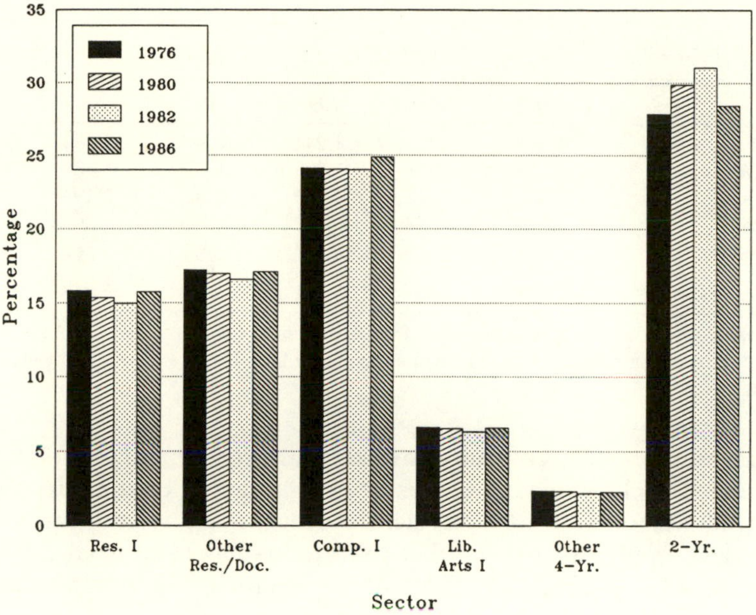

FIGURE 4.2
Percentage Shares of FTE Enrollment by Sector, 1976–86
Source: Appendix Table D.1.

significant share than many might have anticipated: they enrolled 2.4 percent of all FTE students in 1976 and 2.3 percent in 1986. The Other Four-Year institutions have been the most consistent of all, with exactly 6.6 percent of FTE enrollments in three of the four years for which we have data.

On the basis of this analysis, we decided, in the work that follows, to allocate the changes in aggregate FTE enrollments projected in Chapter Three among the major sectors in accord with the percentage shares prevailing in 1986. Since there are no clear trends in shares by sector, this is one instance in which disaggregation is unnecessary. But it is obviously preferable to reach this conclusion on the basis of evidence, rather than to make such an assumption in the absence of data. The resulting projections of FTE enrollment by sector, for each five-year interval from 1987–92 through 2007–12, are shown in Table 4.1.

ENROLLMENT BY FIELD OF STUDY

If stability in shares of enrollment has been the norm for the major sectors of higher education over the last ten years, radical change has been the corresponding rule for fields of study. The shifts in student

TABLE 4.1
Projected FTE Enrollment, by Sector, 1987–2012 (in Thousands)

Sector	*1987*	*1992*	*1997*	*2002*	*2007*	*2012*
Research I	1,341	1,279	1,244	1,327	1,383	1,387
Other Res./Doc.	1,444	1,377	1,339	1,428	1,489	1,493
Comprehensive I	2,127	2,028	1,973	2,105	2,193	2,200
Liberal Arts I	196	187	182	194	203	203
Other Four-Year	564	538	523	558	581	583
Five-Sector Total	5,673	5,408	5,261	5,612	5,849	5,866

Sources and Notes: Total FTE projections are from Chapter Three. Projected enrollment by sector was calculated using enrollment shares in Appendix Table D.1. Detail will not add to total because of rounding.

interest among fields of study have been unprecedented in their magnitude. Simply stated, there has been a large and continuous flight of students from the arts and sciences over the last twenty-five years. It is also important to note that the exodus has been from the arts and sciences defined broadly, not just from the humanities, as is sometimes assumed.

Data showing enrollments by field of study exist only at the level of the individual institution, and even then they are often incomplete or incompatible with data from other institutions. Fortunately, however, there are reliable data describing degrees conferred by field of study at the baccalaureate, master's, and doctoral levels obtained regularly through the "Degrees and Other Formal Awards Conferred" surveys (see Appendix A). Special tabulations have allowed us to supplement published data with more detailed breakdowns of degrees conferred by sector of higher education and field of study for the period since 1976.

Throughout this study, whenever we need to examine particular sectors and fields, we use degrees conferred as a proxy for enrollments. Our use of the degrees-conferred proxy has one obvious shortcoming. It does not allow us to take account of the fact that students who go on to receive one kind of degree can cross-register in courses taught by faculty members who are in other fields of study. For instance, students who will receive engineering and professional degrees enroll in arts-and-sciences courses. Engineering students take courses in mathematics and the physical sciences; medical students enroll in courses in the biological sciences; and business students take courses in the social sciences. All of these students (we hope) also take some courses in the humanities. As a result of such cross-registrations, we almost certainly underestimate shares of enrollment in the arts and sciences when we look only at degrees conferred.

What is most relevant for our purposes, however, is *changes over time,* not *absolute levels* of enrollment. It is reasonable to suppose that trends in enrollment mirror trends in degrees conferred. Unless there is a shift in the underlying relationship, study of trends in degrees conferred should permit reasonably accurate estimates of trends in enrollment by field of study and sector of higher education.

The Flight from the Arts and Sciences

Between 1970–71 and 1984–85, the number of degrees conferred in the arts and sciences dropped from 40.0 percent of all degrees to 24.9 percent (see Fig. 4.3). The rate of decline over this period, however, was by no means uniform. The movement toward other fields was

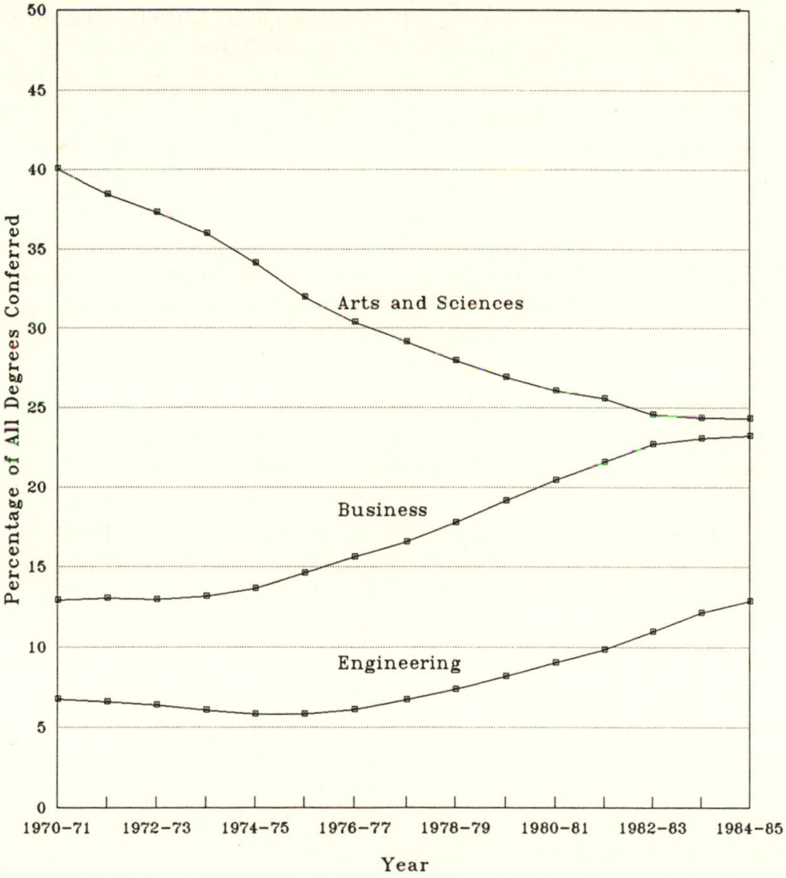

FIGURE 4.3
Trends in Degrees Conferred, 1970–71 to 1984–85
Source: HEGIS Earned Degrees Conferred surveys.

precipitous in the 1970s but much more gradual in the first half of the 1980s. (The arts-and-sciences share of degrees conferred had fallen to 26.7 percent by 1980–81.)

The difficult economic conditions of the 1970s and early 1980s were surely responsible in good measure for this shift. Many parents and students became concerned about job prospects and the "relevance" of the arts and sciences. In addition, rising costs of education almost certainly contributed to skepticism about the value of these fields. And then, of course, the general temper of the times, including the attitudes of politicians, may have discouraged students from pursuing what many came to see as esoteric subjects.

The dramatic fall in the number of arts-and-sciences degrees has been offset by striking increases in the number of business and engineering degrees. The steady upsurge of interest in business is not surprising, but the magnitude of the change is difficult to comprehend: in 1970–71, business degrees were roughly one-third as numerous as degrees in the arts and sciences; by 1984–85, the numbers of degrees were almost equal.

The increased popularity of engineering is equally noteworthy. It is not surprising that interest in engineering was bottoming out at the beginning of the period, in the wake of the Vietnam War. Young people who opposed American military involvement in Southeast Asia often opposed (the study of) science and technology, which they perceived to be a part of the war effort. Following the war, as can be seen from Figure 4.3, degrees conferred in engineering rose significantly.

Business and engineering together accounted for 19.6 percent of degrees conferred in 1970–71 and 36.1 percent in 1984–85. A convenient way to think about the scale of the change in student interests is to recognize that, out of every 100 degrees conferred in 1984–85, 16 fewer degrees were awarded in the arts and sciences than in 1970–71—and approximately 16 more degrees were conferred in business and engineering.

More recently, however, undergraduate interest in engineering has waned. Undergraduate enrollment (full-time students only) peaked at 406,144 in 1983; the comparable figures for 1984 and 1985 were 394,635 and 384,191. Surveys of field interests expressed by entering freshmen show similar trends, as do data showing numbers of applicants to several technical institutions. At the graduate level, the continuing influx of foreign students has masked comparable shifts in interest among U.S. residents.[2]

[2] Undergraduate enrollment data are from *Science and Engineering Indicators—1987*, Table 2–1, p. 42. Field interests of entering freshmen are reported in Astin et al., *The*

Between 1970–71 and 1984–85, there were also significant increases in degrees conferred in communications, public affairs, and the visual and performing arts. The increasing number of programs of this kind has no doubt contributed to the flight from the arts and sciences, but it is also true that these programs have developed because of the growing interest in them.

The other broad field (besides the arts and sciences) to experience a substantial fall-off in student interest was education. Between 1970–71 and 1984–85, the percentage of degrees conferred in education plummeted from 24.7 percent of all degrees conferred to 13.2 percent.[3]

Differences by Level of Degree

The relative number of degrees conferred in the arts and sciences has declined at *all* levels (B.A.'s, M.A.'s, and Ph.D.'s). The drop was steepest, however, at the baccalaureate and master's degree levels (see Fig. 4.4).

The Ph.D. is very important in the arts and sciences (with such large numbers of doctorate holders pursuing academic careers), but less important in most other fields; therefore, it is not surprising that the arts-and-sciences share of Ph.D.'s has held up somewhat better than the arts-and-sciences shares of other degrees. In general, it is clear that more students are pursuing non-academic, professional careers, and that they believe it is more useful (or more marketable) to pursue B.A. and M.A. degrees closely related to their intended vocations.

The degrees-conferred data also reveal another relationship among degrees offered at the different levels. More often than not, students who go on to do graduate work at the master's and doctoral degree levels do so in the general fields of study that they pursued as undergraduates.[4] Therefore, it is reasonable to expect trends in enrollment at the graduate level to follow (with appropriate time lags) trends in

---

American Freshman (ACE-UCLA Cooperative Institutional Research Program, various years). Data on numbers of applicants to selected technical institutions were provided by Peter Likins, president of Lehigh University. Information on graduate degrees is presented in *Science and Engineering Indicators* and *Digest of Education Statistics.*

[3] See *Digest of Education Statistics* 1988, Table 166. In 1985–86, the comparable figure was 13.0%. All of the data cited above are for B.A., M.A., and Ph.D. degrees only and exclude first professional degrees. If we had included these professional degrees in our calculations, the flight from the arts and sciences would have appeared even more pronounced. The number of first professional degrees awarded—in fields such as medicine and law—rose sharply from 38,000 in 1970–71 to 72,000 in 1984–85.

[4] Sarah Turner, in an unpublished undergraduate thesis (Princeton University, Department of Economics, April 1989), found that choice of undergraduate major has a

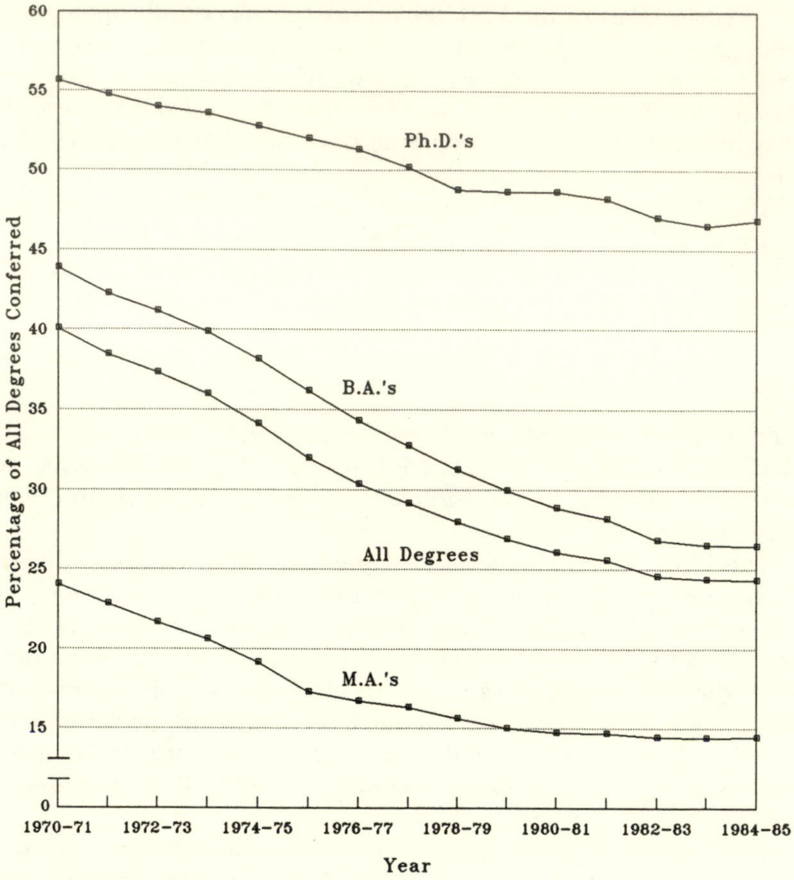

FIGURE 4.4
Percentage Shares of Arts-and-Sciences Degrees, by Level of Degree, 1970–71 to 1984–85
Source: HEGIS Earned Degrees Conferred surveys.

enrollment at the undergraduate level. If there are fewer students completing undergraduate programs in any field, it stands to reason that subsequently there will be a smaller applicant pool available to graduate programs in the same field.

This pattern is evident in the biological sciences. According to the

strong impact on the probability that a student will do graduate work. For example, students who major in physics are ten times more likely to pursue graduate studies in the arts and sciences than are all other students. An implication is that the flight from the arts and sciences at the B.A. level has led to a significant reduction in the number of candidates for M.A. and Ph.D. degrees.

published data, the number of bachelors' degrees conferred in biological sciences increased from 35,743 in 1970 to 54,275 in 1975, when the number of undergraduate degrees began to decline. The peak number of masters' degrees in biological sciences was reached one year later, in 1976, when 7,114 degrees were conferred. The number of doctorates continued to increase through 1981, when 3,743 degrees were awarded. These time lags are roughly consistent with the normal duration of M.A. and Ph.D. programs.

Differences by Field of Study

In many ways, the most important and most interesting findings pertain to particular fields of study. While no component of the arts and sciences has been immune from the general trends noted above, there are significant differences among fields.

Mathematics and the physical sciences are unusual in several respects (see Fig. 4.5). Of all of the individual fields of study, mathematics is the only one to exhibit a U-shaped pattern over the fifteen years surveyed here. While never large in absolute terms (never more than 3 percent of all degrees conferred), the share of degrees conferred in mathematics dropped steadily between 1970–71 and 1980–81, but then recovered significantly in more recent years. The recovery of interest in mathematics may have been triggered by the attention paid to computer science and other fields related to work in applied mathematics.

The physical sciences are unique within the arts and sciences in that their share of degrees conferred has been essentially flat over the last fifteen years. Taken together, the share of degrees conferred in mathematics and the physical sciences has been relatively constant at about 4 percent of all degrees conferred. There has been, if anything, a modest upward trend in the last few years.

Among fields within the arts and sciences, mathematics and the physical sciences have exhibited the smallest decline in share of degrees conferred. This may be explained, at least in part, by the fact that the skills taught in these fields are perceived by some students to be useful in various professional fields outside the arts and sciences. Engineers, computer scientists, and chemists working in industry, for example, all need to be familiar with the basic principles taught in mathematics and science. A perceived utility and practicality may well account for the relative stability of these fields.

The biological sciences and psychology exhibit quite a different pattern (see Fig. 4.6). Both of these fields experienced an upswing in popularity between 1970–71 and the mid-1970s, when a modest, but

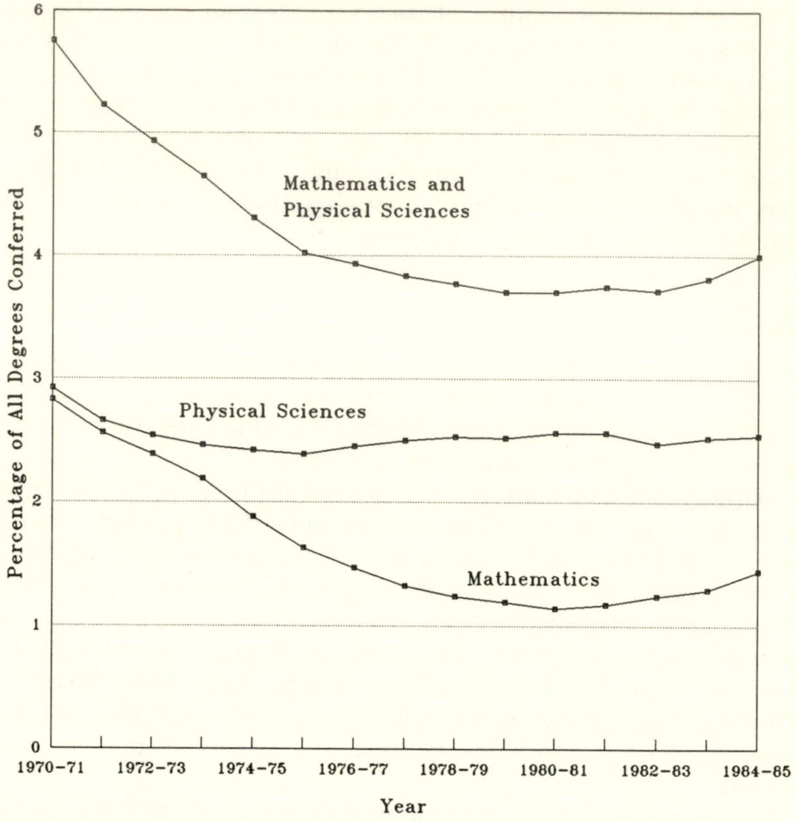

FIGURE 4.5
Percentage Shares of Mathematics and Physical Sciences Degrees, 1970–71 to 1984–85
Source: HEGIS Earned Degrees Conferred surveys.

continuing, decline in share of degrees conferred began. In 1976–77, 9.8 percent of all degrees conferred were in the biological sciences and psychology. By 1980–81, their combined share had fallen to 8.5 percent, and by 1984–85, it had fallen further, to 7.7 percent—which is below where it had been in 1970–71. The downturn in psychology began sooner than the downturn in biological sciences, but the drop in the latter field has been sharper.

Clearly, medicine and the biological sciences share common skills and knowledge. As a point of interest, it is worth noting that fluctuations in interest in medicine have paralleled fluctuations in interest in the biological sciences. Since 1974, the number of people applying to medical school has dropped from 42,624 to 28,123, with the sharpest

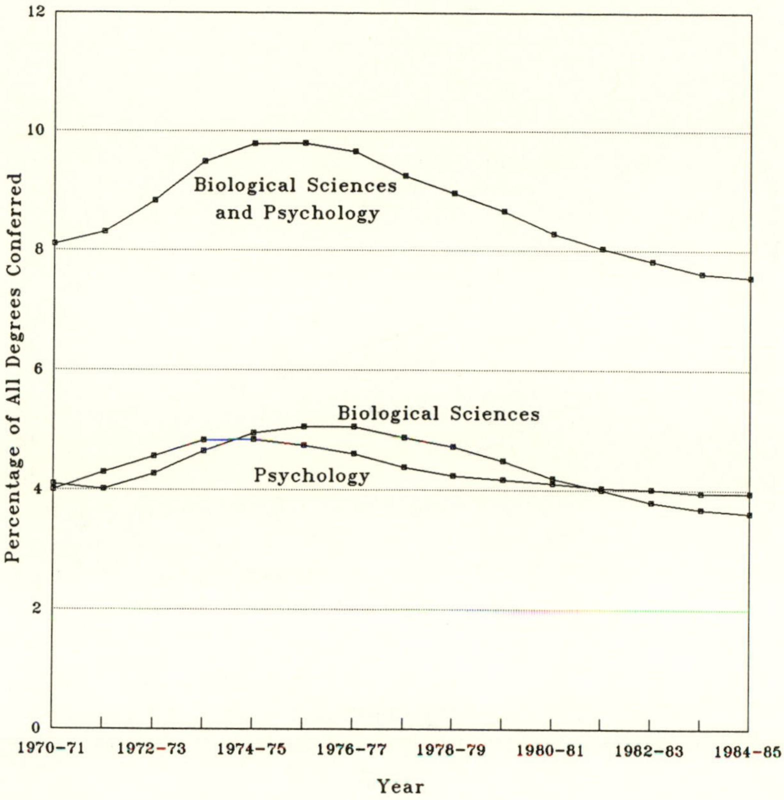

FIGURE 4.6
Percentage Shares of Biological Sciences and Psychology Degrees, 1970–71 to 1984–85
Source: HEGIS Earned Degrees Conferred surveys.

decline coming in the last four years.[5] High tuition in medical school and the somewhat tarnished image of the medical profession may be partly to blame, but the drop in applications probably stems largely from the emergence of what have been perceived as more attractive opportunities in business, computer science, and other fields. In any event, it seems likely that changes in the relative appeal of medicine as a vocation have had a great deal to do with the ups and downs of student interest in both the biological sciences and psychology.

By far the greatest drop in share of degrees conferred has occurred in the humanities and social sciences (see Fig. 4.7). The number of degrees conferred in the humanities, as a percentage of all degrees,

[5] "Medical Education in the United States, 1987–88" (1988, p. 1066).

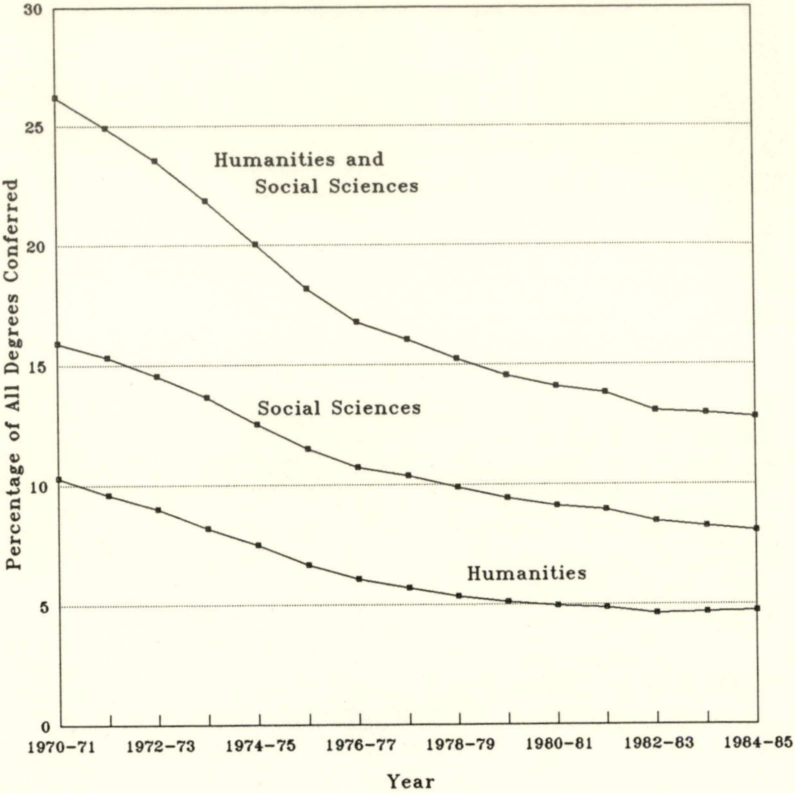

FIGURE 4.7
Percentage Shares of Humanities and Social Sciences Degrees, 1970–71 to 1984–85
Source: HEGIS Earned Degrees Conferred surveys.

fell by more than half between 1970–71 and 1984–85, when *only 4.7 percent of all degrees conferred were in the humanities.* This seems to us a staggeringly low figure. The downward trend is reflected in the experience of sub-fields within the humanities. In English, for instance, the number of B.A. degrees, expressed as a percentage of all B.A. degrees, fell from a high of 7.6 percent in 1967–68 to a low of 2.6 percent in 1984–85.

It should be noted, however, that the steepest part of this decline occurred prior to the end of the 1970s. In recent years, the share of degrees conferred in the humanities has actually increased slightly from the extraordinarily low levels reached in the mid-1980s. Degrees conferred (at all levels) in the field of letters increased from 3.1 percent of degrees in all fields in 1982–83 to 3.3 percent in 1985–86. Similar trends are evident in the responses by entering freshmen to questions concerning fields of interest.[6]

The curve for the social sciences resembles the curve for the humanities, and again we see from Figure 4.7 how sharp the drop in student interest has been. Here, too, there is some evidence that this decline may have stopped by 1985–86.

Differences by Sector and Field of Study

At the beginning of this chapter, we presented data on enrollments in the main sectors of higher education and then commented on the extraordinary degree of stability over time in their relative shares of *aggregate* enrollment. There are, however, major differences among the sectors in the relative importance of the arts and sciences as well as in the extent of the movement away from these fields.

Percentages of arts-and-sciences degrees vary from a low of 19.6 percent of all degrees conferred in the Comprehensive I institutions to a high of 65.1 percent in the Liberal Arts I institutions. Next to the Liberal Arts I institutions, the Research I universities have the highest concentration of degrees in the arts and sciences. Still, only about three of every ten degrees awarded today by these universities are in the arts and sciences (see Table 4.2).

Table 4.2
Percentage Shares of Arts-and-Sciences Degrees, by Level of Degree and by Sector, 1984–85

Sector	*B.A. (%)*	*M.A. (%)*	*Ph.D. (%)*	*Total[a] (%)*
Research I	32.7	17.5	48.0	29.6
Other Research/Doctorate	24.9	16.4	43.8	23.5
Comprehensive I	21.7	11.4	—	19.6
Liberal Arts I	68.2	27.0	—	65.1
Other Four-Year	24.8	11.1	—	23.3
All Institutions[b]	26.4	14.4	45.4	24.9

Sources and Notes: These calculations are based on tabulations from the HEGIS Earned Degrees Conferred surveys. Detail will not add to total because of rounding.

[a]Total of B.A.'s, M.A.'s, and Ph.D.'s. First professional degrees are excluded.

[b]Includes Other and Specialized but not Two-Year institutions.

[6] See Astin et al. 1988. Data reported in a recent publication of the American Council of Learned Societies (George Levine et al. 1989) also suggest increased interest in the humanities among both undergraduate and graduate students.

If we look at trends over time (see Table 4.3), we see that the arts-and-sciences share of all degrees granted declined noticeably between 1976–77 and 1984–85 in all sectors. However, we also see that the

TABLE 4.3
Changes in Percentage Shares of Arts-and-Sciences Degrees, by Field of Study and by Sector

Sector and Field of Study	*1976–77 (%)*	*1980–81 (%)*	*1984–85 (%)*
Research I:			
Humanities/Social Sciences	17.8	15.8	15.7
Mathematics/Physical Sciences	5.1	4.8	5.3
Biological Sciences/Psychology	10.7	9.0	8.5
All Arts/Sciences	33.6	29.6	29.6
Other Research/Doctorate:			
Humanities/Social Sciences	15.6	13.1	12.5
Mathematics/Physical Sciences	3.8	3.6	3.9
Biological Sciences/Psychology	9.3	7.8	7.2
All Arts/Sciences	28.7	24.6	23.5
Comprehensive I:			
Humanities/Social Sciences	15.5	12.2	9.8
Mathematics/Physical Sciences	3.1	2.7	3.1
Biological Sciences/Psychology	8.6	7.4	6.6
All Arts/Sciences	27.2	22.3	19.6
Liberal Arts I:			
Humanities/Social Sciences	41.1	41.2	41.0
Mathematics/Physical Sciences	8.2	8.1	8.3
Biological Sciences/Psychology	18.1	16.8	15.5
All Arts/Sciences	67.3	65.6	65.1
Other Four-Year:			
Humanities/Social Sciences	19.2	14.7	11.4
Mathematics/Physical Sciences	3.4	3.2	3.3
Biological Sciences/Psychology	10.7	9.9	8.5
All Arts/Sciences	33.3	28.0	23.3
All Five Sectors:			
Humanities/Social Sciences	17.4	14.6	13.1
Mathematics/Physical Sciences	4.0	3.7	4.0
Biological Sciences/Psychology	9.8	8.5	7.7
All Arts/Sciences	31.2	26.7	24.8

Sources and Notes: These calculations are based on tabulations from the HEGIS Earned Degrees Conferred surveys. Percentages are of all B.A.'s, M.A.'s, and Ph.D.'s. First professional degrees are excluded. Detail will not add to total because of rounding.

Liberal Arts I institutions and the Research I universities were more successful than the other sectors in maintaining their arts-and-sciences shares. In fact, since 1980–81, the arts-and-sciences shares in these two important sectors have remained essentially constant.

These patterns, of course, reflect institutional priorities, as well as the preferences of students. Many of the leading liberal arts colleges and research universities have wished to continue to concentrate in the arts and sciences. Some have had the luxury to do so because of the size and depth of their applicant pools. Others have experienced declining applicant pools—and, in some cases, even threats to institutional well-being—as a consequence of their commitment to the arts and sciences.

Institutions in other sectors, with different historical commitments and different constraints, have extended their curricula significantly and emphasized fields other than the arts and sciences. These curricular characteristics have both reflected and influenced student preferences. Within the Comprehensive I and Other Four-Year sectors, one consequence has been particularly severe declines in the arts-and-sciences shares of degrees conferred. These shares have continued to fall significantly since 1980–81, and no plateau can yet be identified. The relative number of degrees conferred in the humanities and social sciences has fallen especially rapidly in these sectors.

Inspection of these data leads to the question of whether we are witnessing a movement in American higher education toward greater specialization by sector. If arts-and-sciences degrees become progressively less common in many Comprehensive I and Other Four-Year institutions, the higher education community could become still more polarized between sectors that have a strongly professional/vocational orientation and sectors that give a greater emphasis to the traditional fields within the arts and sciences. Such a development would have ramifications that extend well beyond academic employment.

Projections of Enrollment in the Arts and Sciences

The main purpose of this section is to develop the enrollment projections that will serve as a building block to be used in deriving projections of demand for faculty in the arts and sciences. These projections are based on alternative assumptions about the future course of arts-and-sciences shares of aggregate enrollment.

At the outset, however, we should alert the reader to one factor that could cause our projections of enrollments in the arts and sciences to be slightly high. We have not made any allowance for possible shifts in the ratio of part-time to full-time students. As explained in Chapter Three, the proportion of part-time students is expected to rise only modestly, from 42.0 percent of all students in 1984 to a high of 45.8 percent in 1997, before falling back to 44.4 percent in 2002. Since we suspect that part-time students take relatively fewer courses in the arts and sciences than full-time students, the small increase in the part-time ratio that is expected could depress enrollments in the arts and sciences slightly below the levels that we project.

Consideration must also be given to the significance of the anticipated change in the racial/ethnic mix of the population (see Fig. 3.3). Some believe that this demographic shift will accelerate the movement away from the arts and sciences because minority students are thought to enroll in greater numbers in vocational or other non-arts-and-sciences courses of study.

The data available from the degrees-conferred surveys for 1980–81 and 1984–85 tell a more complex story. In both years, the fraction of all B.A. degrees conferred in the arts and sciences was higher for Hispanic students than for white students (see Table 4.4). The comparable figures for black students were only slightly below the figures for white students (one-tenth of a percentage point in 1980–81 and 1.3 percentage points in 1984–85). These data do not seem to us to justify making any downward adjustments in projections of arts-and-sciences enrollments.

TABLE 4.4
Changes in Percentage Shares of B.A. Degrees, for Selected Racial/Ethnic Groups, by Field of Study

	1980–81			*1984–85*		
Field of Study	*White (%)*	*Black (%)*	*Hispanic (%)*	*White (%)*	*Black (%)*	*Hispanic (%)*
Humanities	5.6	3.7	7.3	5.4	3.8	6.3
Social Sciences	10.6	13.4	13.2	9.3	10.6	11.0
Mathematics	1.2	1.0	0.8	1.5	1.3	1.0
Physical Sciences	2.6	1.5	1.9	2.5	1.4	1.6
Biological Sciences	4.6	3.7	5.2	3.9	3.6	4.8
Psychology	4.3	5.5	6.0	4.1	4.6	5.1
All Arts/Sciences	28.9	28.8	34.5	26.6	25.3	29.8

Sources and Notes: *Digest of Education Statistics 1987*, Table 159; *Digest of Education Statistics 1988*, Table 183. Detail will not add to total because of rounding.

Projecting Arts-and-Sciences Shares

When deriving projections, we must decide first what is likely to happen to the shares of enrollment in each of our three clusters of fields within the arts and sciences. In light of the importance of this judgment, and recognizing that there is no firm basis for insisting on one particular set of assumptions, we have elected to present three basic options: Option A ("Continuing Decline"); Option B ("Steady State"); and Option C ("Recovery"). The parameters of these three options are summarized in Table 4.5.

The first of the three options, *Option A*, is based on the assumption that the steady declines in the arts-and-sciences shares of FTE enrollment that have characterized the recent period will continue, but at a slower rate. While this option allows the arts-and-sciences shares to continue to decline, it does not presume that this pattern will go on indefinitely. We believe that at some point a floor in arts-and-sciences enrollments must be reached, and that is why we moderate

TABLE 4.5
Assumptions Used in Projecting Arts-and-Sciences Shares of Enrollment, by Field of Study

	Humanities/ Social Sciences (%)	*Mathematics/ Physical Sciences (%)*	*Biological Sciences/ Psychology (%)*	*All Arts/ Sciences (%)*
Actual Shares				
1976–77	17.4	4.0	9.8	31.2
1980–81	14.6	3.7	8.5	26.7
1984–85	13.1	4.0	7.7	24.9
Projected Shares, Option A:				
1987–92	12.0	4.0	7.2	23.2
1992–97 and thereafter	11.8	4.0	7.0	22.8
Projected Shares, Option B:				
1987–92 and thereafter	13.1	4.0	7.7	24.9
Projected Shares, Option C:				
1987–92	14.6	3.7	8.5	26.7
1992–97 and thereafter	17.4	4.0	9.8	31.2

Sources and Notes: The actual percentage shares are from the HEGIS Earned Degrees Conferred surveys. These percentages are for five sectors only.

See text for explanation of projected shares. In brief, Option A assumes Continuing Decline; Option B assumes Steady State; and Option C assumes Recovery.

the rate of decline and do not permit any decline beyond the levels stipulated for 1997. The rates of decline proposed in Option A are about one-half the annual rates of decline observed in recent years and are roughly consistent with the slopes of the historical relationships.

In the case of the humanities and social sciences, where the share of degrees conferred (our proxy for enrollment) fell from 17.4 percent in 1976–77 to 14.6 percent in 1980–81 to 13.1 percent in 1984–85, Option A assumes a further drop to 12.0 percent by 1992 and 11.8 percent by 1997, with constant shares thereafter. In mathematics and the physical sciences, shares have been stable recently, and Option A assumes continued stability (at 4 percent of total FTE enrollment). Biological sciences and psychology have fallen off sharply—from 9.8 percent in 1976–77 to 8.5 percent in 1980–81 to 7.7 percent in 1984–85—and Option A stipulates a 7.2 percent share by 1992 and 7.0 percent by 1997 (and constant thereafter).

Option B is a steady-state model. It is based on the assumption that, for each cluster of fields within the arts and sciences, the 1984–85 shares of degrees conferred (and thus, we presume, of enrollments) will remain constant through 2012. Thus, as can be seen from Table 4.5, this option assumes a 13.1 percent share for the humanities and social sciences through this period, a 4.0 percent share for mathematics and the physical sciences, and a 7.7 percent share for biological sciences and psychology.

Unlike Option A, Option B presumes that the drop in the arts-and-sciences shares is essentially over, and that from here on the odds of increases in these shares are as high as the odds of further declines. From the perspective of those concerned about the flight from the arts and sciences, this could be considered a somewhat optimistic possibility in light of recent trends.

Our final option, *Option C*, is, in this sense, still more optimistic. It rests on the assumption that there will be a recovery in the arts-and-sciences shares of enrollment between 1987 and 1997. More specifically, this option assumes not only that there will be a recovery, but that the path of recovery will be the mirror image of the previous path of decline. That is, this option treats the 1984–85 shares (used also for the 1987 projections) as low points; it then assumes that by 1992 the shares will have recovered to their 1980–81 levels, and that by 1997 they will have recovered still further to reach their 1976–77 levels (see Table 4.5).[7]

[7] The intervals of decline and of recovery are of slightly different length—four years versus five years. Thus, while the recovery postulated in this alternative will mirror

It is hard to be confident about the plausibility of this option. Much as those of us committed to the arts and sciences would like to anticipate renewed appreciation of the fundamental importance of these fields—and it is never a good idea to conceal one's biases—there is no obvious reason to believe that such a reversal of recent trends will in fact occur. Still, we never know, and we can hope. In any event, it seems important to bound the projections developed here by bracketing the Steady-State option (Option B) with alternatives on both sides of the status quo.

So far we have been concerned with projections of shares of enrollment for all colleges and universities, considered together, that constitute our five major sectors of higher education. If recent history is any guide, however, we should not ignore differences among sectors. As was pointed out earlier, one of the striking features of the educational landscape over the last ten years or so is that two of our sectors—the Comprehensive I institutions and the Other Four-Year colleges and universities—have experienced much sharper declines in relative interest in the arts and sciences than have the other sectors.

We believe, therefore, that it is most sensible to assume that the further decline in the arts-and-sciences share of enrollments projected in Option A will be concentrated in the Comprehensive I and Other Four-Year sectors.[8] For similar reasons, the recovery projected in Option C is assumed to replicate the sector-by-sector pattern of decline that occurred previously.

Projecting Enrollment by Sector and Field

We are now in a position to project enrollment by separate clusters of fields of study and for the arts and sciences overall within each sector. This is done by multiplying the projections of shares of degrees conferred in each field by the respective enrollment projections for each sector. The result is three sets of projections that are both field- and sector-specific, one corresponding to each of our three options.

A visual summary of the main results of these projections is provided in Figures 4.8–4.10. Each of these figures shows the projected enrollments, by field-of-study cluster, for one of the three options.

---

the previous decline, the rate of recovery will be slightly slower than the previous rate of decline.

[8] Thus, we allocated the projected decline (in Option A) in the humanities and social sciences share exclusively to Comprehensive I and Other Four-Year sectors and allocated the projected decline in the biological sciences and psychology share proportionately among all five sectors. These two allocation assumptions are best seen as a pair that together reflect the general pattern observed in recent years.

(The detailed projections are presented in their entirety as Appendix Tables D.2, D.3, and D.4.)[9]

The first figure in this series, Figure 4.8, makes an important point. It demonstrates that even the moderate continuing declines in arts-and-sciences shares that underlie the Option A projections produce quite large perturbations. Arts-and-sciences enrollments in all fields, for instance, can be seen to fall from 1.4 million in 1987 to 1.2 million

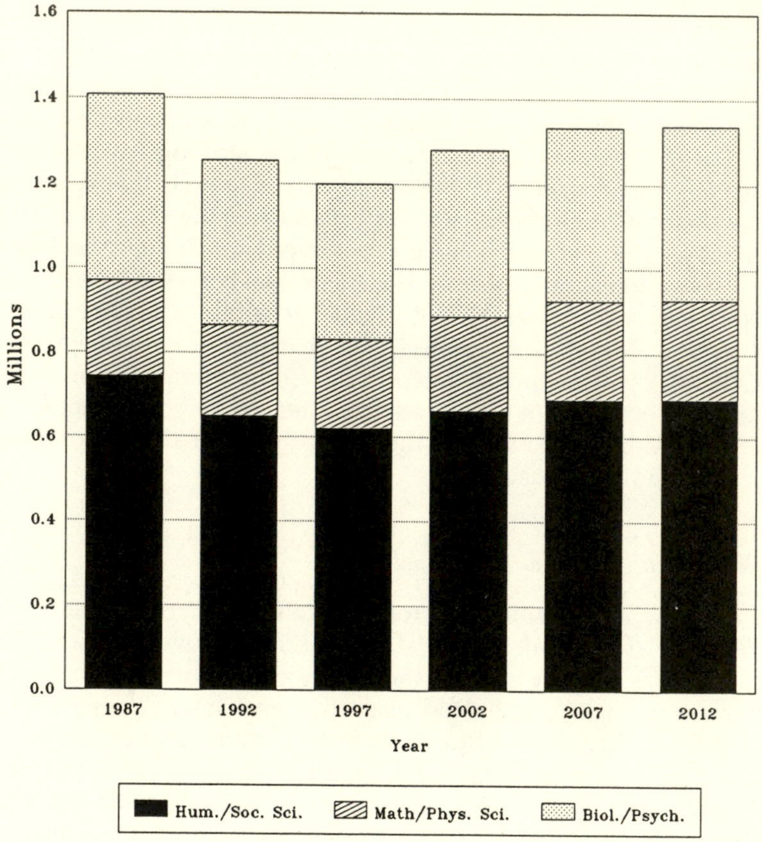

FIGURE 4.8
Projected Arts-and-Sciences Enrollment, Option A (Continuing Decline)
Source: See text.

[9] These tables show, for example, the quantitative effects on different sectors of assuming that further declines in the arts-and-sciences shares of enrollment are concentrated in the Comprehensive I and Other Four-Year institutions.

in 1997. Although arts-and-sciences enrollments later climb back, they never come close to regaining the 1987 levels.

Option B (Steady State) also implies decreases in arts-and-sciences enrollments for the next ten years. This is, of course, a consequence of the aggregate enrollment projections developed in the previous chapter. Unlike Option A, however, this option shows enrollments returning almost to the 1987 level of 1.4 million by 2002 and then rising above the 1987 figures in 2007 and 2012—to approximately 1.45 million (see Fig. 4.9).

The Option C (Recovery) projections are, of course, quite different. They imply a modest increase in arts-and-sciences enrollments right

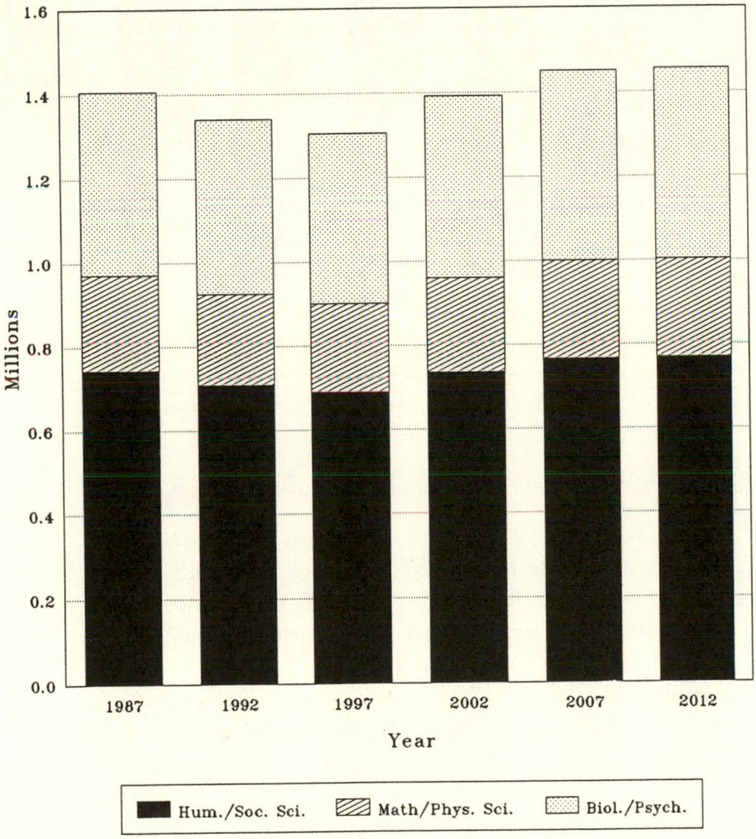

FIGURE 4.9
Projected Arts-and-Sciences Enrollment, Option B (Steady State)
Source: See text.

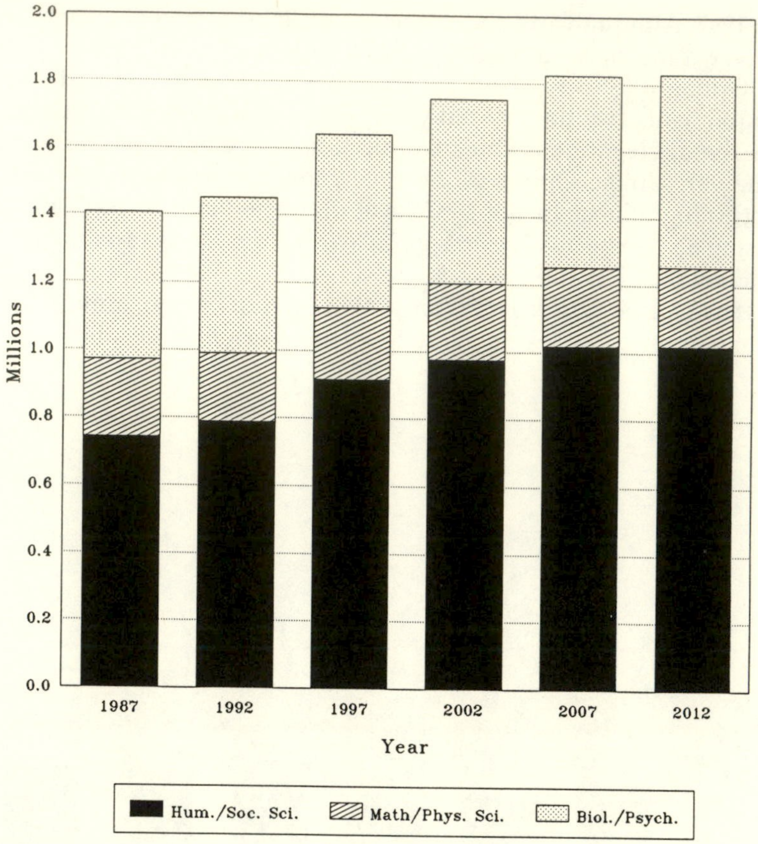

FIGURE 4.10
Projected Arts-and-Sciences Enrollment, Option C (Recovery)
Source: See text.

away—from 1.4 million in 1987 to almost 1.5 million in 1992—followed by an increase of another 200,000 FTE students by 1997 (see Fig. 4.10). The peak enrollment in the arts and sciences under this model is 1.83 million in 2012.

A more direct comparison of the three options is provided in Figure 4.11. Here we see (absent detail for fields of study) how much depends on whether the arts-and-sciences shares continue to decline even moderately, or whether they recover all the ground that they have lost since 1980. The absolute differences between Options A and C rise from 189,000 FTE enrollments in 1992 to 442,000 in 1997 to a high of 471,000 in 2002.

These are dramatic differences. They indicate the magnitude of what is at stake as we consider the vitality of the arts and sciences

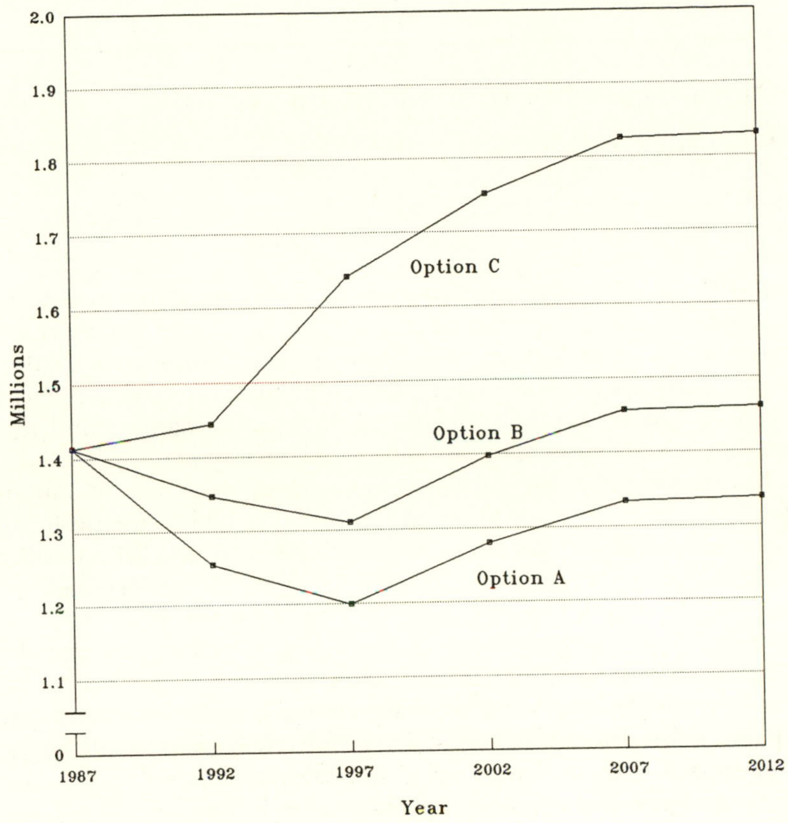

FIGURE 4.11
Projected Arts-and-Sciences Enrollment: A Comparison of Options A, B, C
Source: See text.

over the next two decades. While external forces will be important in determining enrollment patterns, well-conceived efforts by colleges and universities may be able to play at least a moderate role in shaping future events. The quality and the commitment of faculty teaching in the arts and sciences will be extremely important.

Needless to say, it would be foolish in the extreme to invest too much significance in any of these patterns or numbers. We have tried to describe carefully the assumptions on which the enrollment projections are based so that readers can make their own judgments as to their utility as indicators of what could happen under various circumstances. In the next chapter we combine these projections with another critical variable—student/faculty ratios—to arrive at projections of faculty positions by field and sector.

CHAPTER FIVE

Student/Faculty Ratios and Projections of Faculty Positions

IT IS IMPOSSIBLE to interpret past changes in the number of faculty positions or to develop reasonable projections without paying careful attention to student/faculty ratios. Anyone who assumes that student/faculty ratios are relatively inert, and can be treated as constants, runs a serious risk of overlooking one of the most dynamic—and most complex—factors affecting the outlook for faculty staffing.

To illustrate, over the last ten years, striking decreases in student/faculty ratios have been *the* most important single factor protecting the number of faculty positions in the arts and sciences. When student interest in these fields waned, faculty positions did not decrease proportionately—in fact, they increased. This does not mean that "productivity" necessarily declined or that higher education became "less efficient." Lower student/faculty ratios need not imply that faculty were teaching less, or doing less research; teaching seminars and small discussion groups can be every bit as time-consuming as lecturing to large classes. Still, the implications for staffing and for the economics of higher education are undeniable.

Student/faculty ratios, even when specified rigorously, are nothing more than convenient summary measures of the outcomes of decisions made at many levels concerning the staffing of departments and schools. What "critical mass" of faculty members is needed more or less regardless of enrollments? How speedily and fully should faculty numbers be expected to adjust to changes in enrollment? Should institutions simply "chase" enrollments in making staffing decisions? How will the integrity of the curriculum, the continuity of research and teaching, and the morale of the faculty be affected?

More than one institution has discovered through experience that it is usually more difficult and expensive to rebuild a demoralized department than to sustain a fundamentally strong group through lean periods. At the same time, institutions must address the economic consequences of what are clearly long-term trends. All institutions must cope with these issues, and the often complex conclusions reached determine the student/faculty ratios that we observe.

The first part of this chapter is devoted to an examination of the shifts in student/faculty ratios that have occurred over the last decade. In the last part of the chapter, we discuss the implications of alternative student/faculty ratios for projections of the number of faculty positions that will need to be filled in the future.[1]

Basic Concepts

A cautionary flag must be posted. While the student/faculty ratio is of obvious importance in analyzing historical changes in the number of faculty positions and in projecting future demand, it is a slippery concept. First of all, it is misleading to think in terms of a single student/faculty ratio, since there are several useful ways to define both the student numerator of the ratio and the faculty denominator. In addition, student/faculty ratios (however defined) vary across fields of study and sectors of higher education.

We will refer to four kinds of student/faculty ratios in this discussion:

1. FTE enrollments in all fields of study divided by all FTE faculty, including those without doctorates, in all fields of study. This is the most conventional definition. In 1987, this ratio was approximately 18.5 for the five sectors.[2]

---

[1] An early study of student/faculty ratios was made in Radner and Miller 1975, chs. 6 and 7. This work consisted of both historical analyses and a rigorous effort to derive relationships between faculty/student ratios (with which the authors chose to work) and such variables as institutional size and quality. Allan Cartter's well-known (1976) study included a variety of assumptions about student/faculty ratios (see especially chs. 6 and 7). Neither of these studies, however, used what we call "arts-and-sciences" student/faculty ratios.

[2] The conventional student/faculty ratio differs from the arts-and-sciences student/faculty ratios in its faculty denominator. The conventional student/faculty ratio cannot be observed directly from available data and is relevant to this study only as a benchmark. It was calculated as follows.

The number of full-time faculty with doctorates in the five sectors in 1987 was 195,668; this number included faculty teaching in all fields of study, not just in the arts and sciences (see Table 5.3). Two adjustments are needed to move from this definition to an estimate of all FTE faculty teaching those students included in the numerators of these student/faculty ratios. First, we must add those faculty who teach full-time but who do not hold doctorates. According to Table 118 of the American Council on Education's *1986–1987 Fact Book on Higher Education*, 65.1% of all faculty at four-year institutions in 1984 held doctorates. Using this ratio, we calculate that we need to add 104,897 non-doctorates to the faculty base.

Second, we must add part-time faculty. According to Table 118, 92.5% of all faculty at four-year institutions in 1984 were full-time. Using this ratio, and assuming that two part-time faculty members are equivalent to one full-time faculty member, we calculate

2. FTE enrollments in all fields of study divided by *full-time* faculty *with doctorates* in all fields of study. In 1987, this ratio was 29.6; it is appreciably higher than the conventional ratio because part-time faculty and faculty without doctorates are no longer included in the denominator.
3. FTE enrollments in all fields of study divided by full-time faculty with doctorates *in the arts and sciences*. In 1987, this ratio was 41.6. As we saw in the previous chapter, increasingly large numbers of students are studying in programs outside the arts and sciences. Many of the faculty teaching these students are beyond the purview of this study (which is concerned solely with faculty in the arts and sciences) because they list employment specialties such as business, communications, engineering, education, and the arts. The large absolute size of this ratio is due to the inclusion of all students in the numerator but only faculty in the arts and sciences in the denominator.
4. FTE enrollments *in the arts and sciences* divided by full-time faculty with doctorates in the arts and sciences. We call this the "arts-and-sciences" ratio, and it was 10.3 in 1987. This is the most useful ratio for our purposes, and it is the one we use in projecting faculty positions. It is the lowest ratio because the numerator is limited to arts-and-sciences students. (As explained in Chapter Four, these arts-and-sciences enrollment figures were derived from data on degrees conferred.)

In an absolute sense, the arts-and-sciences ratio understates the teaching done by arts-and-sciences faculty measured simply in terms of the number of students served. It gives these faculty no credit for the teaching that they provide to students outside the arts and sciences (e.g., engineering students who take some courses from arts-and-sciences faculty). This deficiency need not impair the use of the ratio in making projections, however, unless the amount of teaching outside the arts and sciences changes significantly *relative* to the amount of teaching within the arts and sciences proper. The available data on changes in the number of faculty positions outside the arts and sciences are reassuring in this regard.

Student/Faculty Ratios in 1987

The pattern of student/faculty ratios in 1987 in each of the major sectors is shown in Table 5.1. Looking first at the all-student/all-faculty

---

that we need to add 12,185 part-time faculty to the faculty base.

Taken together, these adjustments yield a new faculty base for the five sectors of 312,750. Dividing this faculty base into the corresponding FTE enrollment figure for the five sectors in 1987 (5,794,000) results in a student/faculty ratio of 18.5.

TABLE 5.1
Student/Faculty Ratios, by Sector, 1987

Sector	(1) All Student/All Faculty Ratios	(2) All Student/ Arts-and-Sciences Faculty Ratios	(3) Arts-and-Sciences Student/Arts-and-Sciences Faculty Ratios
Research I	21.3	32.7	9.7
Other Research/Doctorate	27.7	40.5	9.5
Comprehensive I	41.4	54.1	10.6
Liberal Arts I	18.0	20.2	13.2
Other Four-Year	39.3	52.7	12.3
All Five Sectors	29.6	41.6	10.3

Sources and Notes: SDR tabluations and enrollment data from Chapter Four. All of these ratios are defined to include only full-time faculty with doctorates. See text for further explanation.

ratios (defined to include only full-time faculty with doctorates), we observe a pattern across sectors that is just what might have been predicted. This ratio is lower for Liberal Arts I (18.0) and Research I (21.3) than for other sectors, in part because many of the institutions in these sectors traditionally have invested relatively heavily in faculty resources per student. A second part of the explanation is that fields in which student/faculty ratios are generally higher (such as business) are more popular in the other sectors.

When the all-student numerators are divided by faculty in the arts and sciences only (Col. 2), all of the ratios of course increase. The increase is smallest in the Liberal Arts I sector since there are relatively few faculty members outside the arts and sciences teaching in these institutions. The other increases are roughly proportional. The high ratios in Comprehensive I and Other Four-Year can be attributed to the relatively heavy emphasis given to professional and technical programs in these sectors. The somewhat lower ratio for Research I than for Other Research/Doctorate is credible, given both the lighter teaching loads and the greater relative emphasis on the arts and sciences characteristic of the major research universities.

The arts-and-sciences student/faculty ratios (Col. 3) are the most revealing. Not only are these ratios much lower in all sectors (since smaller numbers of students in the numerators are being divided by the same faculty denominators), but now the differences across sectors have been muted considerably. Much of the variance among the sectors in the other ratios has been removed by, in effect, "correcting" for differences among the sectors in the relative emphasis given to the arts and sciences.

The remaining differences among sectors also make sense. The research universities have the lowest student/faculty ratios because they do the most graduate teaching (where the numbers of students are ordinarily small) and have the lightest teaching loads, since intense research is an expected part of a faculty member's regular duties. The liberal arts colleges have the highest ratio because they concentrate more heavily on teaching, have few if any graduate programs, and have relatively few students outside the arts and sciences.

Having seen that all of these measures of faculty utilization tell coherent stories, we now extend this analysis of arts-and-sciences ratios to encompass differences among fields of study as well as among sectors of higher education (see Table 5.2). This table contains the matrix of arts-and-sciences ratios that is used in the last part of this chapter as the basic tool for converting projections of future enrollments by field of study and sector into projections of future numbers of faculty positions.

University administrators will not be surprised to see that mathematics and the physical sciences have the lowest ratio—a pattern that is observable within every sector. The humanities and social sciences are intermediate, and the highest ratio is found in biological sciences

TABLE 5.2
Arts-and-Sciences Student/Faculty Ratios, by Sector and Field of Study, 1987

Sector	*Humanities/ Social Sciences*	*Mathematics/ Physical Sciences*	*Biological Sciences/ Psychology*	*All Arts/ Sciences*
Research I	10.7	6.3	10.3	9.4
Other Research/Doctorate	10.2	6.2	10.8	9.3
Comprehensive I	9.8	7.0	15.0	10.4
Liberal Arts I	14.4	7.3	15.2	13.0
Other Four-Year	10.2	8.2	20.8	12.1
All Five Sectors	10.5	6.6	12.7	10.1

Sources and Notes: The student/faculty ratios by sector shown in this table are slightly lower than the corresponding ratios in Table 5.1. The reason is that the enrollment figures for the arts and sciences by field of study are projected enrollments for 1987 rather than actual enrollments in 1986. This small adjustment is necessary in order to obtain student/faculty ratios that can be used consistently with the projected enrollment data to calculate anticipated changes in the number of faculty positions by field and sector.

and psychology. In each instance, the pattern is consistent across sectors.[3]

Recent Shifts in Student/Faculty Ratios

As already indicated, sharp shifts in student/faculty ratios occurred over the last decade. These shifts raise intriguing questions about how higher education responds to major shifts in patterns of enrollment.

Between 1976–77 and 1986–87, total FTE enrollments in the major sectors of higher education increased 7.5 percent. The movement of students away from the arts and sciences was so pronounced that enrollments in the five sectors attributed to those fields *declined* 14.2 percent. Enrollments in other fields (also based on the use of the degrees-conferred proxy, as explained in Chapter Four) increased 17.3 percent (see Table 5.3).

Over the same period, the number of full-time faculty members in

Table 5.3
Interpreting Student/Faculty Ratios, 1977 and 1987

	1977	*1987*	*Change (%)*
FTE Enrollments:			
All Fields	5,391,000	5,794,000	+7.5
Arts and Sciences	1,679,800	1,442,000	−14.2
Other Fields	3,711,200	4,352,000	+17.3
Full-Time Faculty:			
All Fields	156,847	195,668	+24.8
Arts and Sciences	119,863	139,350	+16.3
Other Fields	36,984	56,316	+52.3
Ratios:			
All Std./All Fac.	34.2	29.6	−13.5
All Std./Art-Sci. Fac.	45.0	41.6	−7.6
Arts-Sci. Std./Arts-Sci. Fac.	14.0	10.3	−26.4

Sources and Notes: Faculty data are from SDR tabulations for five sectors only. They include only full-time faculty with doctorates.

Enrollments are from Chapter Four; they are based on degrees-conferred data, and therefore the absolute numbers for the arts and sciences and for other fields need to be interpreted with care.

[3] Psychology is mainly responsible for pulling up the student/faculty ratio for the biological sciences and psychology cluster. The biological sciences are very much like the other fields from the standpoint of student/faculty ratios; psychology, on the other hand, has many more students per faculty member than any of the other arts-and-sciences fields.

the arts and sciences *increased* 16.3 percent. Obviously, if the number of faculty rose while enrollments fell, the arts-and-sciences student/faculty ratio must have declined—and so it did, from 14.0 in 1977 to 10.3 in 1987.

Over this decade, there was a still more pronounced increase in the number of faculty outside the arts and sciences—which is hardly surprising, given the shifts in patterns of enrollment. The number of full-time faculty holding doctorates who were employed outside the arts and sciences increased 52.3 percent (from 36,984 to 56,316), but since this group remained a small fraction of all faculty, overall faculty numbers rose only 24.8 percent (from 156,847 to 195,668). Thus, the arts-and-sciences share of faculty positions fell, but not nearly as much as the arts-and-sciences share of enrollments.

As a consequence of these changes in enrollments and faculty positions, the two student/faculty ratios with all students in their numerators declined over this decade. But these declines (13.5 percent and 7.6 percent) were much more modest than the decline in the arts-and-sciences ratio (26.4 percent).

The implications of these developments for faculty staffing have been profound. One way to appreciate the magnitude of the impact is to ask what would have happened to the total number of faculty positions between 1977 and 1987 if the arts and sciences student/faculty ratio had remained at its 1977 level. Rather than increasing from 119,863 in 1977 to 139,350 in 1987, the number of faculty positions in the arts and sciences would have fallen to about 103,000. In short, there would have been 36,350 fewer faculty positions in 1987—about one-quarter of all positions that actually existed—had it not been for the sharp drop in the arts-and-sciences student/faculty ratio.[4]

The arts-and-sciences ratio declines consistently across sectors (see

[4] It would be easy to exaggerate the effects of these changes on the overall costs of education, especially at a time when this is such a sensitive and politically charged subject. The student/faculty ratio most relevant to the cost question is the conventional ratio (because it is the most inclusive in its definition of faculty members). The limited data available on trends in this ratio do not indicate significant changes over time. We are more confident in our estimates of changes in the ratio that relates students in all fields to full-time faculty with doctorates in all fields. As we saw above, that ratio declined about 13.5% over a ten-year period, which is roughly equivalent to a 1.5% annual rate of change. Instructional expenditures constitute about one-third of all current fund expenditures. Full-time faculty with doctorates constitute just over 60% of all staff (measured in FTE's) on the teaching budget and perhaps 75% of the faculty salary bill. Thus, as a very rough approximation, the decline in the student/faculty ratio between 1977 and 1987 could be said to have contributed between 0.25% and 0.5% of incremental direct cost per year.

Fig. 5.1). The smallest drop in the ratio occurred in Liberal Arts I (from 14.7 in 1977 to 13.2 in 1987), and it is no coincidence, we believe, that the smallest drop in the arts-and-sciences share of enrollment also occurred in this sector (from 67.3 percent in 1977 to 65.1 percent in 1987). The Research I universities rank next both in experiencing a smaller-than-average drop in their student/faculty ratio and in retaining their complement of arts-and-sciences students. The Comprehensive I and Other Four-Year institutions exhibit both an above-

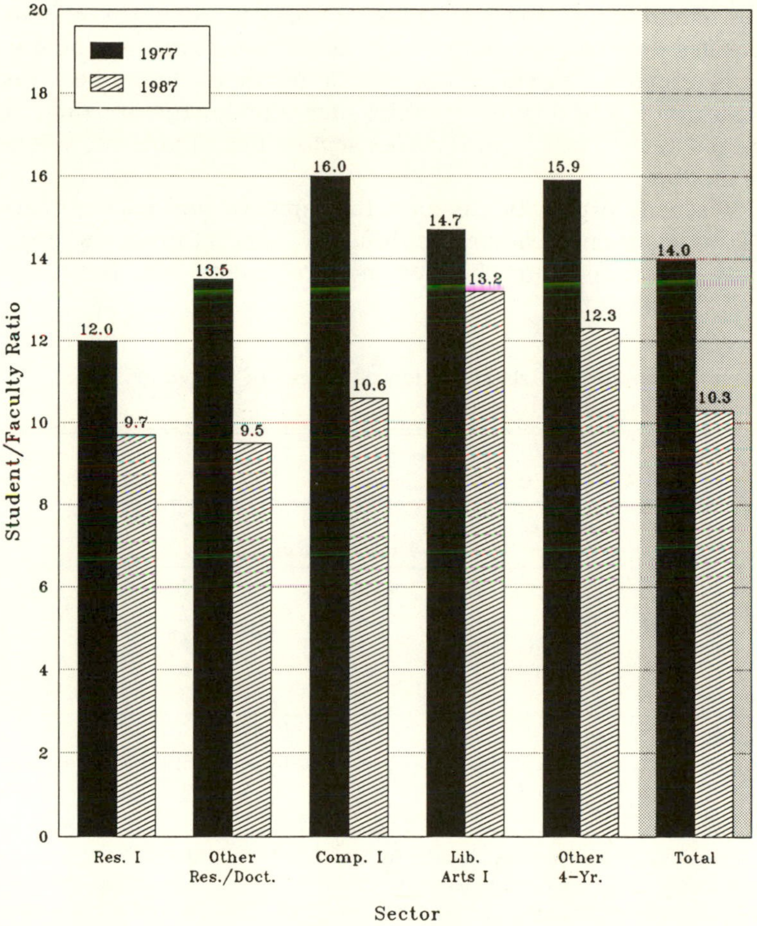

FIGURE 5.1
Arts-and-Sciences Student/Faculty Ratios, by Sector, 1977 and 1987
Source: See text.

average drop in their student/faculty ratios and the greatest drop in their arts-and-sciences shares of enrollment.[5]

There is a striking—and significant—correlation between the drop in the arts-and-sciences ratio by sector and the movement by students in the various sectors out of the arts and sciences. The relevant data are summarized below in Table 5.4.

There are two likely explanations. First, as we observed earlier, some of the teaching responsibilities of arts-and-sciences faculty members involve instruction of students pursuing non-arts-and-sciences degrees. And, of course, the greater the fall-off in the arts-and-sciences share of enrollment, the greater the number of students in other fields who need to be taught—with the arts-and-sciences faculty doing some of this teaching. The student/faculty ratios, then, should be adjusted to take account of this relationship; such an adjustment would bring changes in the "true" ratios across sectors even more into line with one another.

The second explanation is more fundamental and takes us back to an issue mentioned earlier: the difficulty—and at times the undesirability—of translating changes in enrollments into proportional

TABLE 5.4
Comparison of Changes in Arts-and-Sciences Shares of Enrollment and Student/Faculty Ratios, by Sector

	Arts-and-Sciences Enrollment Shares[a]			*Arts-and-Sciences Student/Faculty Ratios*[b]		
Sector	*1984 (%)*	*1976 (%)*	*Change (1984 ÷ 1976)*	*1987 (%)*	*1977 (%)*	*Change (1987 ÷ 1977)*
Liberal Arts I	65.1	67.3	0.97	13.2	14.7	0.90
Research I	29.6	33.6	0.88	9.7	12.0	0.81
Other Res./Doc.	23.5	28.7	0.82	9.5	13.5	0.70
Comprehensive I	27.2	19.6	0.72	10.6	16.0	0.66
Other Four-Year	33.3	23.3	0.70	12.3	15.9	0.77

[a]See Chapter Four.
[b]Arts-and-sciences student/faculty ratios are presented by sector in Table 5.1 and Fig. 5.1.

[5] The reader must be warned that the student/faculty ratios for 1977, by sector, were obtained through an elaborate adjustment process that was inescapable if any believable comparisons were to be made between 1977 and 1987. This adjustment process (which is explained in Appendix C) was necessary because a large number of institutions were reclassified within the Carnegie Classification categories between 1977 and 1987. Because of the complex nature of these adjustments, the ratios for 1977 are only approximate and should not be invested with specious precision. However, they do permit us to examine the pattern of changes in student/faculty ratios by sector.

changes in faculty staffing. Tenure is often cited as one obstacle to reducing faculty positions in fields in which enrollment is shrinking. When the movement away from the arts and sciences started, many departments must have had large numbers of members who had recently received tenure but who were not close to retirement age.[6]

Quite apart from the formal constraints imposed by tenure, there is the natural tendency to retain current staffing complements. This is partly a matter of inertia, and partly a matter of intelligent institutional management, which involves some willingness to wait and see if a recovery in enrollments will occur. It is also partly a response to the need to maintain a critical mass of faculty in a field even if enrollments decline.

There are often larger interests to be served. Certain specialized fields of knowledge need to be protected and sustained because of their broad cultural significance and their national and even international importance. For example, for many decades the academic study of East and Southeast Asia was carried forward as an intellectual and "national" investment by a small number of universities in spite of extraordinarily small student enrollments. By any conventional standard, such programs were utterly cost-ineffective. Yet now considerable numbers of students are studying Chinese, Japanese, and other Asian subjects, partly in response to dramatic changes in the worldwide economic and political climate. Had universities not continued to invest in these fields during the decades of low enrollments, the capacity to respond to current student needs and interests simply would not have been there.

An examination of changes in arts-and-sciences ratios by field of study reveals related forces at work. As can be seen from Figure 5.2, these ratios fell in all fields of study except for the physical sciences, which had the lowest ratio of any field throughout the decade. Mathematics experienced a relatively small drop. Very substantial drops in student/faculty ratios occurred in the humanities and social sciences (from 16.0 to 10.8), in the biological sciences (12.7 to 7.5), and in psychology (19.5 to 14.4).[7]

[6] The effects of tenure on both the efficiency of institutions of higher education and educational costs are frequently misunderstood. Of course, much depends on how tenure systems are administered. A paper by Michael S. McPherson and Gordon C. Winston (1988) concludes that "the tenure/probation system is a reasonable response to the highly specialized nature of academic work and to the long training such work requires" (p. 194).

[7] These ratios differ from those presented elsewhere in this chapter in that they include students and faculty in the Specialized and Other institutions, as well as in

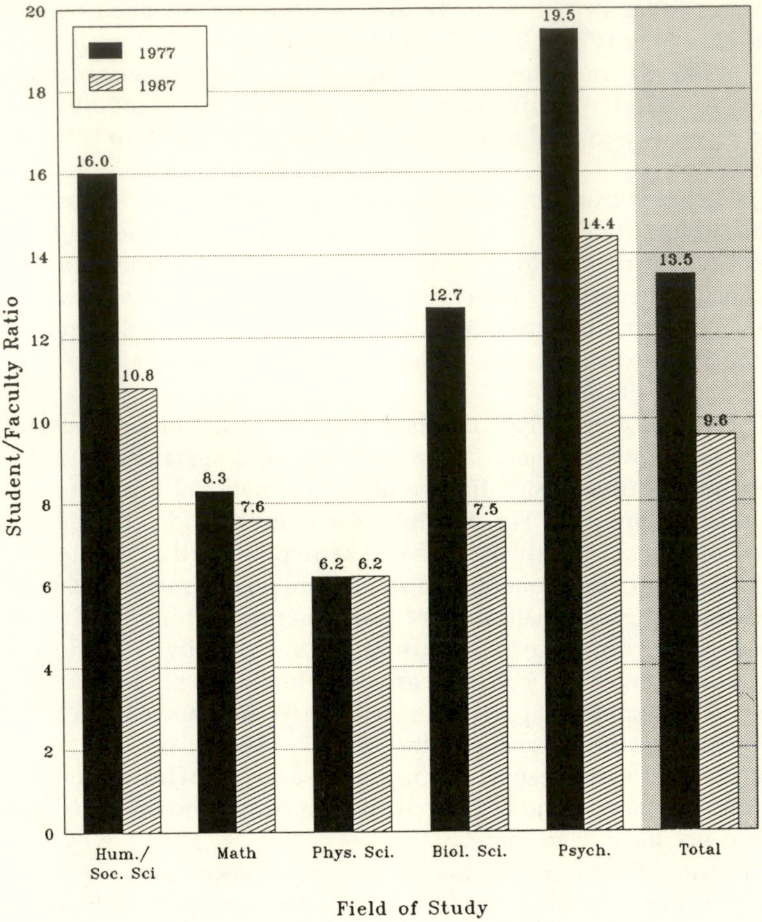

FIGURE 5.2
Arts-and-Sciences Student/Faculty Ratios, by Field
Source: See text.
Note: Ratios are for all sectors except Two-Year institutions.

Failure to allow for the strength of such powerful (and very non-mechanical) characteristics of faculty staffing can lead to errors, including overstatements of the probable adverse effects on academic labor markets of projections of declining enrollments. Therefore, it is

---

our five major sectors. Since Specialized institutions have relatively low student/faculty ratios, all aggregate ratios that include Specialized will be slightly lower. It should also be noted that biological sciences is particularly affected by the inclusion of the Specialized institutions, primarily because this sector includes medical schools with separate campuses.

important to incorporate the lessons of this historical analysis into our projections of future demand for faculty.

Projecting Student/Faculty Ratios and Net New Faculty Positions

The marked decline in student/faculty ratios over the last decade is unambiguous. The implications for the future, however, are far less clear. Time lags in the system, as well as interactions between student/faculty ratios and trends in enrollment, complicate the task of developing projections of faculty positions. Several interpretations of recent experience are possible.

- One inference is that there is a long-term trend toward ever-lower student/faculty ratios, and that we should simply extrapolate the pattern that we have observed.
- An opposite inference is that a very large drop in student/faculty ratios has already occurred, largely as a result of a lagged response in staffing decisions to declining enrollments in the arts and sciences. We might then expect at least a mild movement back toward the higher ratios of earlier years, as institutions reallocate faculty positions away from the arts and sciences to fields where enrollment pressures have become greater.
- An intermediate inference also deserves consideration. We could assume that the forces causing the arts-and-sciences student/faculty ratios to decline have played themselves out, but that there is no reason to expect a reversal of recent trends. Student/faculty ratios could remain rather steady, at their 1987 levels, for the foreseeable future.

There is no compelling evidence that would lead us to choose one of these propositions over the others. Thus, we have chosen to make use of several assumptions that allow us to examine closely the implications of adopting one or another projection of student/faculty ratios. Since student/faculty ratios are a matter for policy determination—and are certainly not determined by some kind of *deus ex machina*—this approach has the further advantage of showing what the consequences of various possible institutional decisions will be for academic employment.[8]

[8] In the analysis that follows, we assume no changes in either the ratio of part-time to full-time faculty or the ratio of faculty holding doctorates to all faculty. In note 2 above, we showed how these ratios can be combined with other data to obtain more conventional student/faculty ratios. The available data show no evidence of any significant trend in the part-time ratio. (See Tuckman and Pickerill 1988, top panel of Fig. 2, p. 105; Brown 1987, Fig. 1, p. 8; and Gappa 1984, Table 3.) Nor is there evidence of

Constant Student/Faculty Ratios

The simplest and perhaps most plausible assumption is that there will be no further changes in arts-and-sciences student/faculty ratios. To generate projections of net new faculty positions, we must combine this assumption with each of the three projections of arts-and-sciences enrollment developed in the previous chapter: Option A (Continuing Decline); Option B (Steady State); and Option C (Recovery).

Looking first at the implications for net new faculty positions in all of the arts and sciences, we see from Figure 5.3 that Options A and B both imply decreases between 1987 and 1992, and then again between 1992 and 1997, when an ascent begins. This projection restores the number of net new positions under the Steady-State option (Option B) essentially to the 1987 level by 2002, with a further increase in 2007. Projected net new positions under the Continuing Decline option (Option A) never regain the 1987 level. In contrast, the Recovery option (Option C) shows quite substantial increases above the 1987 level in every five-year interval.

The variations in projections of net new positions are far greater for the humanities/social sciences than for other fields (see Fig. 5.4). This is because humanities/social sciences is both the largest cluster (slightly larger, in fact, than the other two clusters combined) and has been seen to be more susceptible to sharp swings in student interest.[9]

Declining Student/Faculty Ratios

We now relax the assumption that student/faculty ratios remain constant at the 1987 levels and, instead, permit these ratios to decline. More specifically, we assume that the arts-and-sciences student/faculty ratio declines one percent per year over the 1987–92 interval. This is equivalent to setting the student/faculty ratios for all fields and sectors in 1992 equal to 95 percent of the corresponding ratios in the base year of 1987. There must eventually be some dampening of such declines if faculty costs are to be budgeted properly, and so we also

any significant change between 1975 and 1984 in doctorates as a percentage of all faculty in all institutions of higher education (see *1986–1987 Fact Book on Higher Education*, Table 118).

[9] Projections for all three clusters, under all options, are shown in Appendix Tables D.8 through D.11. These tables also provide separate data by sector and summarize all the projections.

assume that student/faculty ratios will fall 2½ percent more during the next five-year interval (1992–97) and then remain constant.[10]

These assumptions seem plausible when combined with enrollment assumptions that do not project significant increases in enrollments

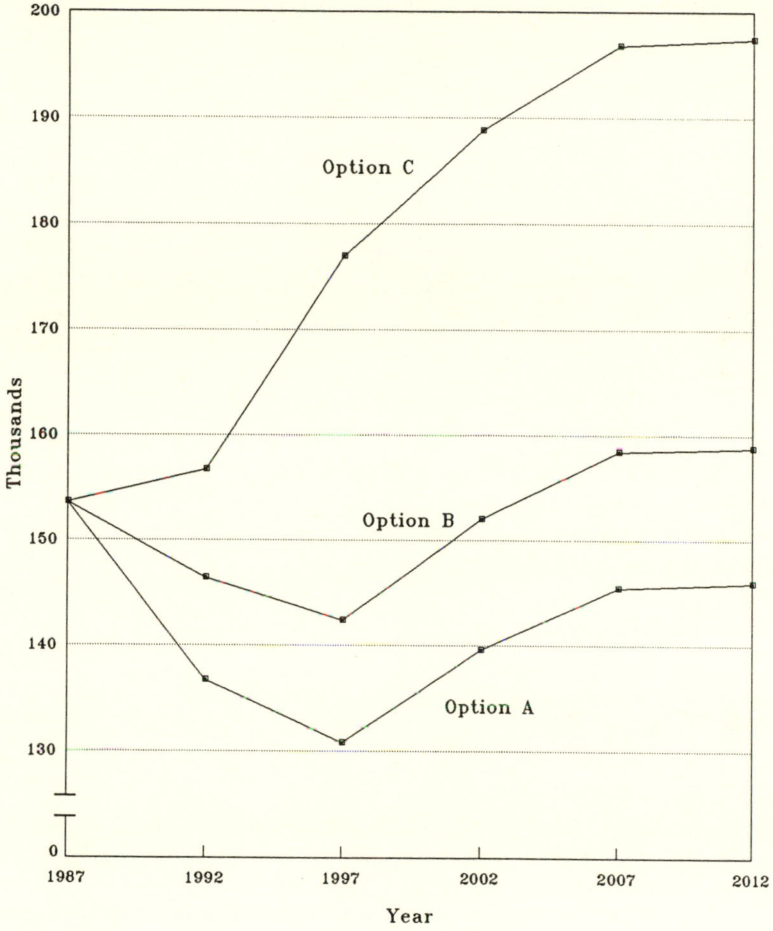

FIGURE 5.3
Projections of Net New Positions in the Arts and Sciences, Assuming Constant Student/Faculty Ratios

Source: See text.

Note: The arts-and-sciences share of enrollment is assumed to vary under each option. Option A assumes Continuing Decline, Option B assumes Steady State, and Option C assumes Recovery.

---

[10] The assumed rate of decline between 1987 and 1992 of 1% per year is roughly equivalent to the average annual rate of decline between 1977 and 1987 in the all-

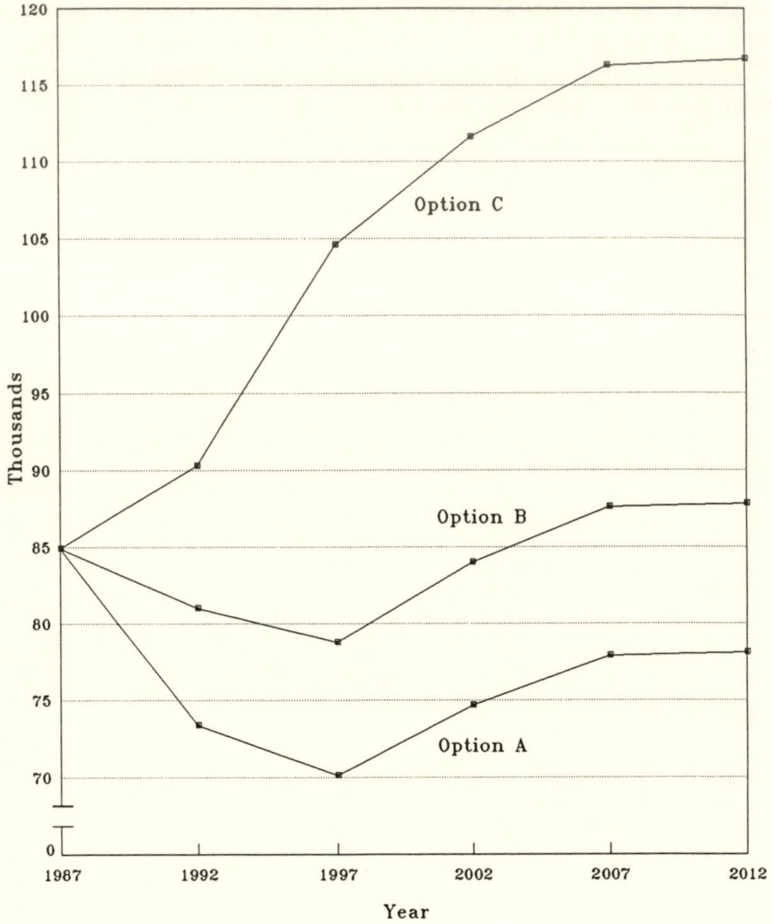

FIGURE 5.4
Projections of Net New Positions in the Humanities and Social Sciences, Assuming Constant Student/Faculty Ratios

Source: See text.

Note: The arts-and-sciences share of enrollment is assumed to vary under each option. Option A assumes Continuing Decline, Option B assumes Steady State, and Option C assumes Recovery.

---

student/arts-and-sciences faculty ratio (see Table 5.3). This is a useful benchmark because it indicates what happened to student/faculty ratios in the recent past independent of the particularly sharp drops in the arts-and-sciences shares of enrollment that dominated the more narrowly defined arts-and-sciences student/faculty ratios. These arts-and-sciences ratios fell roughly three times faster—about 3% per year on average. It seems highly unlikely that this rate of decline can persist, especially in the absence of continued rapid shifts of enrollment away from the arts and sciences.

in the arts and sciences. Figures 5.5 and 5.6 show the implications for faculty staffing. For reasons that will be given below, it seems unlikely that further declines in student/faculty ratios would accompany a real recovery in arts-and-sciences enrollments, and so we do not combine these projections of student/faculty ratios with Option C enrollment projections.

As expected, the lower student/faculty ratios dampen considerably the negative effects of further declines in the arts-and-sciences share of enrollments (Fig. 5.5). The projected decreases in net new faculty

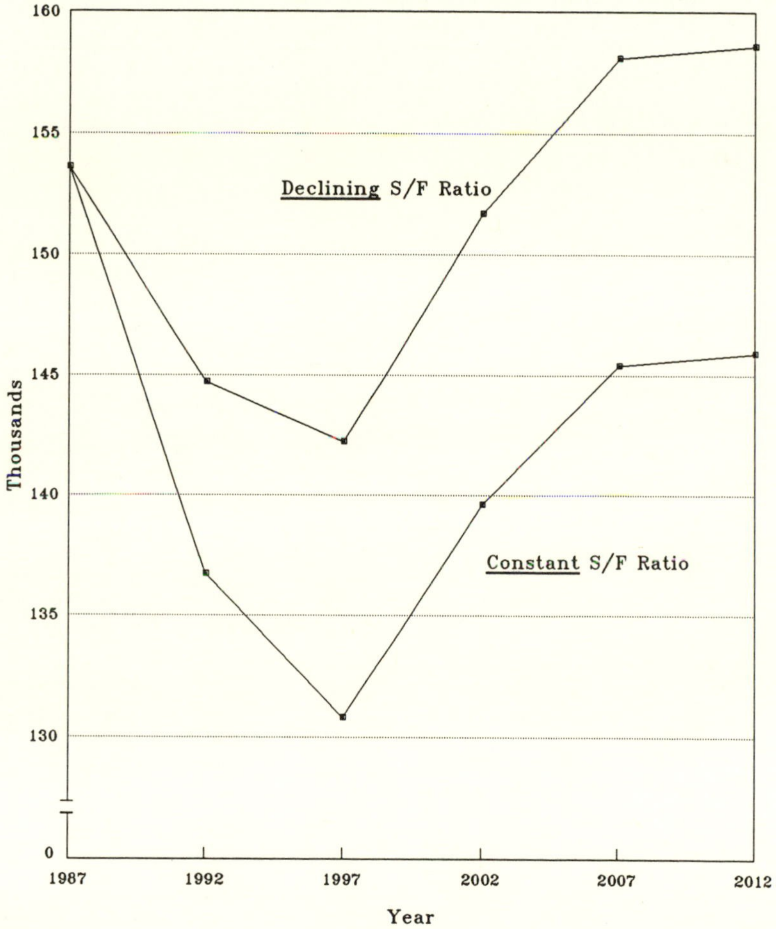

FIGURE 5.5
Projections of Net New Positions, under Option A Enrollment Assumptions and Alternative Student/Faculty Ratios

Source: See text.

Note: Option A assumes Continuing Decline in the arts-and-sciences share of enrollment.

positions are cut essentially in half. Still, this "cushioning" is not great enough to offset fully the effects of the Option A enrollment projections. Under these combined assumptions, we continue to project numbers of net new positions below the 1987 levels for at least fifteen years.

Combining the declining student/faculty ratios with the Steady-State enrollment projections (Fig. 5.6) produces different results. The declines in net new faculty positions between 1987 and 1997 produced by the assumption of constant student/faculty ratios are converted into generally stable faculty complements.

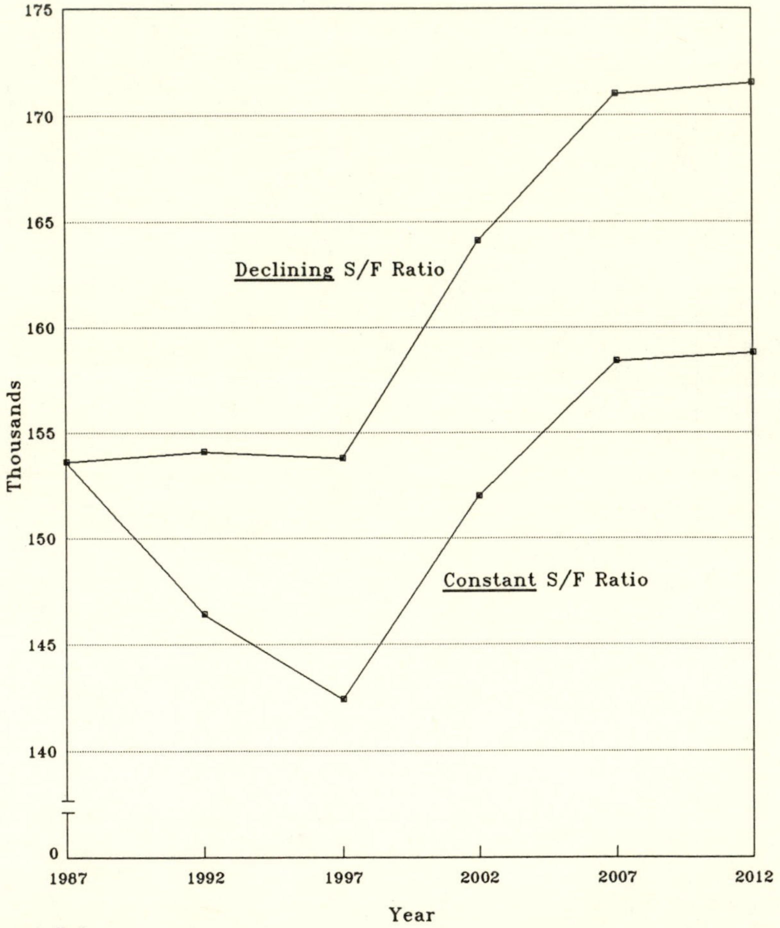

FIGURE 5.6
Projections of Net New Positions, under Option B Enrollment Assumptions and Alternative Student/Faculty Ratios

Source: See text.

Note: Option B assumes Steady State in the arts-and-sciences share of enrollment.

Increasing Student/Faculty Ratios

We do not see a basis either in *a priori* reasoning or in historical evidence for anticipating general increases in student/faculty ratios. If there were a severe financial crisis in higher education, institutions might feel compelled to ask faculty members to teach more students, but that would be a special situation. Of course, anyone who believes that student/faculty ratios will rise should anticipate fewer net new faculty positions than are projected here. As stated above, this is not our expectation.

There is one set of (non-financial) circumstances, however, that could lead to higher student/faculty ratios. If enrollments in the arts and sciences were to increase significantly—in line, for instance, with the assumptions of Option C (Recovery)—then we would expect that some of these additional students would be taught by faculty members who are already employed. Just as faculty staffing decisions tend to be somewhat unresponsive to declining enrollment, so too are they likely to be somewhat unresponsive to increasing enrollment.[11]

Therefore, if—contrary to our expectations—enrollments in the arts and sciences were to increase substantially, we would not expect commensurate increases in staffing. The significant decline in student/faculty ratios that has accompanied the flight from the arts and sciences has produced a situation in which there may be some slack in faculty staffing in these fields.

Since we believe that it would be a mistake to translate projections of increased enrollment into proportionate increases in net new faculty positions, we assumed modest increases in the student/faculty ratio in the context of the rising enrollments called for by the Recovery option. Specifically, these projections envision increases in student/faculty ratios of 5 percent between 1992 and 1997 (when most of the recovery in arts-and-sciences enrollments is projected to occur), and then 2½ percent between 1997 and 2002. Student/faculty ratios are then projected to remain constant.

The consequences of these assumptions for the Option C projections are shown in Figure 5.7. The dampening of the projected increases in net new faculty positions caused by allowing even this modest rise in student/faculty ratios seems right to us. This new projection is more plausible than the earlier Option C projections, which made no provision for any interaction between rising enrollments and rising student/faculty ratios.

[11] There is some historical evidence, and some evidence based on cross-sectional studies, to support this proposition. See Cartter 1976, pp. 102–07, and Radner and Miller 1975, ch. 7.

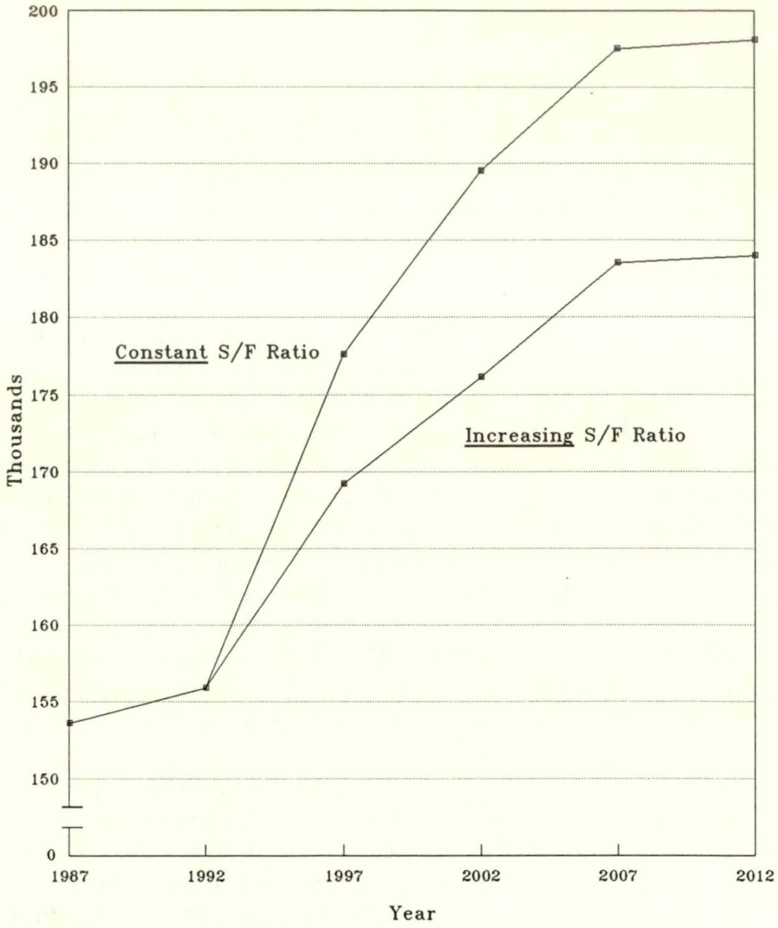

FIGURE 5.7
Projections of Net New Positions, under Option C Enrollment Assumptions and Alternative Student/Faculty Ratios

Source: See text.

Note: Option C assumes Recovery in the arts-and-sciences share of enrollment.

FOUR BASIC MODELS FOR PROJECTING NET NEW FACULTY POSITIONS

Out of the array of possibilities considered in Chapters Four and Five, we have selected four basic models. Each combines a particular enrollment projection with a particular projection of student/faculty ratios. These four models represent, we believe, the most important alternatives for future faculty staffing. Taken together, they define a range of realistic possibilities and form the basis for the supply and demand projections presented in Chapter Seven.

- Model I: Continuing declines in arts-and-sciences shares of enrollment are combined with declining student/faculty ratios.
- Model II: Steady-State projections of arts-and-sciences shares of enrollment are combined with constant student/faculty ratios.
- Model III: Steady-State projections of arts-and-sciences shares of enrollment are combined with declining student/faculty ratios.
- Model IV: Recovery projections of arts-and-sciences shares of enrollment are combined with increasing student/faculty ratios.

The projections of net new faculty positions (which can of course be either positive or negative) implied by these four models are summarized graphically in Figures 5.8–5.11. Each figure shows the projections by clusters of fields for a single model for five-year intervals from 1987–92 through 2007–12. The sum of these field-specific pro-

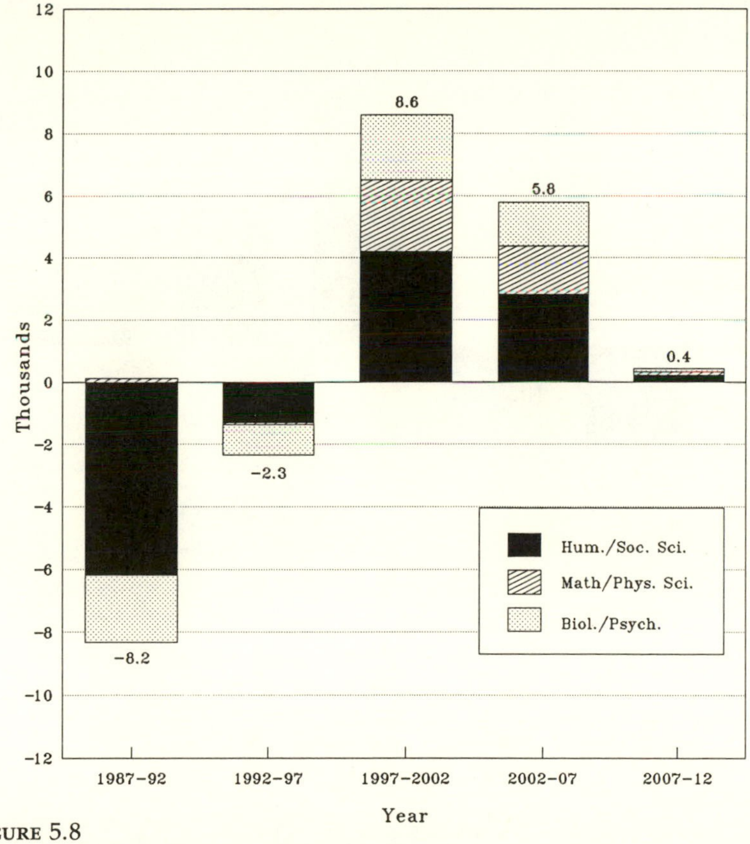

FIGURE 5.8
Projections of Net New Positions: Model I
Source: Appendix Table D.8.
Note: In Model I, continuing declines in the arts-and-sciences share of enrollment are combined with declining student/faculty ratios.

jections, for the arts and sciences as a whole, is indicated at the top or bottom of each bar.

Figures 5.8 and 5.9, which represent Models I and II, are similar in all important respects. This may, at first, seem surprising. The explanation is that the interactions between enrollment trends and student/faculty ratios bring the two sets of projections together. If we had made the same assumption about student/faculty ratios in the two models, Figure 5.8 would have shown much greater drops in projected net new faculty positions until 1997 and then smaller increases. However, the assumption of a declining student/faculty ratio in Model I dampens these swings and brings them closely into line with the Steady-State projections of Model II.

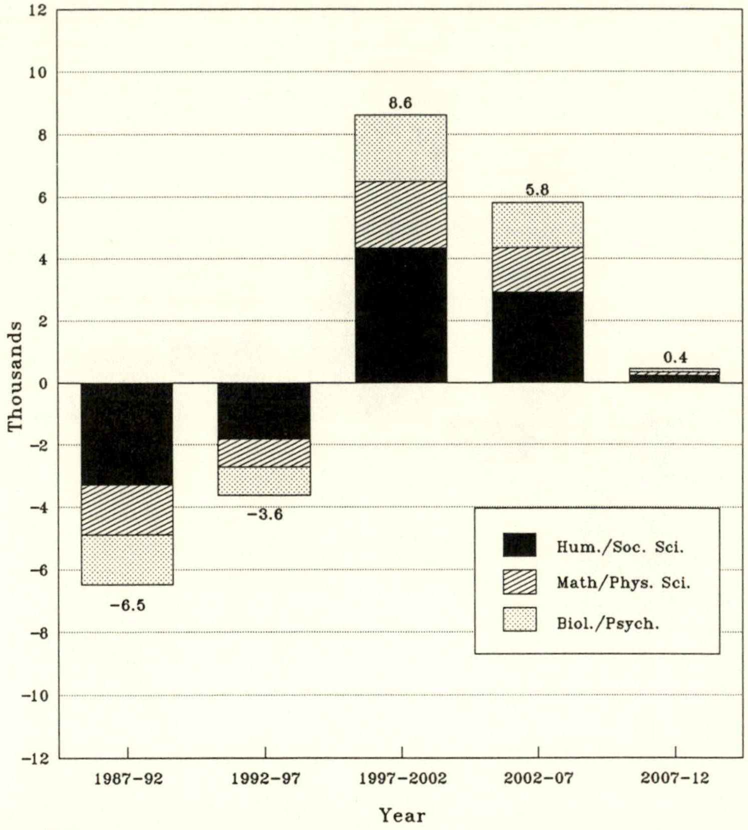

FIGURE 5.9
Projections of Net New Positions: Model II

Source: Appendix Table D.9.

Note: In Model II, steady-state projections of the arts-and-sciences share of enrollment are combined with constant student/faculty ratios.

In these two models, the number of net new faculty positions is projected to decline by slightly more than 10,000 over the combined periods 1987–92 and 1992–97. The number of net new positions is then projected to increase by about 8,600 in 1997–2002 and 5,800 in 2002–07. The final period shows no significant increase or decrease. As is true of all models, the humanities and social sciences cluster consistently accounts for the largest fraction of net new positions.

Model III, which is shown in Figure 5.10, demonstrates clearly the importance of a declining student/faculty ratio when arts-and-sciences shares of enrollment are constant. The projected declines in net new positions implied by Model II are now gone. According to this model,

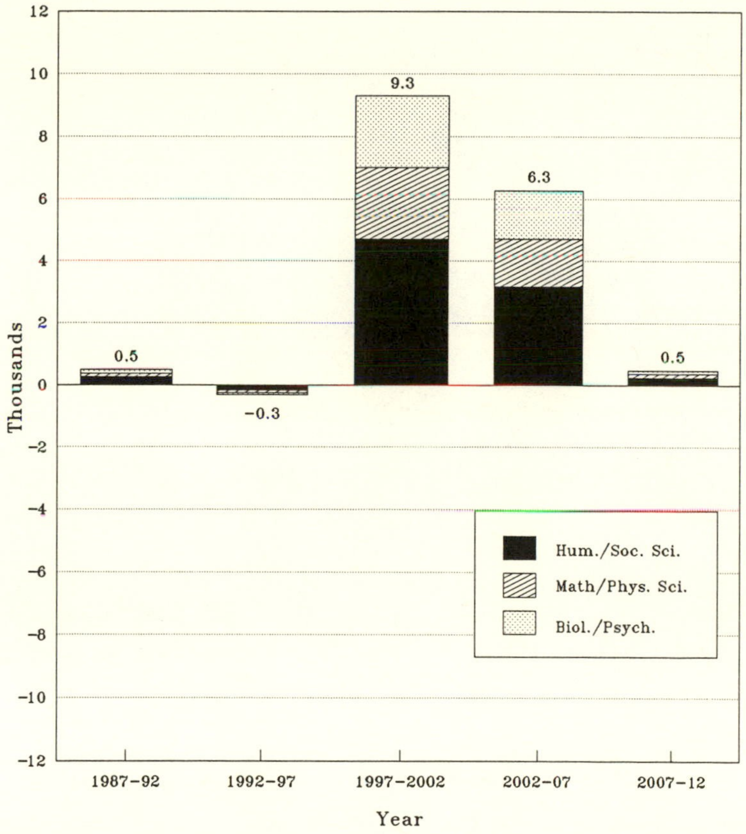

FIGURE 5.10
Projections of Net New Positions: Model III
Source: Appendix Table D.10.
Note: In Model III, steady-state projections of the arts-and-sciences share of enrollment are combined with declining student/faculty ratios.

the number of positions in all clusters can be expected to be stable for the next ten years, when a significant increase is projected.

Model IV, shown in Figure 5.11, demonstrates the powerful effect of allowing the arts-and-sciences shares of enrollment to recover the ground that has been lost. The number of net new positions is now decidedly positive in all periods, in spite of the presumed increase in student/faculty ratios during 1987–92 and 1992–97.

These projections of net new faculty positions will be combined (in

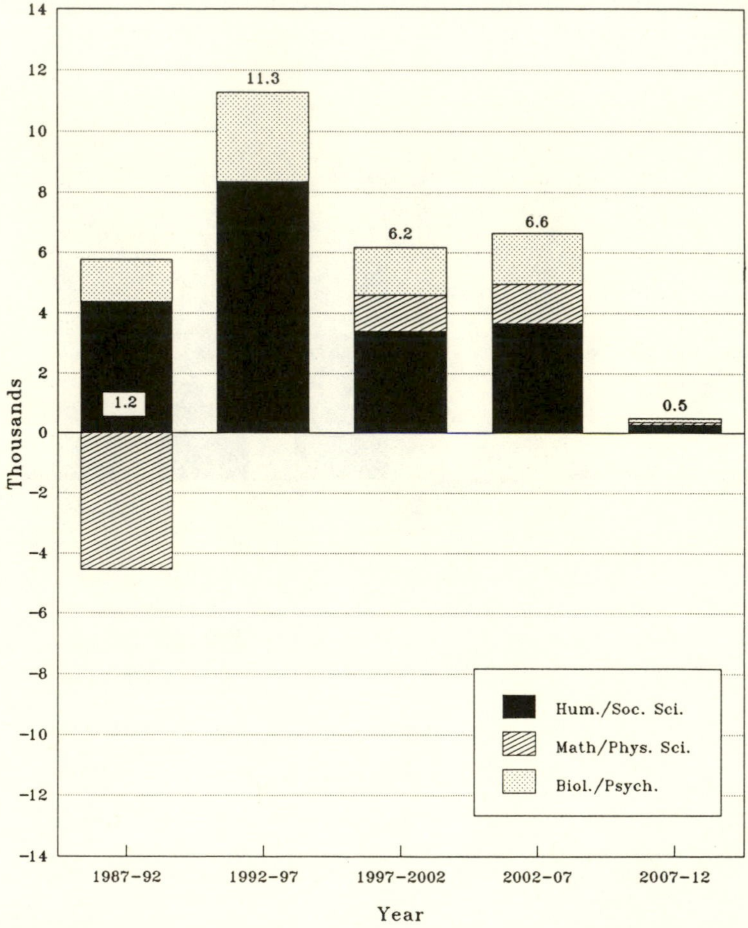

FIGURE 5.11
Projections of Net New Positions: Model IV

Source: Appendix Table D.11.

Note: In Model IV, recovery projections of the arts-and-sciences share of enrollment are combined with increasing student/faculty ratios.

Chapter Seven) with projections of replacement demand and of supply to create what we regard as an informative series of pictures of future academic labor markets. Although there is no reason to anticipate the dramatic changes in population or in aggregate FTE enrollment that had such pronounced effects on higher education in the postwar years, the outlook for the next decades is no less complex. As we have seen, much will depend on evolving student interests in the arts and sciences, as well as on the student/faculty ratios that have such direct implications for faculty positions.

CHAPTER SIX

The Supply of New Doctorates

TRADITIONALLY, a large majority of faculty appointees have been younger people who have recently completed—or are about to complete—their graduate work. Thus, any analysis of the pool of candidates for faculty positions must begin with a careful examination of the number of new doctorates in the relevant fields of study. Over the last thirty years, there have been wide fluctuations in the number of new doctorates, and a principal task of this chapter is to use recent experience to project the supply of new doctorates likely to be available for faculty positions in the arts and sciences.

The total number of new doctorates overstates substantially the number of candidates for such positions. Significant numbers of new doctorates are awarded in fields other than the arts and sciences. In addition, foreign students have earned relatively larger numbers of doctorates in recent years, and non-academic employment has exerted a growing appeal. At the end of this chapter we will also consider reasons why there is increasing concern about the quality of the pool of new doctorates—hard as it is to measure quality.

TRENDS IN THE NUMBER OF NEW DOCTORATES

Fortunately, reliable data can be derived from the Survey of Earned Doctorates (SED), which has been conducted annually since 1958 by the National Research Council. As they complete requirements for their doctoral degrees, graduate students provide a considerable amount of basic information—such as year of Ph.D., elapsed time between B.A. and Ph.D., gender, race, citizenship status, field of study, and type of graduate institution attended.[1]

Over the past three decades, there has been nearly a four-fold increase in the number of doctorates earned annually. However, almost

[1] See Appendix A. In this discussion, we use "doctorates" and "Ph.D.'s" interchangeably. While the SED data include doctorates of all kinds, the number of doctorates other than Ph.D.'s is small in the arts and sciences. The largest group by far consists of Doctorates of Music (328 in 1987). For reasons explained in Appendix A, we excluded these doctorates from the SED data used to examine trends in doctorates in the arts and sciences.

all of this phenomenal increase occurred in the first half of the period. Between 1958 and 1972, the number of doctorates awarded each year by U.S. universities in all fields of study rose from 8,800 to 33,000. This extraordinary growth—which coincided with a boom in hiring and may also have been related in part to draft deferments—then ended as abruptly as it started. For the last 15 years or so, the number of doctorates awarded annually has fluctuated within a relatively narrow range—from about 30,000 to about 33,000 (see Fig. 6.1).

In recent years, there has been some increase in the number of new doctorates in nearly all fields, but the annual increments have been quite small. Recipients numbered 32,278 in 1987, an increase of just 1.4 percent over the previous year. Moreover, while the number of doctorates awarded in 1987 was the largest since 1976, the number

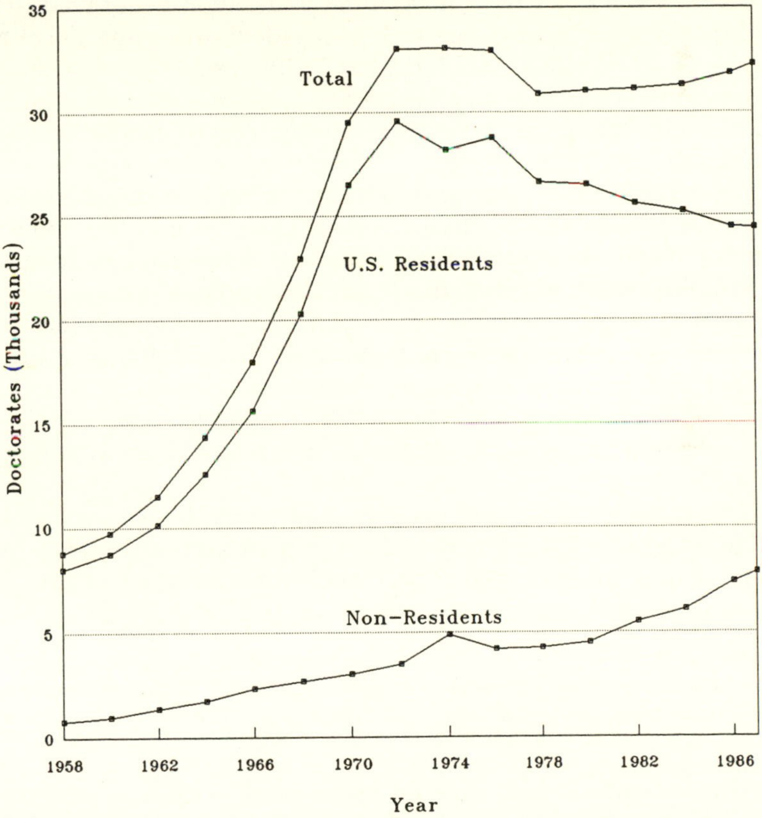

FIGURE 6.1
Doctorates Awarded in All Fields, 1958–87
Source: SED surveys.

of recipients still fell short of the peak reached in 1973, when 33,755 doctorates were earned.

Citizenship

In the last twenty-five years, the composition of the group receiving doctorates, classified by citizenship, has changed significantly. The percentage of all doctorates awarded to U.S. residents fell from 85.6 percent in 1962 to 72.3 percent in 1987. That is, almost one-quarter of all recipients of doctorates in 1987 were not residents of the United States. The raw numbers tell the story even more emphatically: in 1958, 600 non-residents earned doctorates in U.S. universities; by 1987, this number had risen to 5,600.[2]

The rough stability in the overall number of doctorates awarded annually since 1972 can be misleading if attention is not paid to the citizenship mix. The number of U.S. residents receiving doctorates has declined steadily since the early 1970s, and only now may be reaching a plateau. The number of non-residents receiving degrees, on the other hand, has increased steadily, almost exactly offsetting the decline in U.S. recipients.

Major questions of policy are raised by the mix of doctoral recipients classified by citizenship status. To what extent is it in this country's interest to educate citizens of other nations? Do we have an obligation to make this kind of contribution? Are there political as well as other benefits to be gained? What are the effects of foreign graduate students on the education of students from this country and on the overall academic programs of our universities? If there are benefits to both the United States and the "home" countries, how should the costs of providing graduate education to foreign nationals be apportioned?[3]

Though important, these questions fall outside the scope of this study. More relevant to our immediate purposes is the much narrower issue of how the presence of such significant numbers of non-residents in the pool of earned doctorates affects the supply of candidates

[2] We use the term "U.S. residents" to include not only respondents who are U.S. citizens, native or naturalized, but also permanent residents. "Non-residents" are those who are in this country on temporary visas. We also include under this heading those whose citizenship is "unknown," since trends in these numbers parallel trends for "temporary residents." This is hardly surprising, in that we would presume that non-residents are more likely than residents to decline to answer a question about citizenship. These citizenship data are from the SED, including both regularly published summaries and special tabulations prepared for this study.

[3] There is considerable literature on this subject. See, for example, National Research Council 1988c; and Barber 1985.

for faculty positions in U.S. colleges and universities. Needless to say, relatively smaller numbers of these recipients remain in this country, and their status is at times dependent on such factors as the state of international relations and the policies of both this country and other countries concerning immigration and emigration. The percentage of temporary residents who reported in 1986 that they intended to remain in the United States following graduation was 35.6; the corresponding percentages for U.S. citizens and permanent residents were, respectively, 92.4 and 74.5.[4]

The number of non-residents, and their inclinations to pursue academic careers in this country, vary significantly by field of study. Accordingly, we will defer the question of how to take account of citizenship mix until we have examined trends in the number of doctorates by field of study.

Trends in New Doctorates by Field of Study

One of this country's greatest resources is its human capital, and for that reason alone there is independent interest in the number of new doctorates in fields of study ranging from mathematics to foreign languages and literatures.

Doctorates in the arts and sciences as a whole comprise about one-half of all doctorates conferred today in the United States. (See Fig. 6.2 for a comparison of doctorates awarded in the arts and sciences with doctorates awarded in all fields from 1958 through 1987, along with corresponding data for U.S. residents only.) Those whose experience is primarily in the arts and sciences may be surprised to learn how many doctorates are awarded in other fields—and how much of an increase there has been in doctorates awarded outside the arts and sciences.

In 1987, for example, there were 17,123 doctorates awarded in the arts and sciences—including 3,004 in the humanities, 2,620 in the social sciences, 6,922 in biological sciences and psychology, and 4,577 in mathematics and the physical sciences. In that same year, there were approximately 6,500 doctorates awarded in education, about 3,700 in engineering, about 1,100 in agriculture, and nearly 1,000 in business.

While the general shape of the historical trend in the number of

[4] Survey of Earned Doctorates 1986, p. 5. It should be noted, however, that these percentages were derived from that component of the population of doctorates which reported definite post-graduate plans (about two-thirds of all recipients). We have no way of knowing what these percentages would have been if it had been possible to obtain reliable information for the other one-third of the population.

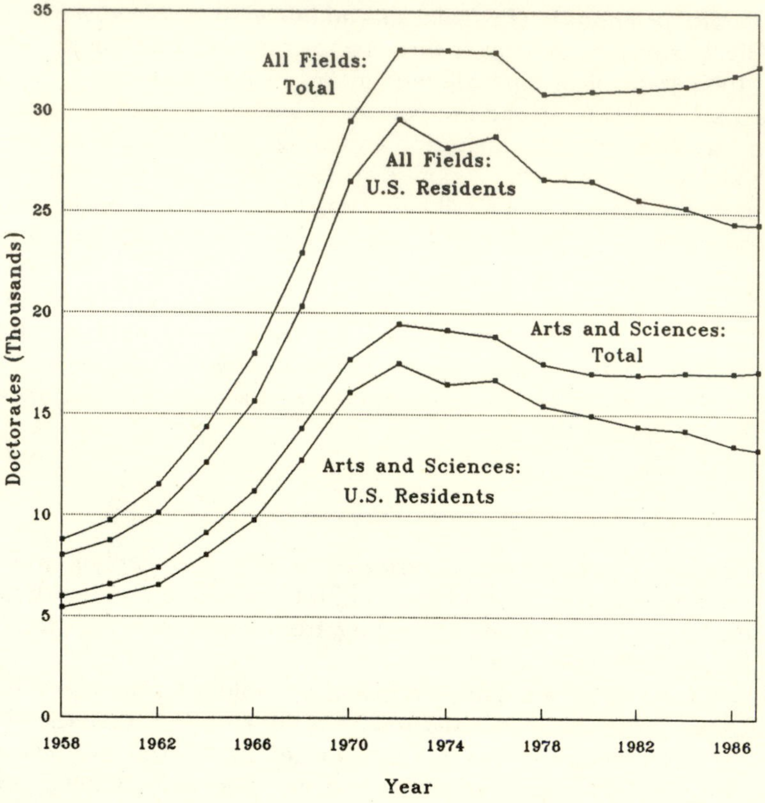

FIGURE 6.2
Doctorates Awarded in the Arts and Sciences and in All Fields, 1958–87
Source: SED surveys.

doctorates awarded in the arts and sciences is similar to the trend for all doctorates, there are also some interesting variations—especially over the last six or seven years. Figure 6.2 shows that the gap between the number of doctorates in all fields and the number of doctorates in the arts and sciences has widened. Put another way, while the total number of doctorates in all fields has shown at least a mild upward trend since 1978, the number of doctorates in the arts and sciences has at best remained constant over this interval. The most significant fact is that the number of doctorates awarded *to U.S. residents* in the arts and sciences has declined rather steadily right through 1987.

Job candidates and prospective employers are most interested in what is happening in particular fields, such as physics and history, and Figures 6.3–6.10 show recent trends for the main fields of study within the arts and sciences. An even finer breakdown is provided

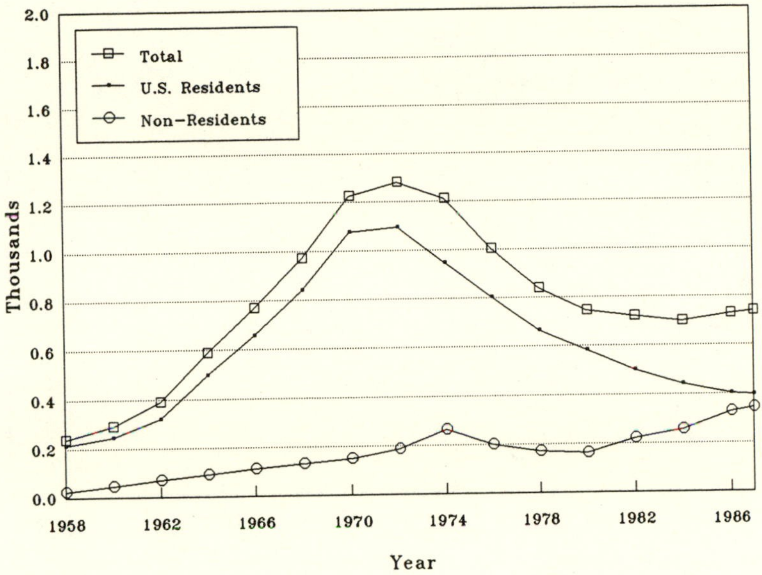

FIGURE 6.3
Doctorates Awarded in Mathematics, 1958–87
Source: SED surveys.

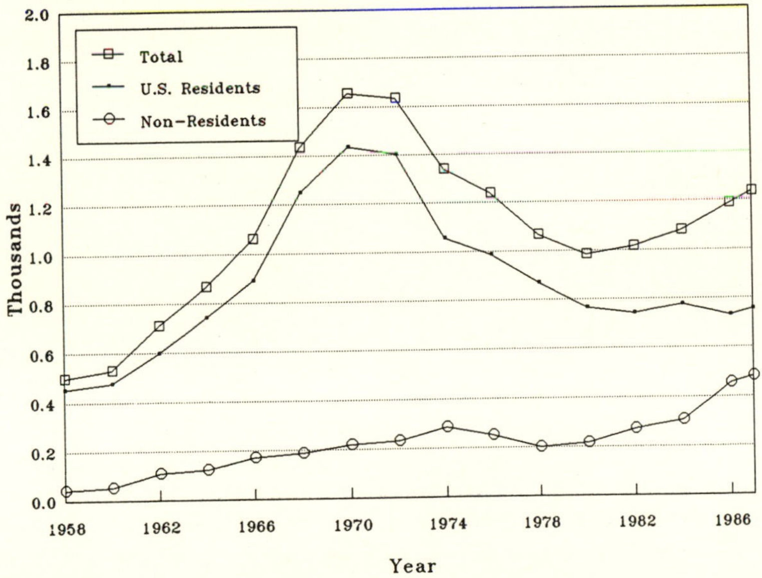

FIGURE 6.4
Doctorates Awarded in Physics/Astronomy, 1958–87
Source: SED surveys.

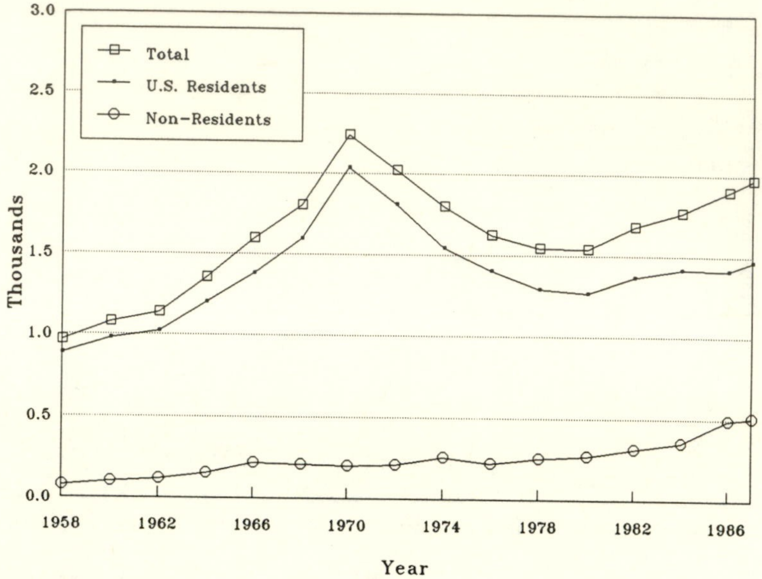

FIGURE 6.5
Doctorates Awarded in Chemistry, 1958–87
Source: SED surveys.

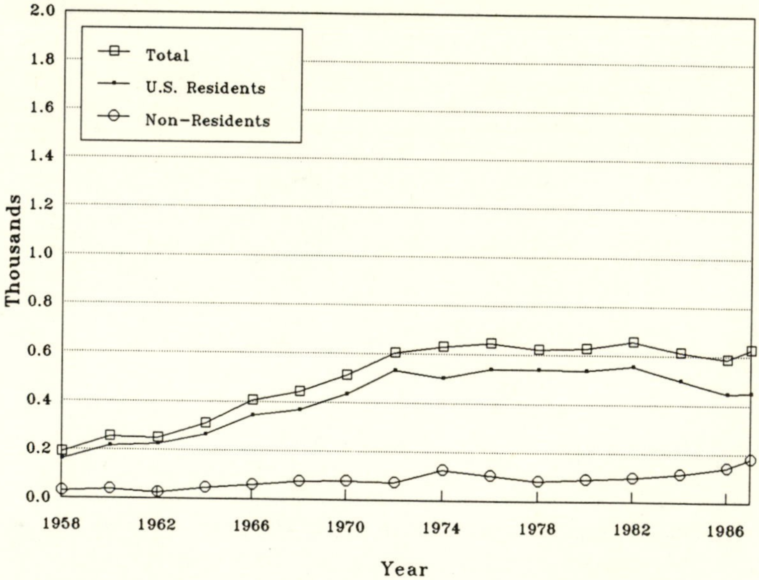

FIGURE 6.6
Doctorates Awarded in Earth Sciences, 1958–87
Source: SED surveys.

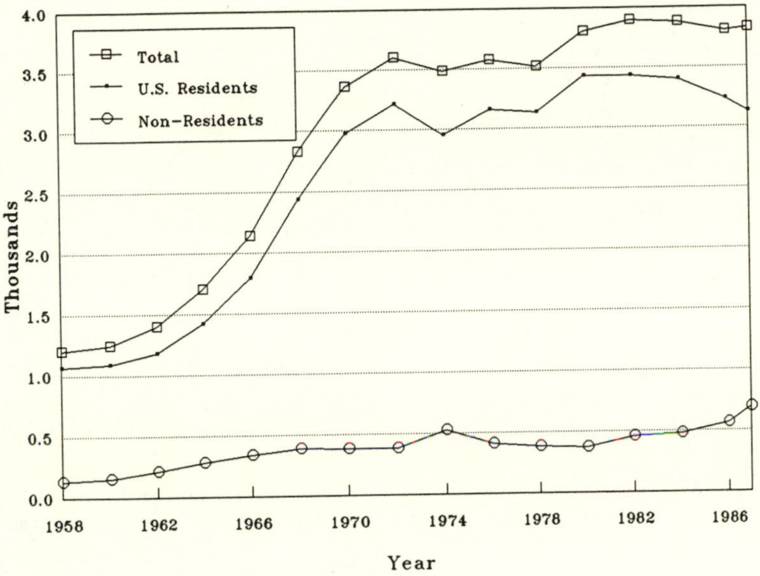

FIGURE 6.7
Doctorates Awarded in Biological Sciences, 1958–87
Source: SED surveys.

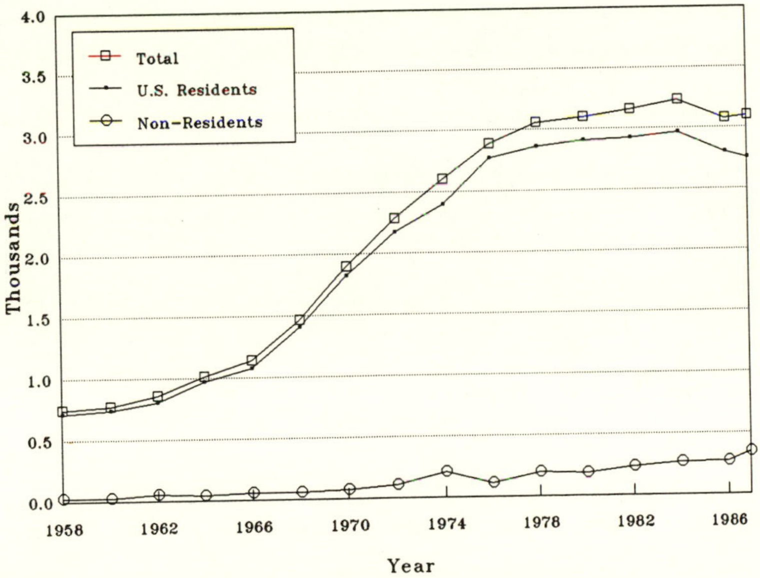

FIGURE 6.8
Doctorates Awarded in Psychology, 1958–87
Source: SED surveys.

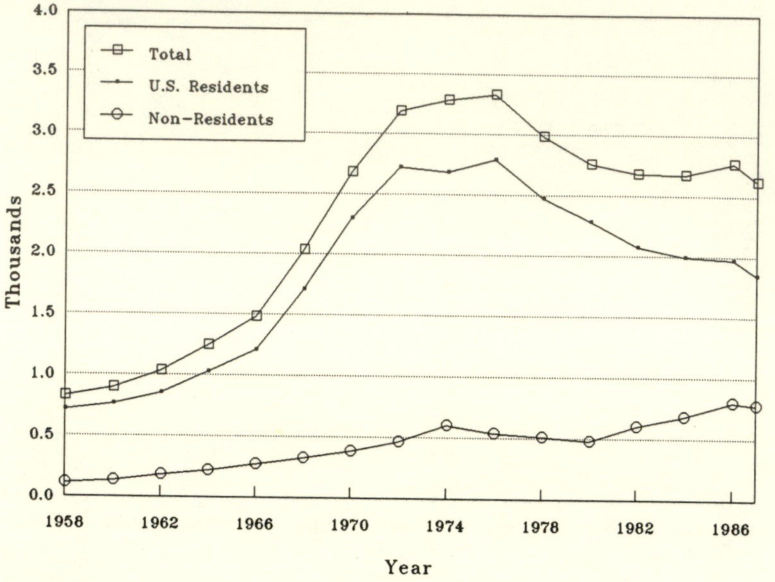

FIGURE 6.9
Doctorates Awarded in Social Sciences, 1958–87
Source: SED surveys.

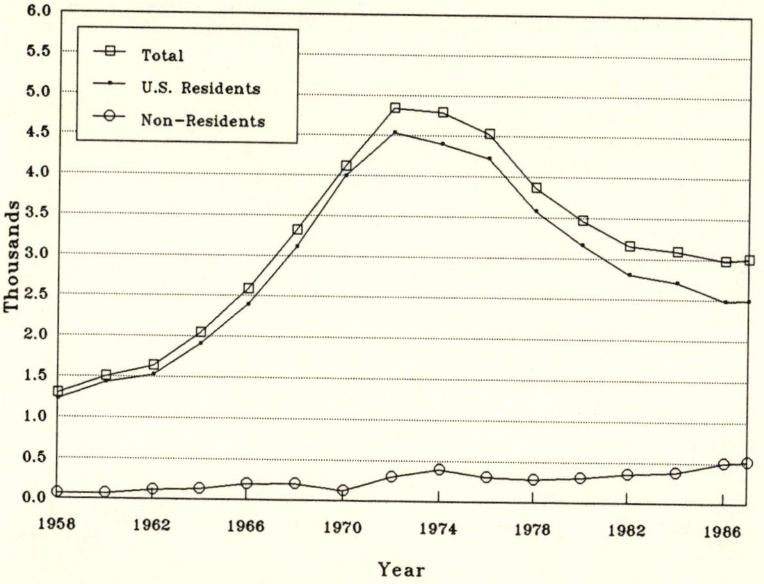

FIGURE 6.10
Doctorates Awarded in Humanities, 1958–87
Source: SED surveys.

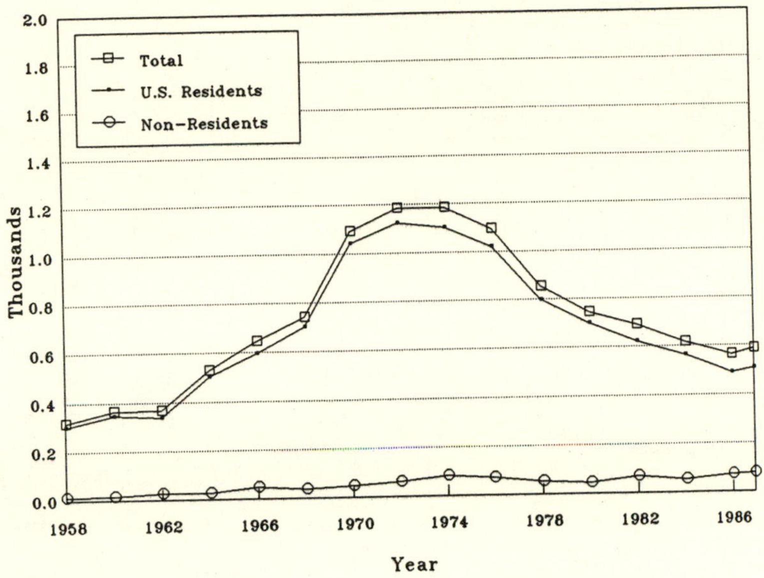

FIGURE 6.11
Doctorates Awarded in History, 1958–87
Source: SED surveys.

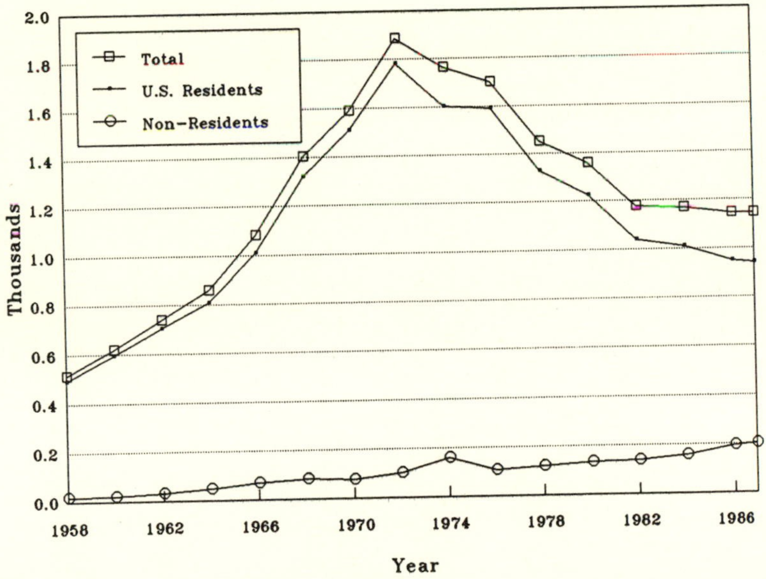

FIGURE 6.12
Doctorates Awarded in Letters, 1958–87
Source: SED surveys.

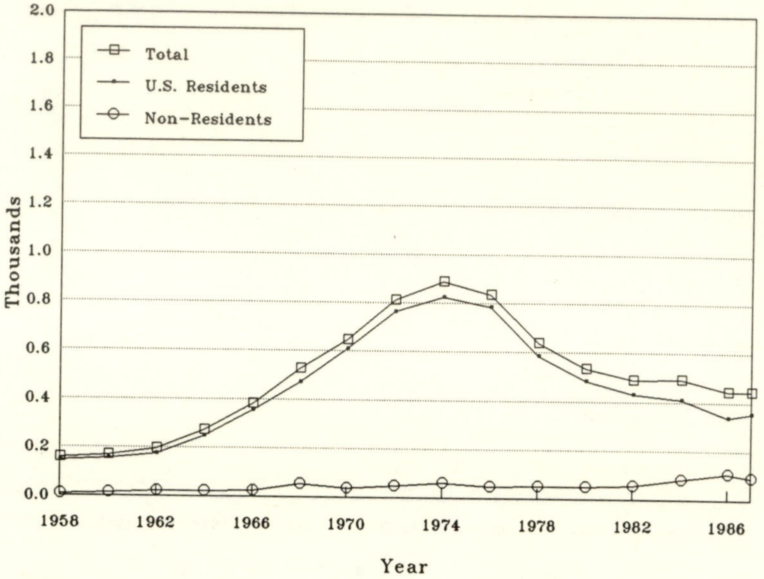

FIGURE 6.13
Doctorates Awarded in Foreign Languages and Literatures, 1958–87
Source: SED surveys.

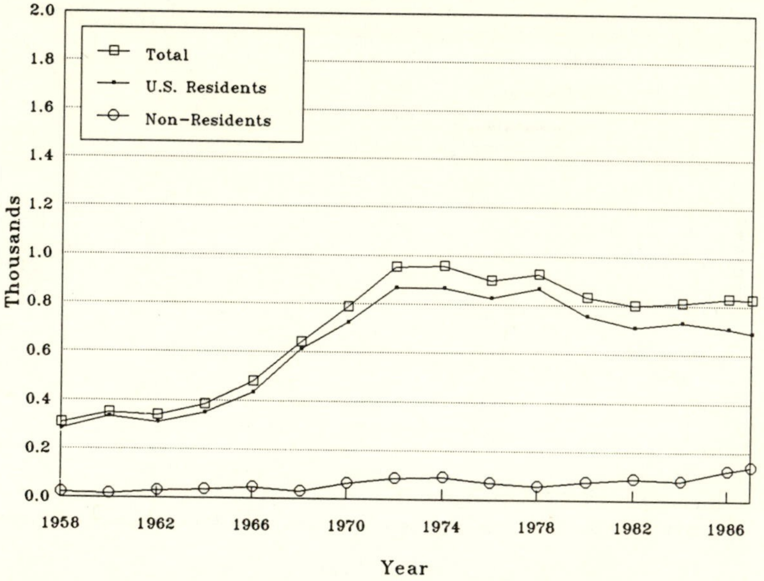

FIGURE 6.14
Doctorates Awarded in Other Humanities, 1958–87
Source: SED surveys.

for the humanities in Figures 6.11–6.14.[5] In all cases, separate data are provided for U.S. residents and non-residents.

One way to gain an overall impression of the similarities and differences among fields is by making a three-way comparison of the number of doctorates awarded in: (1) the base year of 1958; (2) the peak year for the field in question (when the largest number of doctorates was awarded); and (3) 1987. This is done in Table 6.1, which also contains relevant ratios.

The extraordinary rate of increase in new doctorates is shown in this table. For example, the number of new doctorates in mathematics in its peak year of 1972 was 5.4 times greater than the number in its base year of 1958. The subsequent declines are equally striking: in mathematics, the number of new doctorates in 1987 was just 58 percent of the number in the peak year. Then, in the final column, we see the number of doctorates in 1987 in relation to the number in 1958 (eliminating the intervening peak and subsequent decline). In mathematics, the number of new doctorates in 1987 was 3.1 times the number in 1958.

TABLE 6.1
New Doctorates, by Field of Study, 1958–87

	Doctorates Awarded (N)			*Ratio*		
Field of Study	*1958*	*Peak (Year)*[a]	*1987*	*Peak/ 1958*	*1987/ Peak*	*1987/ 1958*
Humanities	1,292	4,796 (1974)	3,004	3.7	0.63	2.3
History	317	1,186 (1972–74)	587	3.7	0.49	1.9
Letters	513	1,885 (1972)	1,146	3.8	0.61	2.2
Foreign Lang./Lit.	157	887 (1974)	444	5.6	0.50	2.8
Other Humanities	305	958 (1974)	827	3.1	0.86	2.7
Social Sciences	825	3,331 (1976)	2,620	4.0	0.79	3.2
Mathematics	238	1,281 (1972)	740	5.4	0.58	3.1
Physics/Astronomy	497	1,655 (1970)	1,236	3.3	0.75	2.5
Chemistry	965	2,238 (1970)	1,974	2.3	0.88	2.0
Earth Sciences	190	657 (1982)	627	3.5	0.95	3.3
Biological Sciences	1,201	3,893 (1982)	3,824	3.2	0.98	3.2
Psychology	743	3,230 (1984)	3,098	4.3	0.96	4.2

Source: SED tabulations.
[a]The peak number of doctorates awarded in any one year during the period 1958–87, with the year, or years, in ( ).

[5] One of the sub-fields of the humanities is called "letters." In the 1987 SED specialties list, letters includes classics, comparative literature, linguistics, English and American languages and literatures, speech and debate, letters–general, and letters–other.

The "roller-coaster" behavior of Ph.D. output is most pronounced in foreign languages and literatures, one of the sub-fields within the humanities. It is a matter of no small concern that the number of doctorates awarded in foreign languages and literatures has fallen from a peak of 887 in 1974 to 444 in 1987—having been just 157 in 1958. In 1987, the number of Ph.D.'s awarded in French, German, and Spanish was only about half the number awarded in 1974. Russian and Slavic languages and literatures is an even more dramatic case: the number of Ph.D.'s fell from 64 in 1974 to 24 in 1987—glasnost notwithstanding.

Elsewhere in the humanities, we see comparable fluctuations in letters and in history. The omnibus sub-field called "other humanities," however, incorporates divergent trends; more traditional fields such as philosophy behave much the same as letters and history, while there has been some growth in multidisciplinary fields such as American studies.

The social sciences differ from the humanities in that the number of new doctorates peaked later (1976) and then declined more moderately. Within the sciences, mathematics (as already noted) had the widest fluctuations, with chemistry and physics/astronomy showing the same general up-and-down pattern as mathematics, but in muted form. Biological sciences, psychology, and earth sciences, on the other hand, have all experienced longer-lasting periods of increase (with peaks between 1982 and 1984), and then little subsequent decline.

Projections of New Doctorates

Anyone studying the historical data summarized above—with such sharp movements in both directions—would have to feel more than the normal degree of humility in developing projections. Changing conditions in academic labor markets have been an important part of the explanation for the marked fluctuations in the number of new doctorates awarded. Undergraduates considering whether to apply to Ph.D. programs are affected by their sense of future job prospects, and by the advice they receive from their teachers.

Universities offering doctoral degrees make commitments for fellowship support and for other forms of assistance to graduate programs at least partly in response to their perceived sense of the need for larger (or smaller) numbers of Ph.D.'s. Prospective students, in turn, are influenced by what the graduate schools decide, just as the graduate schools are influenced by how many good candidates apply.

If all signals seem positive, as they did in the 1950s and 1960s, the number of new doctorates can be expected to increase. When the outlook is gloomier, we would surely expect some retrenchment—which is what took place in so many fields of study from about 1972 to the present. In any labor market, changes in market conditions affect both quantities demanded and quantities supplied. Academic labor markets, while peculiar in many respects, are hardly immune from the application of this simple truth. We will return to the question of how academic labor markets adjust, and equilibrate, in Chapter Eight.

At this stage in the analysis, we have adopted the simplifying assumption that there will be no change in the number of U.S. residents obtaining doctorates in most of the major fields of the arts and sciences.[6] Close inspection of Figures 6.3–6.14 suggests that in general the number of new doctorates awarded seems to have reached at least a temporary plateau in 1987. In addition, the size of the pool of undergraduates majoring in the relevant fields seems to have stabilized, following a period of substantial decline in the arts-and-sciences share of enrollment. The assumption that the number of new doctorates will be constant may not be far off the mark—at least until there are changes in market conditions or other incentives to pursue graduate study.

In the case of non-residents, recent data offer reason to anticipate continuing increases in the number of new doctorates, especially in certain fields. Accordingly, we have assumed that the 1987 level of new doctorates received by non-residents increases by 100 in 1992 in both mathematics and physics/astronomy; we assume an increase of 50 above the 1987 level in earth sciences; and we assume an increase of 150 in biological sciences. We thought it imprudent to assume any changes past 1992, since so many unknown, and unknowable, events can affect attendance by foreign nationals in U.S. graduate programs.

Combining these assumptions leads to the projections of new doctorates by both field and citizenship status summarized in Table 6.2. In brief, our 1992 projections for the arts and sciences show a very

[6] We have made three modest exceptions to the general rule of treating the number of U.S. residents receiving new doctorates in 1987 as the number to project into 1992 and beyond. In chemistry, the continuing recovery in the number of new doctorates that is evident in Fig. 6.5 suggests raising the 1987 number by 100 in 1992 and then maintaining that level. In biological sciences, the trend is clearly in the other direction (see Fig. 6.7), and so we have assumed a decrease of 250 doctorates in 1992, with no further decline after that. In the social sciences, there is also reason to expect some further decline (see Fig. 6.9), and so we have reduced the 1987 number by 150 in 1992 (with the number of new doctorates constant thereafter). All of these adjustments are relatively small—about 5% at most.

TABLE 6.2
Projections of New Doctorates, by Field of Study and Citizenship Status

	1987			*1992 and thereafter*		
Field of Study	*U.S. Residents*	*Non-Residents*	*Total*	*U.S. Residents*	*Non-Residents*	*Total*
Humanities[a]	2,395	490	2,885	2,395	490	2,885
Social Sciences	1,842	778	2,620	1,692	778	2,470
Hum./Soc. Sci.	4,237	1,268	5,505	4,087	1,268	5,355
Mathematics	396	344	740	396	444	840
Physics/Astronomy	754	482	1,236	754	582	1,336
Chemistry	1,467	507	1,974	1,567	507	2,074
Earth Sciences	449	178	627	449	228	677
Math/Phys. Sci.	3,066	1,511	4,577	3,166	1,761	4,927
Biological Sciences	3,130	694	3,824	2,980	844	3,824
Psychology	2,753	345	3,098	2,753	345	3,098
Biol. Sci./Psych.	5,883	1,039	6,922	5,733	1,189	6,922
All Arts/Sciences	13,186	3,818	17,004	12,986	4,218	17,204

Sources and Notes: Based on SED data for 1987 and trends. See text.

[a]The 1987 base-year numbers shown in this table for the humanities (and thus for the humanities and social sciences and for all arts and sciences) differ very slightly from the corresponding numbers cited earlier in this chapter because doctorates in theatre (82) and in speech and debate (37) have been subtracted from the SED figures presented previously. These subtractions were made for reasons explained in Appendix A.

modest decline in the number of U.S. residents receiving doctorates (from 13,186 in 1987 to 12,986 in 1992). This drop is slightly more than offset by a modest increase in the number of non-residents receiving doctorates. The total number of new doctorates in the arts and sciences projected for 1992 is 17,204.[7]

NON-ACADEMIC EMPLOYMENT

The next step is to consider how many new doctorates will have an interest in academic employment. The supply of potential faculty members depends on (among many other things) the inclinations of non-residents to seek academic positions in this country and the appeal of non-academic employment to U.S. holders of doctorates.

[7] As is explained in detail in the footnote to Table 6.2, the 1987 base-year numbers used to make projections differ slightly from the numbers used earlier in this chapter when we were discussing historical trends. Because of the many factors that could intervene, these projections of new doctorates should be regarded as useful in the process of further analysis, and *not* as predictions of what will in fact occur.

In the case of non-residents, we must estimate the likelihood that an individual holding a doctorate will both remain in the United States and seek academic employment. Available data do not permit separate estimates of these two sets of probabilities. However, it is possible to obtain at least rough estimates of the combined probability that a non-resident holder of a doctorate in a particular field will simultaneously remain in the United States and elect academic employment. The results of the relevant calculations are summarized in Table 6.3.[8]

Not surprisingly, the number of non-resident holders of doctorates on faculties varies considerably by field of study. These data suggest that non-residents can be expected to comprise approximately 9 to 10 percent of all full-time faculty members holding Ph.D.'s in mathematics and the physical sciences (except for chemistry, where the corresponding figure is about 5 percent). In other areas of the arts and sciences, the fractions of non-resident Ph.D.'s holding full-time

TABLE 6.3
Academic Employment of Non-Resident Doctorates, by Field of Study

Field of Study	*(1)* *Non-Resident Ph.D.'s (% of All Ph.D.'s)*	*(2)* *Percentage of Faculty Positions Held by Non-Resident Ph.D.'s*	*(3)* *Percentage of Non-Resident Ph.D.'s Seeking Academic Employment*
Humanities	17.0	4.0	24.0
Social Sciences	29.7	6.5	22.0
Mathematics	46.5	9.0	19.0
Physics/Astronomy	39.0	9.5	24.0
Chemistry	25.7	5.0	19.0
Earth Sciences	28.4	10.0	35.0
Biological Sciences	18.1	4.5	25.0
Psychology	11.1	2.5	23.0

Sources and Notes: Column (1) data are from SED tabulations for 1987. See text for further explanation.

Column (2) data are a rough estimate of faculty positions likely to be filled by non-resident Ph.D.'s over the next decade. The raw data are age-specific SDR tabulations for 1977 and 1987, which we have extrapolated.

Column (3) = Column (2)/Column (1)

[8] In brief, these estimates were obtained by combining SED data showing the percentages of all new recipients of doctorates who are non-residents with SDR surveys for 1977 and 1987 that indicate the percentages of all faculty positions held in those years by non-residents classified by age. As indicated in the notes to Table 6.3, we divide the percentage of all positions likely to be held by non-residents (based on an extrapolation of the SDR data) by the relative numbers of new doctorates who are non-residents to estimate the percentage of non-resident new doctorates likely to seek academic positions in this country.

faculty positions range from about 2.5 percent in psychology to 6.5 percent in the social sciences.

We also know that the number of non-resident recipients of Ph.D.'s is significantly higher in some fields than in others (see Table 6.3). The final column of Table 6.3 shows the percentage of all non-resident holders of Ph.D.'s who can be expected to seek academic employment in U.S. colleges and universities. Needless to say, these are very rough estimates. They range from a low of 19 percent in mathematics and chemistry, where there are many attractive non-academic positions in both the U.S. and other countries, to a high of 35 percent in earth sciences, where there are fewer non-academic jobs in this country and relatively fewer opportunities in the "home" countries of non-residents. In any event, these estimates have a relatively small effect on the overall projections of the future supply of Ph.D.'s for academic positions developed below.

U.S. recipients of doctorates of course constitute the primary pool of candidates for academic appointments in this country. Fortunately, there are good longitudinal data showing the percentages of these holders of doctorates who are employed as full-time faculty members in the arts and sciences (see Appendix Table D.5).

When we rank fields of study by the relative percentages of doctorates employed in academia, we find that the humanities and mathematics both place significantly higher than any of the other fields, with 73 to 74 percent of doctorates in these fields working in higher education in 1987. This high concentration of humanities doctorates in academic institutions is not unexpected. The equally heavy concentration of mathematics Ph.D.'s in academia may come as more of a surprise. Yet, at its most theoretical and speculative, mathematics is a very abstract subject without immediate applications, and that is in part why mathematicians are often employed by academic institutions.

At the other end of the spectrum are chemistry and psychology, with, respectively, just 31 percent and 34 percent of their doctorates holding academic appointments in 1987. Opportunities for employment in industry (especially for chemists) or in a variety of health-care fields (especially for psychologists) clearly create a powerful set of alternatives to academia.

These percentages are hardly static. Particularly noteworthy is the trend *away* from academia. As can be seen from Figure 6.15, the percentage of all holders of doctorates employed by colleges and universities declined significantly between 1977 and 1987 in every field except earth sciences. Especially large declines in academic employment as a percentage of all employment have occurred in the social

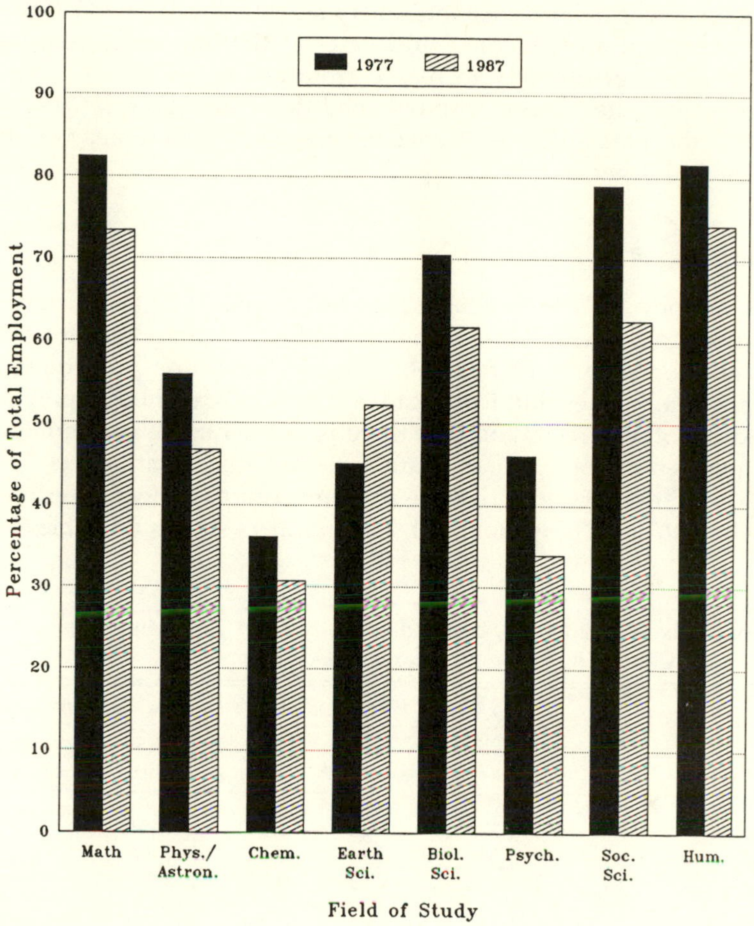

FIGURE 6.15
Academic Employment as a Percentage of Total Employment, by Field of Study, 1977 and 1987
Source: SDR tabulations.

sciences and in psychology. In general, industry, government, and other non-academic sectors are employing larger numbers of holders of Ph.D.'s. More recipients of doctorates have been pursuing such opportunities, as academic positions have become both harder to find and (at least for some) less attractive.[9]

The most recent profile of humanities doctorates published by the

[9] See various studies of the employment of doctorate recipients published by the National Research Council and other government agencies. A relatively early study of interest is National Research Council 1983.

National Research Council indicates that between 1985 and 1987, the percentage of all holders of doctorates in the humanities employed by business or industry increased from 8.7 to 9.8 percent. Among recent graduates (those who obtained doctorates between 1981 and 1986), the percentage employed in business or industry was even higher: 11.3 percent.[10]

Projections of Potential New Academics

We are now able to assemble the various pieces of the supply-side analysis into overall projections of numbers of candidates for faculty positions. We present two sets of projections, one presuming that there is no further shift from academic to non-academic employment, and the other presuming that there is at least some continuation in the movement of doctorates into non-academic vocations.

The first set assumes that the academic shares of doctorates remain at the 1987 level (see Table 6.4). The numbers shown on Table 6.4 are

Table 6.4
Projections of New Academics, by Field of Study and Citizenship Status, Assuming No Change in Academic Shares of Doctorates

	1987			*1992 and thereafter*		
Field of Study	*U.S. Residents*[a]	*Non-Residents*[b]	*Total*	*U.S. Residents*[a]	*Non-Residents*[b]	*Total*
Humanities	1,775	118	1,893	1,775	118	1,893
Social Sciences	1,151	171	1,322	1,058	171	1,229
Hum./Soc. Sci.	2,926	289	3,215	2,833	289	3,122
Mathematics	291	65	356	291	84	375
Physics/Astronomy	352	116	468	352	140	492
Chemistry	450	96	546	481	96	577
Earth Sciences	234	62	296	234	80	314
Math/Phys. Sci.	1,327	339	1,666	1,358	400	1,758
Biological Sciences	1,931	174	2,105	1,839	211	2,050
Psychology	933	79	1,012	933	79	1,012
Biol. Sci./Psych.	2,864	253	3,117	2,772	290	3,062
All Arts/Sciences	7,117	881	7,998	6,963	979	7,942

[a]Obtained by multiplying number of new doctorates in Table 6.2 by the 1987 column of Appendix Table D.5.
[b]Obtained by multiplying number of new doctorates in Table 6.2 by Column (3) of Table 6.3.

[10] See National Research Council 1989, Tables 9 and 11.

derived from the projections of new doctorates in Table 6.2 and the previous discussions of citizenship mix and academic versus non-academic employment. Because of the steady-state nature of the assumptions underlying these projections, we show only the 1987 base figures and projections for 1992.

The most important data in Table 6.4 are the absolute numbers of new doctorates expected to be available for academic employment in 1992 by field of study: 375 in mathematics, for example, and 1,893 in the humanities. Overall, this model envisions 7,942 new doctorates available for appointment in the arts and sciences in 1992 and in each subsequent year. This total is slightly lower than the corresponding figure for 1987. This comparison masks differences by field, however: the number of new doctorates expected to be available in mathematics and the physical sciences is projected to increase modestly, while the corresponding numbers for biological sciences/psychology and for humanities/social sciences are slightly lower in 1992 than they were in 1987.

We can now relax the assumption that the academic share of new doctorates will remain constant. As we saw earlier, the academic share declined between 1977 and 1987 in every field except earth sciences. The second set of supply-side projections, shown in Table 6.5, allows the academic shares to continue to decline, but less rapidly than they did over the last decade.[11]

All of our supply-side projections are summarized in Table 6.6, which has been constructed to facilitate comparisons. When we allow the shares of new doctorates in academia to decline even modestly, the projected number of new doctorates available for employment in the arts and sciences declines from 7,998 in 1987 to 7,571 in 1992 and then to 7,394 in 1997. The projected declines are relatively larger in fields such as the social sciences, where the movement away from academia has been most pronounced.

Qualitative Considerations

Before bringing together the demand-side and supply-side projections—the principal task of Chapter Seven—it is important to ask if there is evidence concerning the quality of the new doctorates in various fields. Anecdotes abound, including frequent comments by heads of departments and deans that there are surprisingly few strong candidates for vacant faculty positions, although there are numerous applications. But it is one thing to hear such comments—or to make

[11] See Appendix Table D.5 for the precise assumptions in each field of study.

TABLE 6.5
Projections of New Academics, by Field of Study and Citizenship Status, Assuming Continuing Decline in Academic Shares of Doctorates

	1992		*1997 and thereafter*	
Field of Study	*U.S. Residents*[a]	*Total*[b]	*U.S. Residents*[a]	*Total*[b]
Humanities	1,727	1,845	1,703	1,821
Social Sciences	973	1,144	922	1,093
Hum./Soc. Sci.	2,700	2,989	2,625	2,914
Mathematics	279	363	267	351
Physics/Astronomy	329	469	314	454
Chemistry	450	546	434	530
Earth Sciences	234	314	234	314
Math/Phys. Sci.	1,292	1,692	1,249	1,649
Biological Sciences	1,749	1,960	1,690	1,901
Psychology	851	930	851	930
Biol. Sci./Psych.	2,600	2,890	2,541	2,831
All Arts/Sciences	6,592	7,571	6,415	7,394

[a]Projections for U.S. residents were obtained by multiplying the projected numbers of new doctorates in Table 6.2 by projected percentage shares in academia in Appendix Table D.5.

[b]The "Total" columns are simply the sum of the projections for U.S. residents and the projections for non-residents in Table 6.4.

them—and quite another to produce anything purporting to be evidence in support of them.

Measuring "quality" is notoriously difficult in almost any context. It is particularly tricky when seeking to evaluate individuals who may be good at one thing and not quite so good at another, whose capacity for growth is hard for anyone to judge, and whose future performance will almost certainly depend as much on personal strengths as on pure academic competence, defined narrowly. No one who has made hiring decisions and then observed the consequences will gainsay the problems or minimize the subjective nature of the judgments that must be made. In short, all of the usual caveats need to be underscored.

One source of evidence is the Graduate Record Examination (GRE) administered by the Educational Testing Service. A 1984 report by the Study Group on the Conditions of Excellence in American Higher Education noted that performance on 11 of 15 major Subject Area Tests declined between 1964 and 1982—with the sharpest declines occurring in subjects requiring high verbal skills. Since 1982, however, scores on the verbal part of the general test have improved steadily.

TABLE 6.6
Summary of Projections of New Academics

Field of Study	1987 Base	Constant Academic Shares, 1992 and thereafter	Declining Academic Shares	
			1992	1997 and thereafter
Humanities	1,893	1,893	1,845	1,821
Social Sciences	1,322	1,229	1,144	1,093
Hum./Soc. Sci.	3,215	3,122	2,989	2,914
Mathematics	356	375	363	351
Physics/Astronomy	468	492	469	454
Chemistry	546	577	546	530
Earth Sciences	296	314	314	314
Math/Phys. Sci.	1,666	1,758	1,692	1,649
Biological Sciences	2,105	2,050	1,960	1,901
Psychology	1,012	1,012	930	930
Biol. Sci./Psych.	3,117	3,062	2,890	2,831
All Arts/Sciences	7,998	7,942	7,571	7,394

Sources and Notes: Data are for U.S. residents and non-residents combined. The 1987 data and the constant-academic-shares data are from Table 6.4. The declining-academic-shares data are from Table 6.5.

Moreover, scores on the quantitative and analytical parts of the GRE have improved as well.[12]

The number of students across the country taking the GRE is also significant, since the size of this pool indicates how many individuals are interested enough in considering graduate school to take the examination. Between 1974–75 and 1981–82, the number of test-takers fell from 298,470 to 258,361—a drop of more than 13 percent. Subsequently, however, there was a recovery. In 1986–87, 293,560 students took the GRE—almost the same number as in 1974–75.

These two complementary sets of data can be read as indicating that there was indeed a general fall-off in interest in graduate education from the mid-1970s through about 1982—manifested in declines in both average test scores and the overall number of prospective graduate students. It is reassuring, however, to note that 1982 appears to have been a low point, with both scores and number of test-takers rising in more recent years.

Perhaps the most direct evidence of a decline in the attractiveness of graduate education to the ablest undergraduates is found in a study

[12] *Involvement in Learning* 1984, p. 9. See also *Digest of Education Statistics* 1988, Table 217, p. 250.

of "highest achievers" carried out by the Consortium on Financing Higher Education (COFHE). In analyzing the post-baccalaureate plans of graduating classes between 1956 and 1981, the COFHE study found that the proportion of highest achievers (usually defined as the top 3 to 5 percent of the graduating class) enrolling in graduate school reached a peak in 1966—59.3 percent—and subsequently declined until 1976, when it stabilized at about 35 percent. It would be interesting to know what has happened to this percentage in the years since 1981, but we are unaware of any data that would allow us to answer the question.[13]

Another COFHE study (1982) examined graduate admission records from 1972 to 1980 at 20 research universities. The main finding was that admission was offered to larger proportions of shrinking applicant pools. In the social sciences, the number of applications declined by 28 percent over this period, while the proportion of applicants admitted rose from 25 percent in 1972 to 33 percent in 1980. In the humanities, the number of applications declined by 47 percent, while the number of acceptances increased from 38 percent in 1972 to 43 percent in 1980.

A study of the careers of members of Phi Beta Kappa showed a sharp decline in the number intending to enter the field of "educator" at the college level. Between 1945 and 1949, 20.6 percent expressed such intentions, and a high point was reached between 1960 and 1964 (24.2 percent). Interest in becoming an educator plummeted during the early 1970s, with the corresponding percentage dropping to 8.6 percent. Data for 1980–83 show a further decline to 2.4 percent.[14]

In addition to the above indices of quality, it is useful to examine what has happened to the relative numbers of doctorates awarded by various categories of universities over the last three decades. There is, of course, ample evidence to indicate that excellent students obtain doctorates from universities in all categories, just as we know that the most prestigious universities, on more than a few occasions, confer doctorates on individuals of very ordinary accomplishments. In short, no one would claim that there is anything approaching a perfect correlation between the quality of recipients of doctorates and the quality (real or perceived) of the universities conferring the doctorates.

Surely, however, there is some positive relationship. Differences in the quality of educational opportunities correlate with library hold-

[13] The COFHE study (1985) surveyed the top graduates of 14 selective colleges and universities, of which 11 were private institutions.

[14] These results, derived from a sample survey, are reported in Bowen and Schuster 1986, Table 11–18, p. 227. The results for 1980–83 may not be comparable with earlier figures because some students were still in graduate school.

ings, laboratory facilities, and the excellence of faculty members. The universities thought to offer the strongest graduate programs in particular fields generally attract the ablest applicants. It is also the case that the availability of fellowships and other forms of support for graduate study tends to correlate, at least roughly, with the perceived quality of graduate programs; both are functions of institutional resources and the ability to compete successfully for external funding.

The distribution of Ph.D.'s awarded has in fact changed significantly. In 1958, the Research I universities conferred 81.3 percent of all doctorates awarded in the arts and sciences. In 1987, these same Research I universities conferred only 62.8 percent of arts-and-sciences doctorates. As Figures 6.16 and 6.17 illustrate, much of the dramatic growth in the overall number of doctorates awarded between 1958 and 1972 occurred outside the Research I sector. More than one-third of the increase was accounted for by the other (non–Research I) universities, which together awarded less than one-fifth of the doctorates in the arts and sciences in 1958.[15]

These statistics reflect the strong demand for Ph.D.'s during the 1960s, which led to a proliferation of new graduate programs and a significant expansion of small programs. Not surprisingly, the more established programs accounted proportionately for much less of the substantial increase in doctorates awarded.[16]

Universities outside the Research I sector continued to increase their share of all doctorates conferred even after the expansion of graduate education ended in 1972 and the total number of new doctorates began to decline. From 1958 to 1987, the non–Research I universities were responsible for almost precisely half of the increase in doctorates awarded. This is why the percentage share of doctorates awarded by Research I universities fell from over 80 percent at the start of the period to just over 60 percent at the end.

It also should be noted that the share of doctorates in the arts and sciences awarded by the *private* universities within the Research I classification fell far more precipitously than the share of doctorates awarded by the public Research I universities. Between 1958 and 1987, the annual number of new doctorates awarded by the private Research

[15] These data, taken from special SED tabulations, are for U.S. residents only. Including non-resident recipients of doctorates does not change any of the trends. The coverage of these data differs slightly from the data presented for all institutions earlier in this chapter in that we are unable here to exclude doctorates in music.

[16] Between 1955–59 and 1970–74, the number of institutions granting doctorates in mathematics and in psychology more than doubled; there was an 80% increase in the number of doctorate-granting institutions in the life sciences and in the social sciences. (See National Research Council 1978, Table 39.)

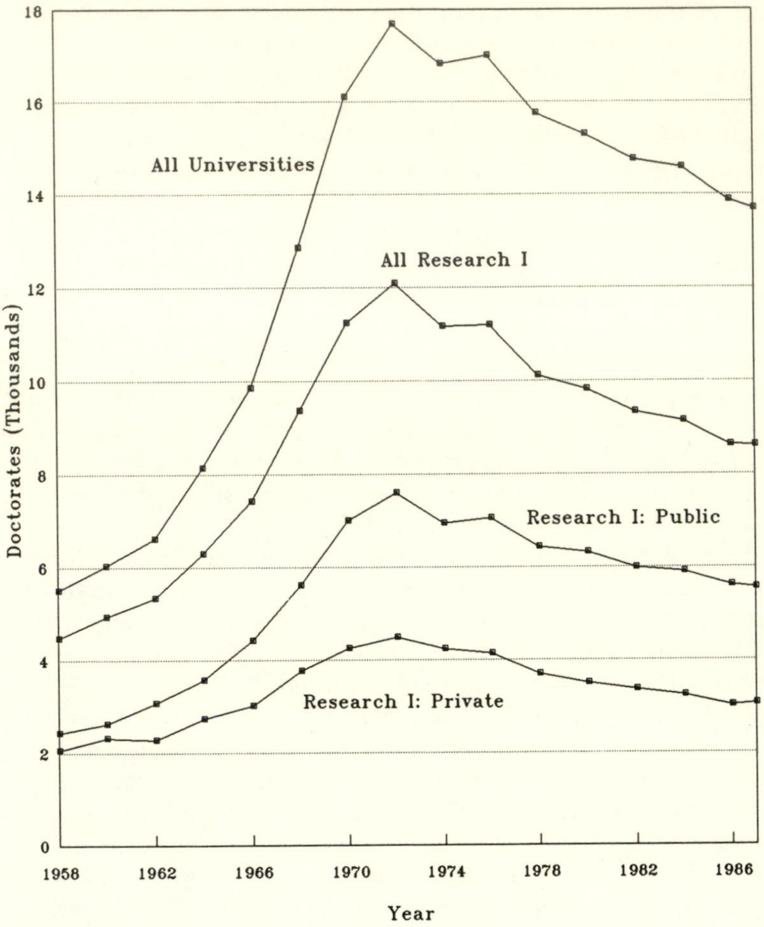

FIGURE 6.16
Arts-and-Sciences Doctorates, Research I Universities, 1958–87
Source: Special SED tabulations.

I universities went up by 999—whereas the comparable increases for the public Research I universities and the non–Research I universities (public and private) were, respectively, 3,135 and 4,167. In 1958, the private Research I universities awarded 37.3 percent of all doctorates in the arts and sciences; in 1987, these same universities awarded just 22.3 percent of all doctorates in these fields.

Undoubtedly, there were a number of considerations that combined to produce this differentiated pattern. Deliberate policy decisions made by many private Research I universities to curtail the sizes of their graduate programs in the face of a (correctly) perceived shrinking

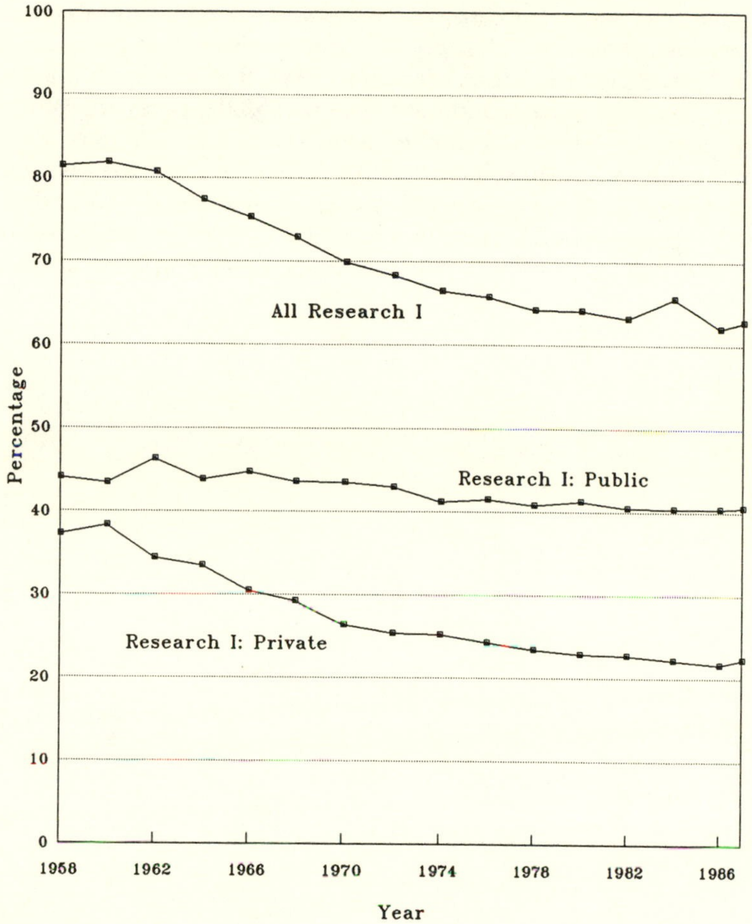

FIGURE 6.17
Percentage Shares of Arts-and-Sciences Doctorates, Research I Universities, 1958–87
Source: Special SED tabulations.

job market were one factor. Many of the very best departments cut their intake of new graduate students dramatically, in the belief that there would not be enough positions open to incoming graduate students when their studies were concluded. Some public university systems also made cuts in their graduate programs for similar reasons, but the aggregate figures indicate a measurable gap between the two sectors in this respect.

The change in relative shares of doctorates awarded by various groups of universities is even more pronounced when the humanities and social sciences are considered separately. While the Research I universities still awarded approximately two-thirds of all doctorates in the humanities and social sciences in 1987, this share was markedly smaller than the corresponding share in 1958 (84 percent). Whereas the private Research I universities contributed almost half of all doctorates awarded in these fields in 1958, they contributed just under 28 percent in 1987. As Figure 6.18 reveals clearly, the dramatic decline in the relative importance of this sector occurred primarily between 1958 and 1980. Since 1980, the share of doctorates in the humanities

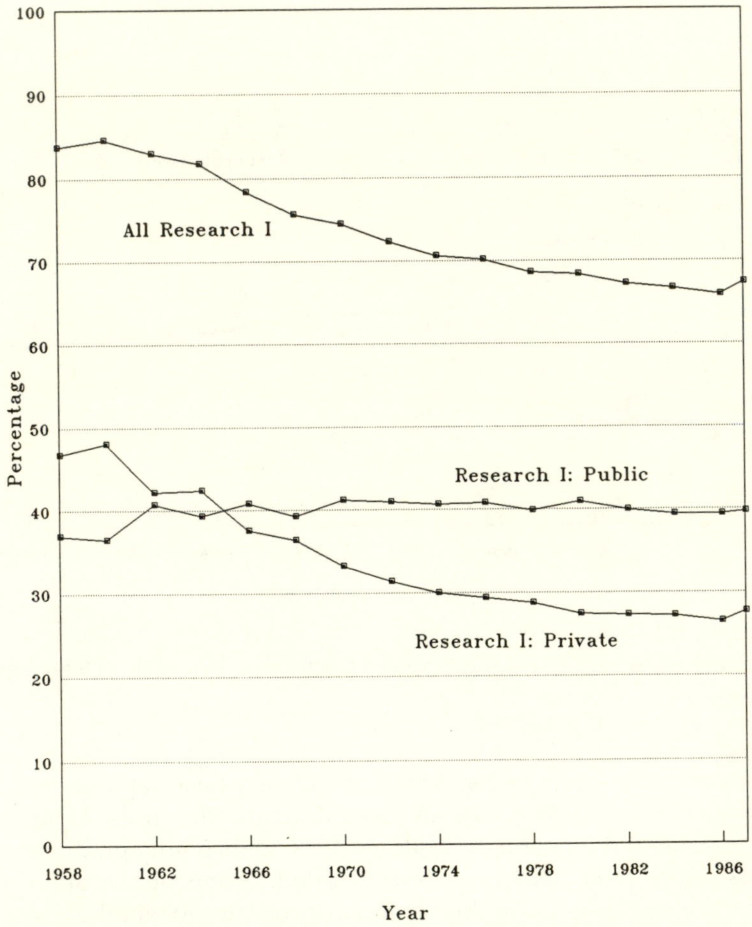

FIGURE 6.18
Percentage Shares of Humanities and Social Sciences Doctorates, Research I Universities, 1958–87
Source: Special SED tabulations.

and social sciences awarded by the private Research I universities has been steady, remaining within the 27 to 28 percent range.

To repeat an important caveat, no one should exaggerate the correlations among institutional quality, quality of doctorate recipients, and institutional classification. But it would be just as wrong to ignore the realities as they are seen by knowledgeable observers of American higher education. Many of the universities with the highest-ranked graduate programs are private Research I universities, and the share of all doctorates in the arts and sciences contributed by these universities has fallen by 40 percent over the last three decades.[17] One possible implication of this shift is that the number of exceptional new Ph.D.'s being trained is indeed smaller in absolute terms—and smaller as a proportion of all new Ph.D.'s—than was the case in the 1960s and early 1970s.

We believe that qualitative considerations may account for part of the apparent conflict between what is heard anecdotally about shortages of talent and what is observed quantitatively. This is a question of major importance, to which we shall return—recognizing all of the sensitivities embedded within it—after we bring together the projected number of positions to be filled and the projected number of candidates for them.

[17] The most recent study of the ranking of American universities with respect to the quality of faculty and graduate programs was published in 1982. For the fields of study within the arts and sciences, this study revealed a quite consistent pattern: on average, 7 of the 10 top departments and 12 of the top 20 were at private Research I universities. See Jones, Lindzey, and Coggeshall 1982.

CHAPTER SEVEN

The Changing Balance between Supply and Demand

THE OVERALL BALANCE between supply and demand in academic labor markets will shift markedly, we believe, over the next few decades. The most dramatic changes will occur in the 1997–2002 period, when we project a *substantial* excess demand for faculty in the arts and sciences. If present trends persist, we would expect that there would be roughly four candidates for every five positions—a condition that could continue in subsequent years unless significant adjustments occur or policy changes are made. Although we project no comparable imbalance during the 1987–92 period, we do expect some appreciable tightening of academic labor markets to begin as early as 1992–97.

Particularly striking are the projected imbalances between supply and demand in the humanities and social sciences. Our analysis suggests that competition for faculty members in these fields may become even keener than competition in the rest of the arts and sciences—contrary to what is often assumed. Of course, much will depend on whether student interest in the arts and sciences recovers, on how institutions allocate faculty positions among fields, and on other factors affecting student/faculty ratios.

These questions, and others pertaining to differences among fields of study, sectors, and periods, are explored in this chapter. First, however, we need to explain carefully the assumptions and methods used to generate the projections of supply and demand on which our conclusions rest.

Supply-side Projections

Following the analysis presented in the last chapter, we project that—unless circumstances change—approximately 33,000 new doctorates will be available for academic employment during the 1987–92 period. Just under 45 percent are expected to be in the humanities and social sciences. Projections for all three clusters of fields, and for all periods, are shown in Table 7.1, which also illustrates the sensitivity of these

TABLE 7.1
Alternative Supply-side Projections, by Field of Study

	1987–92	1992–97	1997–2002 and thereafter
Humanities/Social Sciences:			
Academic Share Constant	14,643	14,643	14,647
Academic Share Declining	14,335	13,633	13,460
Declining/Constant[a]	0.98	0.93	0.92
Mathematics/Physical Sciences:			
Academic Share Constant	7,749	7,957	7,957
Academic Share Declining	7,603	7,567	7,471
Declining/Constant	0.98	0.95	0.94
Biological Sciences/Psychology:			
Academic Share Constant	10,915	10,826	10,826
Academic Share Declining	10,600	10,099	10,003
Declining/Constant	0.97	0.93	0.92
All Arts/Sciences:			
Academic Share Constant	33,307	33,209	33,209
Academic Share Declining	32,538	31,299	30,934
Declining/Constant	0.98	0.94	0.93

Sources and Notes: All of these projections are for five sectors only. The "Academic Share Constant" entries are from Appendix Table D.6; the basic assumption is that the shares of new doctorates available for academic appointments will remain constant at their 1987 levels. The "Academic Share Declining" entries are from Appendix Table D.7; the assumption is that there will be modest declines in the shares of new doctorates available for academic appointments.

[a]Obtained by dividing the projections that assume that academic shares of doctorates decline by the projections that assume constant shares. Thus, these calculations show how much difference is made by adopting the declining-share assumptions.

projections to different assumptions about trends in the non-academic employment of doctorates.[1]

The general lack of any significant trajectory in these projections is due mainly to the relative stability in recent years of the overall number of Ph.D.'s awarded (with some decline in U.S. residents receiving

[1] All of these data pertain to the five main sectors of higher education. They differ, therefore, from the figures in Chapter Six, which were for all of academia. To align the supply and demand sides of our analysis, we adjusted the overall numbers of new doctorates presumed to pursue academic careers to reflect the interest of some of these individuals in positions outside the five sectors (in the Two-Year, Specialized, and Other sectors). Overall, about 84% of arts-and-sciences faculty in academia were employed in our five sectors in 1987. The percentages for individual fields of study are given in Appendix Table D.6, which also shows the derivation of the five-sector figures presented here.

Ph.D.'s offset by significant increases in Ph.D.'s awarded to nonresidents). The flatness of this pattern is particularly marked, of course, in the first set of projections, which holds constant the shares of new doctorates expected to seek academic employment.

The second set of projections, based on the assumption of declining shares, allows for a modest continuation of the movement away from academia that has been evident for some time now. If we adopt this second set of assumptions, the projected supply of new doctorates in all of the arts and sciences falls from 32,538 in 1987–92 to 30,934 in 1997–2002 and thereafter. The projections of supply that result from this set of assumptions are roughly 2 percent lower in the 1987–92 period than those which assume that academic shares will remain constant. By 1992–97 and 1997–2002, the differences average between 6 and 7 percentage points. These are small variations by any reckoning, and they certainly do not justify employing two sets of supply-side projections throughout this chapter.

The declining-shares set of projections appears to be the more realistic of the two, given current labor market conditions, and it is the one that we use in the main part of this analysis. (The reader who believes that the trend away from academia is over can readily substitute the slightly higher supply-side projections that result from holding academic shares constant.) In any event, as we shall see shortly, the variations on the demand side of the market—both over time and from model to model—are so much greater that they dominate any small differences on the supply side.

One final comment pertaining to supply. The historical record indicates that the supply of new doctorates is influenced significantly by labor market conditions and the outlook for academic employment. In short, there is a definite slope to the supply curve. We will examine this important adjustment mechanism in Chapter Eight and then consider the potential effects of policy decisions on the number of new doctorates in Chapter Nine. The point to emphasize is that the projections of supply utilized here are far from immutable; the number of new doctorates seeking academic employment could increase markedly in response to tightening labor markets and strengthened fellowship programs.

Demand-side Projections

The demand-side projections are much more complicated than the supply-side projections. For that reason, before we present the numbers, we will first explain what they measure and how these projections were generated.

As indicated at the end of Chapter Five, we employ four models on the demand side based on different combinations of assumptions about trends in arts-and-sciences enrollments and in student/faculty ratios. For each of these models, the demand for faculty is composed of: (1) *net-new-positions demand;* and (2) *replacement demand.* Replacement demand, in turn, can be subdivided into: (a) replacements for the faculty who were present in the base year (1987 in this case)—a group that we call "starters"; and (b) replacements for the faculty who were added along the way, either as replacements for the starters or to fill new positions—a group called "new entrants."

Whereas replacement demand is by our definition always positive, the net-new-positions demand can be positive or negative, depending on whether the number of faculty is expanding or contracting. If the faculty is expanding, it is necessary to hire new faculty both to replace those who leave and to fill new positions. On the other hand, if the faculty is contracting, it is unnecessary even to replace all those faculty members who are leaving. Decisions not to replace, but rather to leave positions open, are assumed in this analysis to reflect a negative net-new-positions demand rather than a negative replacement demand. There are definite interactions between projections of net new positions and projections of replacement demand. Failure to recognize that some new entrants must also be replaced can lead to serious underestimates of the overall demand for faculty.

Applying the Methodology: An Illustrative Case

This general methodology, and the detailed process of deriving estimates, are so important to all that follows that we will work through a sample case to illustrate how the demand projections have been made. For this purpose we work with just one model—namely, Model II from Chapter Five. This is our Steady-State model (which assumes that the arts-and-sciences shares of enrollment that prevailed in 1987 hold steady), with constant student/faculty ratios.

We will only derive projections for faculty in the arts and sciences in the five sectors considered together. Since there are four basic models, four categories of fields of study (the three regular clusters of fields, plus the all-arts-and-sciences total), and six categories of sectors (the five sectors plus the five-sector total), the sample case we present is only one of 96 cases for which equally detailed calculations have been made. The methodology, however, is the same for all cases.[2]

We begin with the age distribution of faculty present in 1987 (see Table 7.2). To recapitulate the process described in detail in Chapter Two, we calculate the number of faculty members within each age group who are expected to have quit, retired, or died by 1992. The overall exit rates for each age cohort are derived from these three probabilities, and they are shown in the column headed "Faculty Gone by 1992."

When we multiply each exit rate by the size of its age group, we

TABLE 7.2
Deriving Demand Projections for Model II: 1987–92

Age Group	*Total Faculty in 1987 (N)*	*Faculty Gone by 1992 (%)*	*Faculty Gone by 1992 (N)*	*Faculty Continuing[a] in 1992 (N)*
Under 30	736	16.9	124	612
30–34	9,590	16.9	1,621	7,969
35–39	19,904	12.0	2,388	17,516
40–44	26,361	8.3	2,188	24,173
45–49	28,427	8.0	2,274	26,153
50–54	20,806	11.4	2,372	18,434
55–59	16,460	24.3	4,000	12,460
60–64	11,172	59.4	6,625	4,547
65–69	5,020	93.3	4,684	336
Over 69	587	100.0	587	0
Total	139,063[b]	19.3	26,863	112,200

Net New Positions	−6,485[c]
New Entrants (1992)	20,378[d]

Sources and Notes: The age distributions are from SDR tabulations. See Chapter Two for the derivation of assumptions. Data in this table and in Table 7.3 are for all faculty in the arts and sciences in five sectors only.

[a]"Faculty Continuing" means the number of faculty who will continue into the next period.

[b]This total is very slightly smaller than the corresponding total shown in Table 2.4 because "no reports" (by age breakdown) are excluded here. This comment also applies to the corresponding total in Table 7.3.

[c]The number for "Net New Positions" is from Chapter Five, Fig. 5.9, Model II.

[d]The number of "New Entrants (1992)" is also the projected demand for this model in this period. It is obtained by combining the estimate of the "Faculty Gone by 1992" with the projected number of net new positions —which is negative in this instance.

[2] The following discussion is inevitably somewhat tedious, but it is important because it describes the basic "machine" that we have built in order to generate projections of demand for faculty by field and sector. Readers who wish to do so may skip ahead to the more substantive part of the chapter.

obtain an estimate of the number of faculty that will have exited by 1992 within each age group, and (by subtraction from the total in the age group) the number that will continue. For example, we see that within the 40–44 age group, there were 26,361 faculty in 1987; that the exit rate for this age group was 8.3 percent (for the entire five-year period); that 2,188 are projected to be gone by 1992; and that 24,173 would thus continue. The summary figures show that the combined exit rate for all age groups was 19.3 percent, and that 26,863 faculty members are projected to be gone by 1992. These faculty members would have to be replaced *if the total number of faculty positions were to remain constant* between 1987 and 1992.

We now make use of the projections of net new positions summarized at the end of Chapter Five (following the earlier discussion, in Chapters Three and Four, of projections of population, enrollment, and trends in degrees conferred). In the case of Model II, the projected net new positions for the arts-and-sciences faculty in all five sectors between 1987 and 1992 was *negative* 6,485 (see Fig. 5.9). That is, because this model presumes that faculty size will contract somewhat during this period—by just under 5 percent of the total number of faculty at the start of the period—all of those who will leave need not be replaced.

The number of net new positions is entered below the sum of the "Faculty Gone by 1992" on Table 7.2 and is then combined with this figure to obtain the number of new entrants (26,863 *minus* 6,485 = 20,378). In short, 20,378 faculty are expected to be hired over this interval. This is the demand projection generated by Model II for the 1987–92 period, and it will be compared below with both the relevant supply projection and the demand projections generated by other models.[3]

We now move forward to the next period (see Table 7.3) and introduce a new complication. We must distribute the new entrants (who were assumed to start work on January 1, 1992) among the age

[3] One other assumption of a technical nature should be noted. While some of these new entrants would of course be hired at each point in time during the interval, we have assumed for the sake of simplicity that all 20,378 are hired at midnight on December 31, 1991 and that all begin the new five-year period at their posts. This simplifying assumption introduces a bias into the estimates. Since it fails to recognize that some of the new entrants would in fact have been hired earlier, it does not allow any of these new people to leave and be replaced during the period in question. Some (still smaller) fraction of these second-round replacements should be expected to leave in their turn and be replaced during the same period, and so on. We have no way of quantifying this bias with precision, but it is probably not far off to assume that it causes us to understate demand by 1,000 positions over the five-year period. That is, we believe that the upper limit of this bias is about 5% of total demand.

TABLE 7.3
Deriving Demand Projections for Model II: 1992–97

Age Group	*New Entrants in 1992 (N)*	*Total Faculty in 1992 (N)*	*Faculty Gone by 1997 (%)*	*Faculty Gone by 1997 (N)*	*Faculty Continuing in 1997 (N)*
30–34	9,782	10,393	16.9	1,756	8,637
35–39	6,521	14,490	12.0	1,739	12,752
40–44	2,038	19,553	8.3	1,623	17,930
45–49	1,223	25,396	8.0	2,032	23,364
50–54	815	26,968	11.4	3,074	23,894
55–59	—	18,434	24.3	4,479	13,955
60–64	—	12,460	59.4	7,389	5,071
65–69	—	4,547	93.3	4,242	305
Over 69	—	336	100.0	336	0
Total	20,378	132,578	20.1	26,671	105,907
			Net New Positions	−3,617	
			New Entrants (1997)	23,054	

Sources and Notes: See notes to Table 7.2.

groups so that we will know at what rates to exit them from the system. We elected to assume that 48 percent of the new entrants are in the 30–34 age group, 32 percent are 35–39, 10 percent are 40–44, 6 percent are 45–49, and 4 percent are 50–54. We are satisfied that a different distribution of new entrants by age group would not change the results significantly—the main effect would be on the time-path of exits.[4]

Once the number of continuing faculty (who progress from one age group to the next) has been calculated, new entrants are added in order to obtain the total number of faculty in 1992 in each age group.

[4] We assigned 80% of the new entrants to the 30–39 age groups because most of the new hires are likely to be young faculty members who have just received their Ph.D.'s. Since some new entrants will be older, we entered the remaining 20% of the new entrants across a greater portion of the age distribution.

To allocate the 80% of the new entrants assumed to be under 40 between the 30–34 and 35–39 age groups, we elected to use a 3:2 ratio; that is, we assumed that 48% of all new entrants would be age 30–34 and 32% would be age 35–39. The reasoning behind this assumption is as follows. First, the median age upon receipt of the doctorate in 1986 was 33.5 years, according to data taken from the 1986 SED. Second, 22% of new Ph.D.'s in all fields planned postdoctoral study. (See SED 1986, Appendix A, Table 5, p. 56; and Table H, p. 17.) Assuming that the mean length of postdoctoral fellowships is approximately 2.5 years, postdoctoral study should add, on average, approximately 0.5 years to the median age of entry to the faculty. The median age of entry into the faculty, therefore, would be 34. This conclusion implies that roughly half of all new entrants would enter during the 30–34 age interval.

The same exit rates are applied, resulting in estimates of "Faculty Gone by 1997" and "Faculty Continuing in 1997." The number of net new positions for the period is entered at the bottom of the table (*negative* 3,617 in this instance) and combined with the number of faculty who will exit to arrive at the overall estimate of the number of new entrants—the projected demand—for the 1992–97 period. As Table 7.3 shows, this number is higher than the corresponding number for the 1987–92 period: 23,054 as compared with 20,378.

This same estimating process is applied to the 1997–2002 period. The relevant number of new entrants (23,054) is distributed across age groups, continuing faculty are assigned to the proper age groups, and a new figure for net new positions (now decidedly *positive* because of enrollment trends) is incorporated. The logic of the process is clear, we hope, and we will not reproduce here more tables like Tables 7.2 and 7.3 for subsequent five-year periods. What we have tried to illustrate is the methodology by which we have obtained projections of demand, seen as the algebraic sum of demand associated with net new positions and demand associated with the number of vacancies created by the exits of individuals (starters and new entrants) who were employed at the start of the period. Enough! We now return to the results and their implications.

Net New Positions versus Replacement Demand

It is instructive to compare the relative importance of net new positions and replacements as sources of demand for new faculty. Taking the arts and sciences as a whole, and looking only at totals for all five sectors, we find that replacements are by far the dominant determinant of demand in all four of our basic models and in all five of the time periods (see Table 7.4).

The differences among the models and over time are explored in detail below, when we combine these projections of demand with projections of supply. Here it is sufficient to note that the number of net new positions is significantly negative only in the first period (1987–92), and then only for Models I and II. Otherwise, the general pattern is one of positive contributions to demand from net new positions as well as from replacements.

Even in the model with the most optimistic assumptions about increases in arts-and-sciences enrollments (Model IV), however, we see that replacement demand is far greater than the number of net new positions. If we sum the replacement demand in this model for all five time periods, we obtain a total replacement demand of 155,484; the corresponding total for net new positions is 25,831. In other

TABLE 7.4
Components of Demand Projections: Net New Positions and Replacement Demand, Four Models

	1987–92	*1992–97*	*1997–2002*	*2002–07*	*2007–12*	*Total 1987–2012*
Model I:						
Replacements	26,863	26,436	28,453	32,026	32,450	146,228
Net New Positions	−8,193	−2,349	8,590	5,781	439	4,268
Total Demand	18,670	24,087	37,043	37,807	32,889	150,496
Model II:						
Replacements	26,863	26,671	28,472	32,086	32,553	146,645
Net New Positions	−6,485	−3,617	8,619	5,800	440	4,757
Total Demand	20,378	23,054	37,091	37,886	32,993	151,402
Model III:						
Replacements	26,863	27,630	29,706	33,355	34,059	151,613
Net New Positions	501	−323	9,305	6,263	475	16,221
Total Demand	27,364	27,307	39,011	39,618	34,534	167,834
Model IV:						
Replacements	26,863	27,727	31,379	34,313	35,202	155,484
Net New Positions	1,209	11,286	6,181	6,650	505	25,831
Total Demand	28,072	39,013	37,560	40,963	35,707	181,315

Sources and Notes: For definitions of models, see Chapter Five, pp. 84–85. In brief:
In Model I, continuing declines in arts-and-sciences shares of enrollment are combined with declining student/faculty ratios;
in Model II, steady-state projections of arts-and-sciences shares of enrollment are combined with constant student/faculty ratios;
in Model III, steady-state projections of arts-and-sciences shares of enrollment are combined with declining student/faculty ratios;
in Model IV, recovery projections of arts-and-sciences shares of enrollment are combined with increasing student/faculty ratios.
Net new positions are from Chapter Five. Replacements are estimated as explained in text.

words, less than 15 percent of the total demand projected over this twenty-five year period is attributable to increases in the number of positions; more than 85 percent is attributable to replacement demand. And, to repeat, these figures are for the model that makes the most generous assumptions about the likelihood of new positions. For the other models, the share of total demand associated with replacements ranges from 90 to 98 percent.

We should emphasize that replacement demand is much more stable over time than many have assumed. A principal factor is the behavior of retirements. While it is true that the pattern of retirements over time significantly affects the changing balance between supply and demand in certain sectors, we find that peaks and valleys in the number of retirements have relatively little to contribute to our understanding of shifts in the overall balance between supply and demand.

There are, we suspect, two underlying reasons for this result (which is discussed in Chapter Eight). First, age distributions of faculty seem to have become more normalized, with less bunching in the younger age ranges. Whereas in 1977, the percentage of faculty under age 40 in all arts-and-sciences fields within the five sectors was 41.7 percent, the comparable percentages in 1987 and then in 1992 (under Model II) are 21.7 percent and 18.8 percent. The second reason is more fundamental. The "flow through the system" of young people generates a reasonably steady replacement demand that is largely independent of the age distribution of continuing faculty members.

A final point should be made about the respective roles played by replacement demand and net new positions. While replacements are the dominant determinant of the *level* of total demand in every period and for every model, the number of net new positions is the dominant determinant of period-to-period *changes* in total demand.

The projected numbers of net new positions swing from decidedly negative to positive between the 1992–97 and the 1997–2002 periods in all models except Model IV, and this explains why the sharpest fluctuations in projected demand occur then. Also, relatively small fluctuations in net new positions lead to relatively large shifts in total demand. For instance, under Model II assumptions, the number of net new positions for all arts-and-sciences faculty is projected to increase 6.5 percent between 1997 and 2002—and this leads directly to a 37 percent increase in the demand for faculty during the 1997–2002 period, relative to the demand during the previous period.[5]

To understand why relatively small swings in net new positions have such a large impact on total demand, it is instructive to consider an analogy with the demand for capital goods in the broader economy. In the capital goods industry, the need to replace existing equipment is a relatively stable source of demand; new orders derived from the need to expand or contract production in response to changes in consumer behavior are a much more dynamic component. Whereas replacement demand for faculty is, as we have just seen, a relatively stable part of the total demand for faculty, net new positions are analogous to new orders in the capital goods industry.[6]

[5] These calculations are based on data in Tables 7.3 and 7.4. The 6.5% increase is obtained by dividing 8,619 by 132,578; the 37% increase is obtained by dividing 8,619 by 23,054.

[6] Cartter 1976, p. 19, suggested the analogy with the capital goods industry and gave this numerical example: "If, for example, replacement needs in a stationary state are

Supply and Demand Relationships

The principal objective of this study has been to develop congruent projections of supply and demand. Our projections for all of the arts and sciences, for each five-year period from 1987–92 through 2007–12, are summarized in Table 7.5.

The projected levels of supply and demand, and thus the absolute differences (supply minus demand), are summarized in Figures 7.1–7.4, with each figure presenting the results for one of our four models.

Table 7.5
Supply and Demand Projections, All Arts and Sciences: Comparison of Four Models

	1987–92	*1992–97*	*1997–2002*	*2002–07*	*2007–12*
Projected Supply[a]	32,538	31,299	30,934	30,934	30,934
Model I:					
Projected Demand	18,670	24,087	37,043	37,807	32,889
Supply − Demand	13,868	7,212	−6,109	−6,873	−1,955
Supply/Demand[b]	1.74	1.30	0.84	0.82	0.94
Model II:					
Projected Demand	20,378	23,054	37,091	37,886	32,993
Supply − Demand	12,160	8,245	−6,157	−6,952	−2,059
Supply/Demand	1.60	1.36	0.83	0.82	0.94
Model III:					
Projected Demand	27,364	27,307	39,011	39,618	34,534
Supply − Demand	5,174	3,992	−8,077	−8,684	−3,600
Supply/Demand	1.19	1.15	0.79	0.78	0.90
Model IV:					
Projected Demand	28,072	39,013	37,560	40,963	35,707
Supply − Demand	4,466	−7,714	−6,626	−10,029	−4,773
Supply/Demand	1.16	0.80	0.82	0.76	0.87

Sources and Notes: All data are for five sectors only. The demand projections are taken from Appendix Tables D.8–D.11. The supply projections are from Table 7.1 and Appendix Table D.7.

[a]We use the same supply projections with every model. These are the supply projections that assume continuing decline in the shares of new doctorates seeking academic careers.

[b]The supply projection divided by the demand projection is the number of candidates per position.

5 percent annually, and then consumer demand begins to grow at a 5 percent rate, the demand for investment goods doubles."

Ratios showing the projected number of candidates per position (supply/demand) are brought together for all models in Figure 7.5.

These figures reveal a number of important findings, which must be interpreted carefully. Models II and III, both of which assume steady-state shares of arts-and-sciences enrollments, differ only in that Model II assumes constant student/faculty ratios while Model III assumes continuing declines in these ratios. These models show supply exceeding demand over the 1987–92 period by about 12,000 (Model II) and 5,000 (Model III). This is a significant difference, and

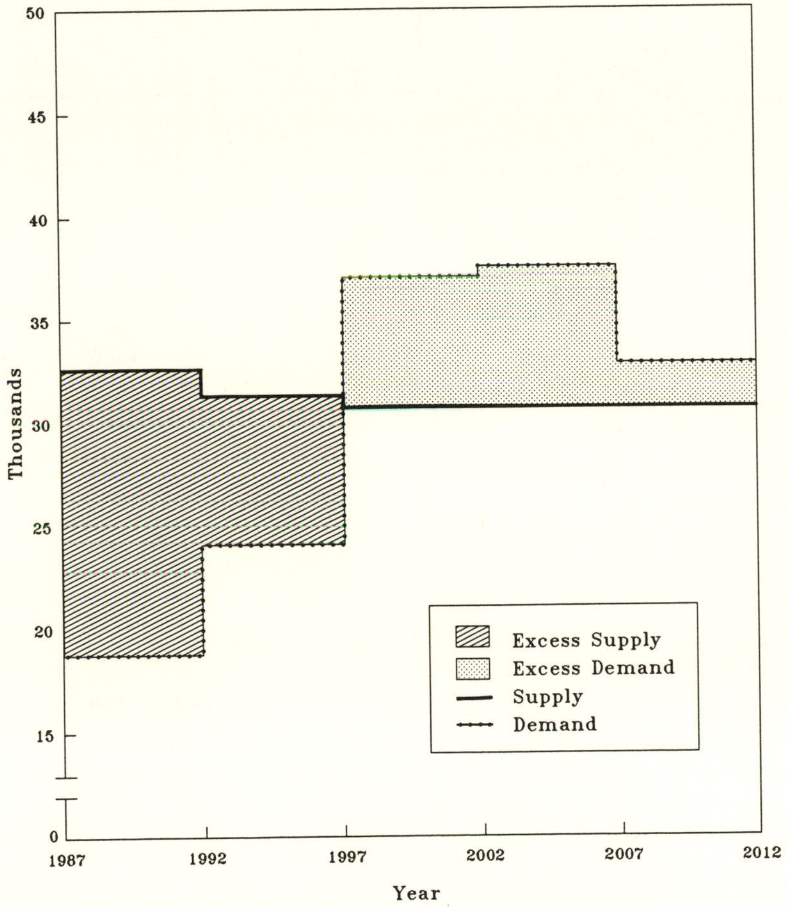

FIGURE 7.1
Supply and Demand Projections, All Arts and Sciences: Model I

Source: See text.

Note: In Model I, continuing declines in arts-and-sciences shares of enrollment are combined with declining student/faculty ratios.

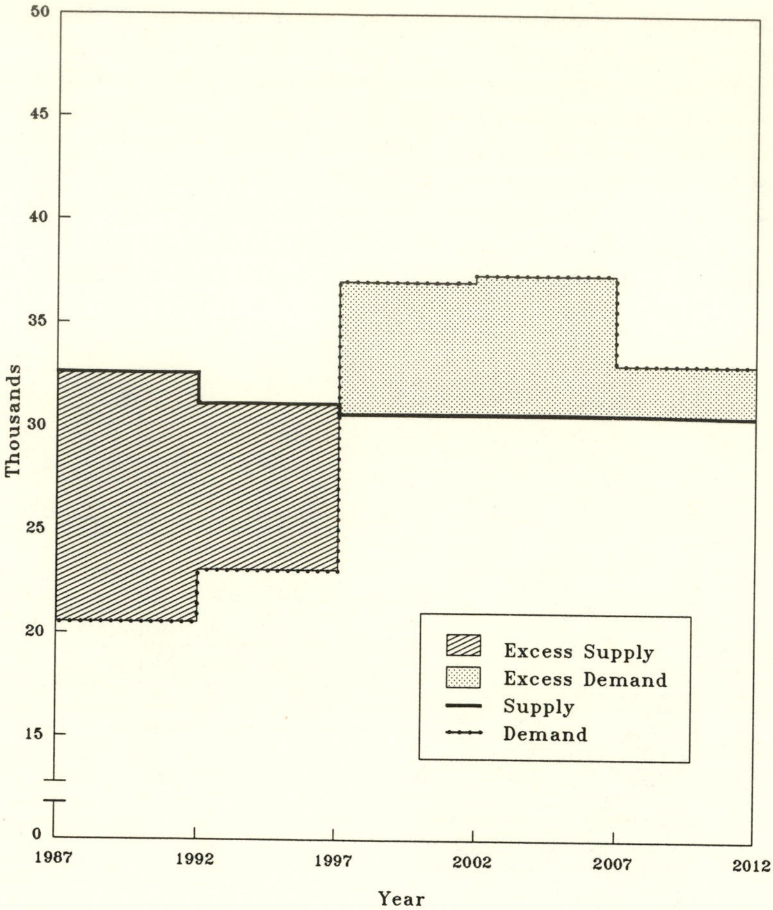

FIGURE 7.2
Supply and Demand Projections, All Arts and Sciences: Model II
Source: See text.
Note: In Model II, steady-state arts-and-sciences shares of enrollment are combined with constant student/faculty ratios.

it indicates the importance of the student/faculty ratio. These results are equivalent to saying, in Model II, that there will be 1.60 candidates per position between 1987 and 1992; in Model III, there will be 1.19 candidates per position.

Models I and IV, the two boundary models, also project supply to exceed demand during the 1987–92 period. The differences between this pair of models and Models II and III are significant but by no means overwhelming. Model I, which assumes continuing decline in the arts-and-sciences share of enrollment and a partially offsetting

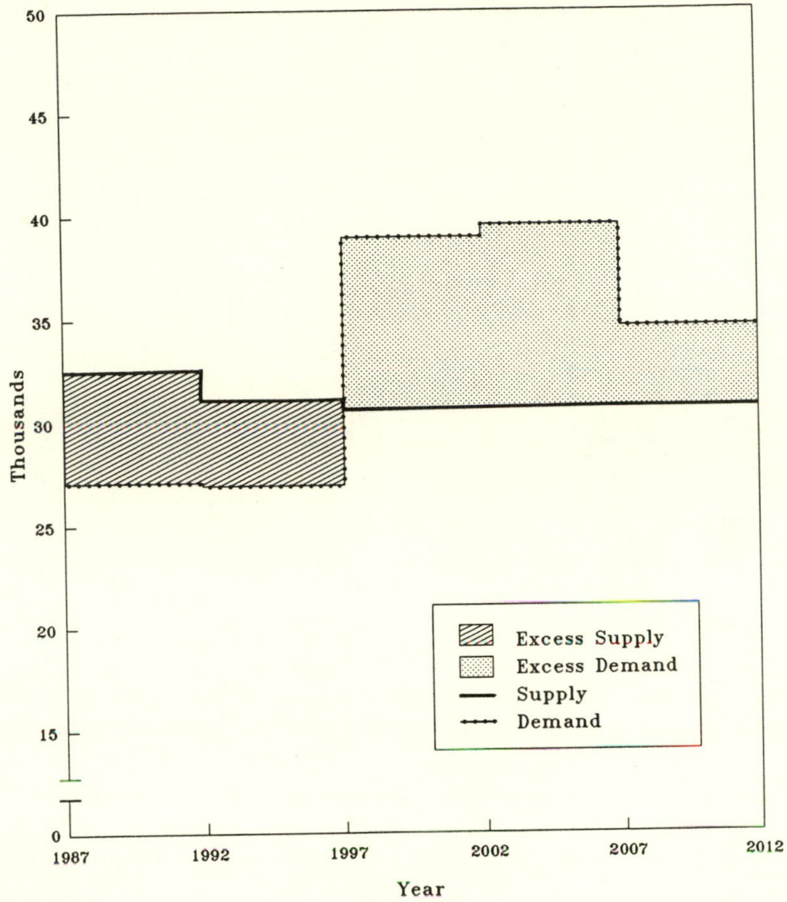

FIGURE 7.3
Supply and Demand Projections, All Arts and Sciences: Model III

Source: See text.

Note: In Model III, steady-state arts-and-sciences shares of enrollment are combined with declining student/faculty ratios.

decrease in the student/faculty ratio, projects an excess supply of about 14,000 between 1987 and 1992 (1.74 candidates per position). Model IV, which assumes recovery in the arts-and-sciences share of enrollment and a partially offsetting increase in the student/faculty ratio, projects an excess supply of about 4,500 (1.16 candidates per position).

Before proceeding to the critical question of how the balance between supply and demand can be expected to change as we move through time, it is useful to pause and compare the general tenor of

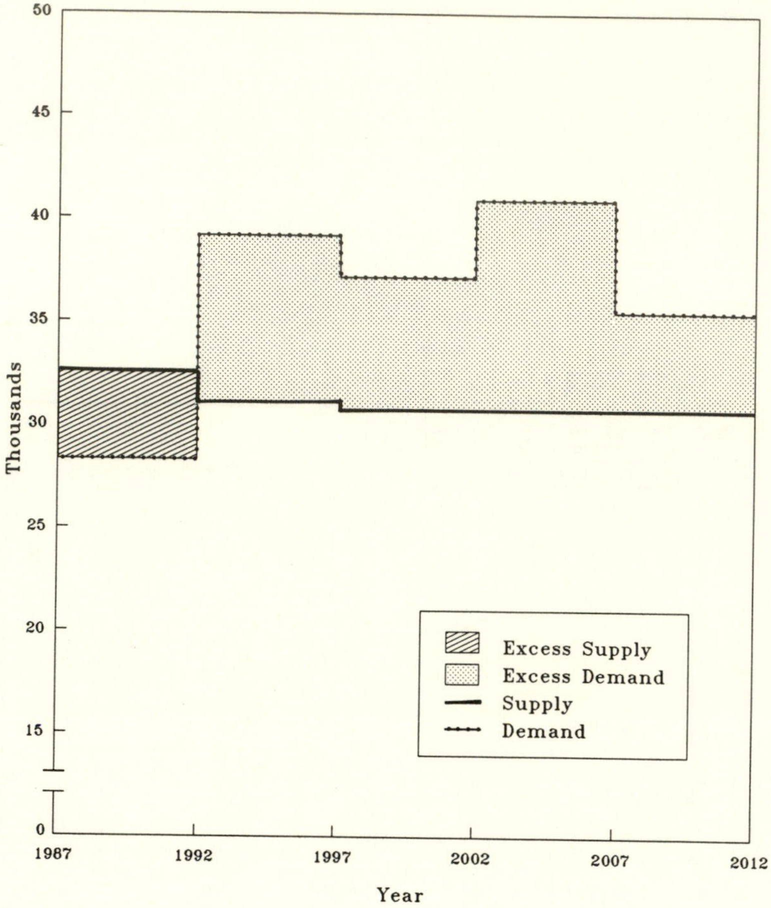

FIGURE 7.4
Supply and Demand Projections, All Arts and Sciences: Model IV

Source: See text.

Note: In Model IV, recovery in arts-and-sciences shares of enrollment is combined with increasing student/faculty ratios.

the projections for the 1987–92 period with what we know, or can infer, about the recent past. In any analysis of this kind, there is always the danger that some unnoticed peculiarity in the data, or some conceptual error, will generate projections that are wildly "off" and fail to track reality. To obtain some sense of the reliability of our results, we went back to 1977 and replicated our analysis of projected supply/demand relationships for the period 1977–87. That is, we carried out a parallel, retrospective analysis of supply, replacement demand, and

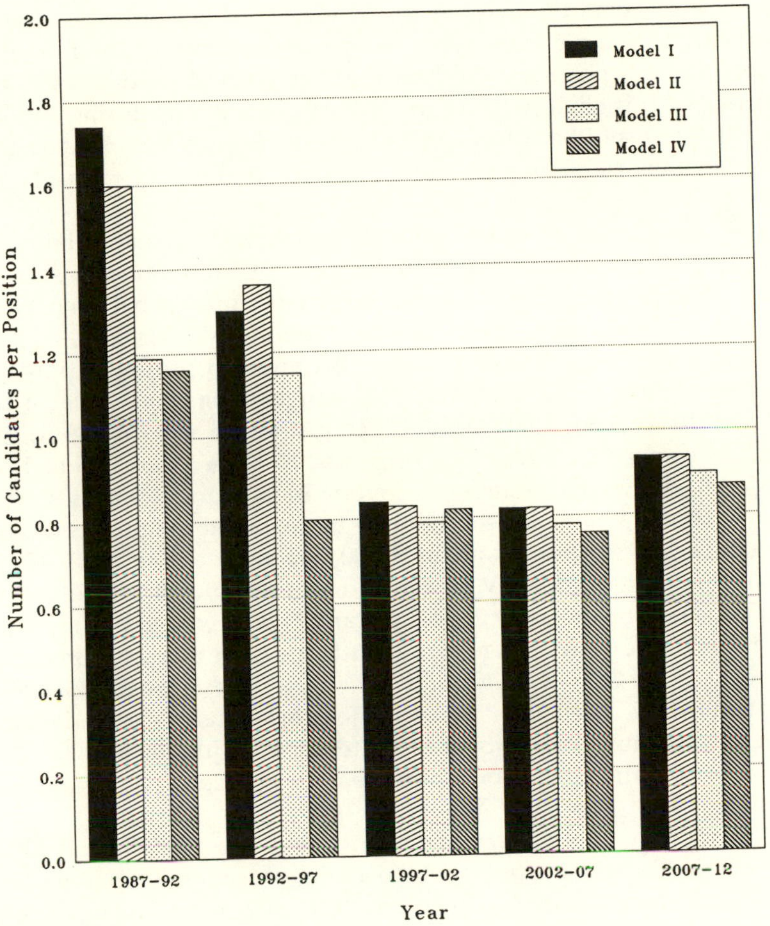

FIGURE 7.5
Projected Number of Candidates per Position, All Arts and Sciences: Comparison of Four Models
Source: Table 7.5.

net new positions, using the *actual* data on age distributions of faculty, changes in the number of faculty positions, and doctorates awarded.

This exercise proved to be most interesting—and reassuring. For 1977–87, we find that the average number of candidates per position in the arts and sciences was 1.60. This "historical" ratio of supply to demand (astonishingly) turns out to be exactly the same as the ratio for Model II in 1987–92. We conclude that the general level of our projections is believable.

A second conclusion is more substantive. There is no reason to expect the overall tightness of the academic labor market to change markedly in the next few years. Using the average of the four projections as a benchmark, we find that the ratio of candidates to positions (1.42) is slightly lower in 1987–92 than it was during the last decade—a result that is consistent with the impression of many that some modest tightening of academic labor markets has already occurred.

We now turn to an examination of trends in the balance between supply and demand in subsequent years. All four models show a more definite tightening of the academic labor market between 1987–92 and 1992–97. Also, the differences among Models I, II, and III narrow appreciably. While all three continue to project supply exceeding demand, the excess supply ranges from just under 4,000 (Model III) to about 7,000 (Model I) to just over 8,000 (Model II); the candidates-per-position ratio is projected to range from 1.15 to 1.36.

Model IV, which assumes recovery in arts-and-sciences enrollments, shows a more acute tightening in the market. It projects a very significant *excess demand*—about 8,000—as early as the 1992–97 period. Under the Model IV assumptions, the ratio of candidates to positions falls below unity in 1992–97 and is projected to be only 0.80.

The most dramatic change in the academic labor market is projected to occur *in the 1997–2002 period when all four models project demand to exceed supply by a significant amount.* The projections of excess demand range from a high of just over 8,000 to a low of just over 6,000, and the corresponding ratios of candidates per position range from 0.79 to 0.84.

This same general pattern prevails through the 2002–07 and 2007–12 periods. While some (relative) loosening of academic labor markets is projected for the last period shown, the change is not strong enough to move the candidates-per-position ratios back to unity, and certainly not back to anything like the ratios in the 1987–92 period.

The similarities among the models from the 1997–2002 period forward are attributable to the cautious nature of our assumptions for periods so far away. We were reluctant to make sweeping assumptions about changes in either arts-and-sciences shares of enrollments or student/faculty ratios beyond 1997, although we did make quite pointed assumptions for earlier periods. Of course, readers who wish to ask "what if" questions can certainly do so. For instance, it is possible to consider what would happen if student/faculty ratios continued to decline significantly past 1997 by extrapolating the differences between Models II and III in the earlier periods into 1997–2002 and later periods. Such an extrapolation obviously would produce projections of still tighter labor markets in those years.

There is a stronger reason for recognizing that our projections of demand may understate the tightness of labor markets. The underlying projections of aggregate enrollment assume constant age-specific enrollment rates. If enrollment rates for the 18–21 age group were to continue to rise in line with past trends, projected demand would be about 2 percent greater in 1987–92 and about 6 percent greater by 2007–12. In the 1997–2002 period (where substantial imbalances appear for the first time), substituting the rising-enrollment assumption in Model II increases projected demand by about 3 percent and therefore reduces the ratio of candidates per position from 0.83 to 0.81. This is obviously not a big change, and it indicates the limited degree to which the projected imbalances are sensitive to these particular assumptions about enrollment rates.[7]

Differences among Fields of Study

The projected relationships between supply and demand are by no means uniform across fields of study. Since staffing decisions by institutions and career decisions by individuals are field-specific, it is important to look carefully at these variations. Appendix Tables D.12 through D.14 are intended for the reader interested in detailed projections by field. To highlight the major differences, we have drawn together in Table 7.6 the projections for all three clusters of fields generated by a single model (Model II).

The biological sciences and psychology consistently show higher ratios of supply to demand than do the other clusters. In 1987–92, the projections indicate that there will be 2.2 candidates per faculty position in these fields (with an excess supply of nearly 6,000). Although the labor market for biological sciences and psychology is then expected to tighten, as it is in other fields, this ratio stays above unity in all periods.[8]

The results for mathematics and the physical sciences mirror those for all of the arts and sciences. Significant shortages (excess demand) are projected only from 1997–2002 onward, with projected ratios of 0.80 candidates per position in 1997–2002, 0.80 in 2002–07, and 0.95 in 2007–12.

From our perspective, the most striking conclusions pertain to the

[7] For a discussion of the methodology used to obtain the rising-enrollment assumption for the 18–21 age group, see Chapter Three, note 6. Other enrollment-rate assumptions could of course be substituted for this one.

[8] Colleagues in psychology with whom we have discussed this result suggest that it is skewed by the inclusion of clinical psychology, which has a growing number of students.

TABLE 7.6
Supply and Demand Projections, by Field of Study: Model II

	1987–92	1992–97	1997–2002	2002–07	2007–12
Humanities/Social Sciences:					
Projected Supply	14,335	13,633	13,460	13,460	13,460
Projected Demand	10,536	11,758	18,935	19,452	16,795
Supply − Demand	3,799	1,875	−5,475	−5,992	−3,335
Supply/Demand[a]	1.36	1.16	0.71	0.69	0.80
Mathematics/Physical Sciences:					
Projected Supply	7,603	7,567	7,471	7,471	7,471
Projected Demand	5,024	5,800	9,312	9,380	7,903
Supply − Demand	2,579	1,767	−1,841	−1,909	−432
Supply/Demand	1.51	1.30	0.80	0.80	0.95
Biological Sciences/Psychology:					
Projected Supply	10,600	10,099	10,003	10,003	10,003
Projected Demand	4,818	5,495	8,844	9,054	8,295
Supply − Demand	5,782	4,604	1,159	949	1,708
Supply/Demand	2.20	1.84	1.13	1.10	1.21
All Arts/Sciences:					
Projected Supply	32,538	31,299	30,934	30,934	30,934
Projected Demand	20,378	23,054	37,091	37,886	32,993
Supply − Demand	12,160	8,245	−6,157	−6,952	−2,059
Supply/Demand	1.60	1.36	0.83	0.82	0.94

Sources and Notes: All data are for five sectors only. The supply projections are from Table 7.1 and Appendix Table D.7. The demand projections are from Appendix Table D.9.

[a]The supply projection divided by the demand projection is the number of candidates per position.

humanities and social sciences. Contrary to what seems to be the general impression, our projections imply that these fields will exhibit by far the tightest labor market conditions. To be sure, projected supply exceeds projected demand in 1987–92 and then again in 1992–97 (but with much smaller margins). Once we reach the 1997–2002 period, the projected gaps between supply and demand are staggering: demand exceeds supply by almost 5,500 in 1997–2002, by nearly 6,000 in 2002–07, and by over 3,300 in 2007–12.

These projected differences for the humanities and social sciences are nearly as large as the differences for *all* of the arts and sciences in the 1997–2002 and 2002–07 periods—and they are almost 1½ times as large in 2007–12. It follows that the corresponding ratios of candidates per position must be very low, and so they are: 0.71, 0.69, and 0.80 in these three periods. If the assumptions used to derive these projections hold, there will be only seven candidates for every ten openings in the humanities and social sciences for roughly a ten-year period.

Because of the significance of the overall results for these fields, we have replicated for the humanities and social sciences the graphical analysis used earlier for all of the arts and sciences (Figs. 7.6–7.9). These figures show how much difference is made when we employ the assumptions of each of the four models.

Not surprisingly, the Model I projections (Fig. 7.6) show even sharper swings than the Model II projections. This is a direct con-

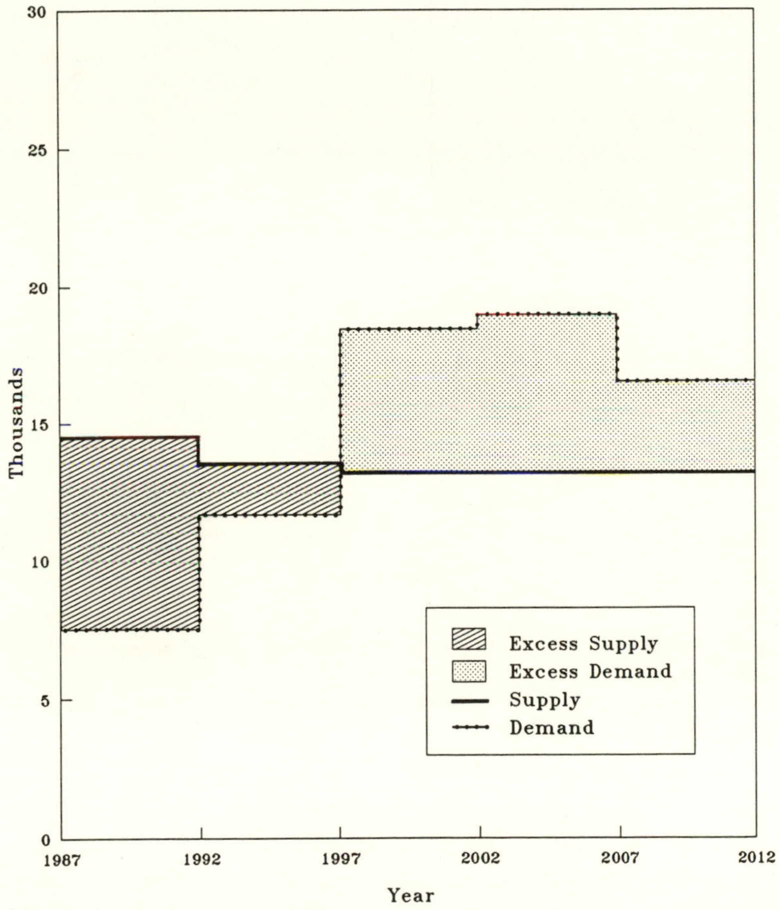

FIGURE 7.6
Supply and Demand Projections, Humanities and Social Sciences: Model I

Source: See text.

Note: In Model I, continuing declines in arts-and-sciences shares of enrollment are combined with declining student/faculty ratios.

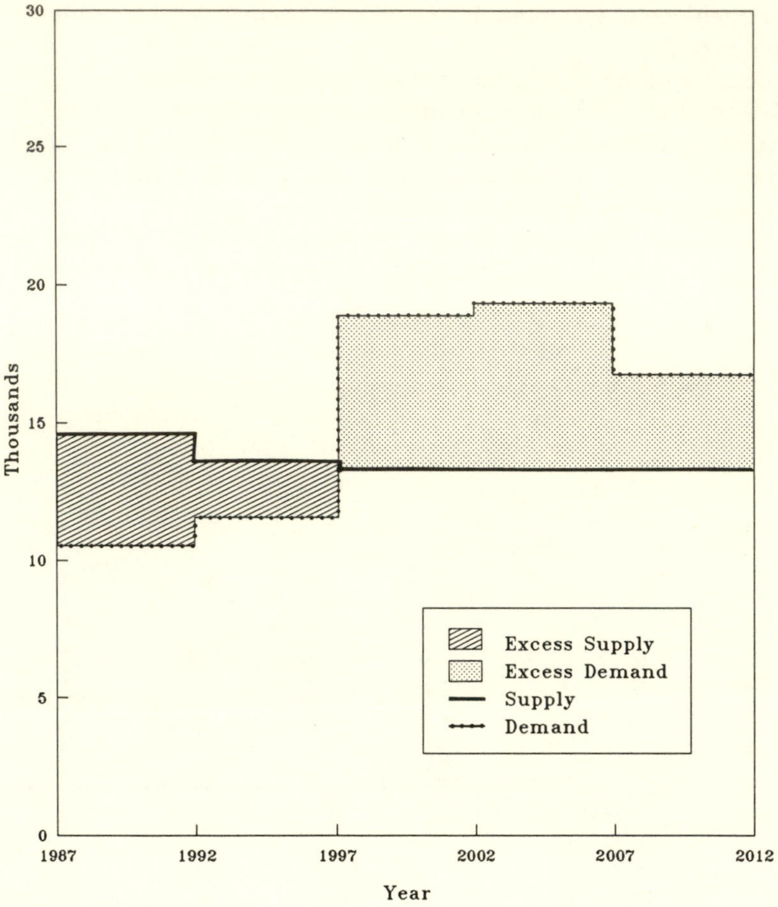

FIGURE 7.7
Supply and Demand Projections, Humanities and Social Sciences: Model II
Source: See text.
Note: In Model II, steady-state arts-and-sciences shares of enrollment are combined with constant student/faculty ratios.

sequence of allowing the arts-and-sciences share of enrollment (including the humanities and social sciences share) to continue falling through 1997, after which these ratios are assumed to reach a plateau.

Model III (Fig. 7.8) is perhaps the most revealing. Under the far-from-extreme assumptions of this model—which include a modest continuing decline in the student/faculty ratio—projected demand in the humanities and social sciences exceeds projected supply right from the start of our analysis in 1987. We also observe the same

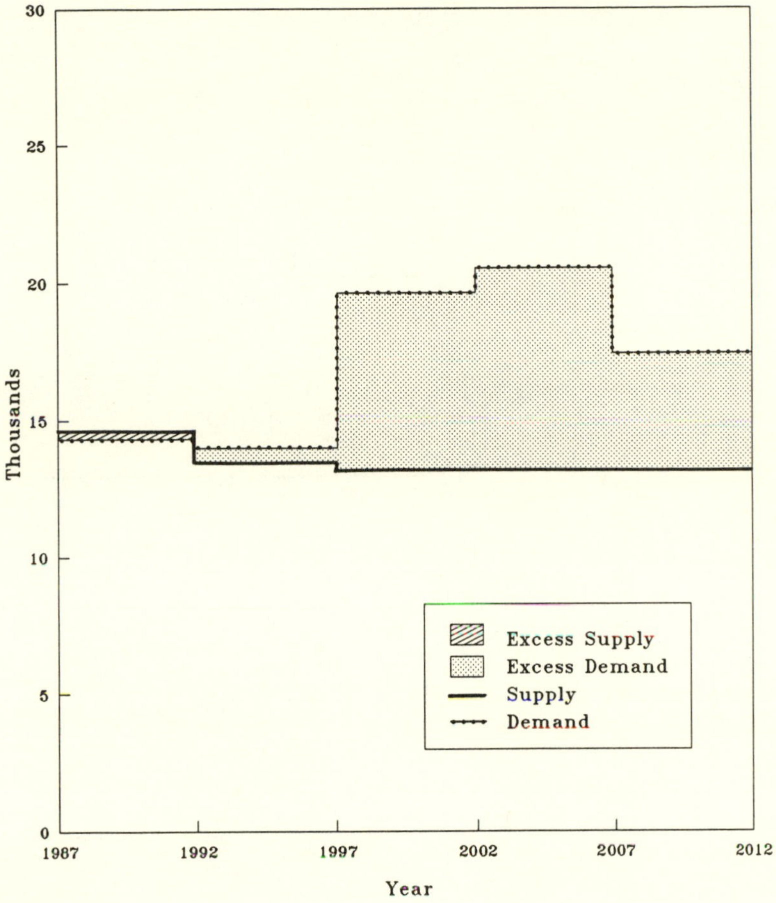

FIGURE 7.8
Supply and Demand Projections, Humanities and Social Sciences: Model III
Source: See text.
Note: In Model III, steady-state arts-and-sciences shares of enrollment are combined with declining student/faculty ratios.

dramatic increase in excess demand between the 1992–97 and 1997–2002 periods that characterizes Models I and II.

Model IV, with its assumption of recovery of the arts-and-sciences share of enrollment, yields projections of excess demand for the humanities and social sciences that are both very large in absolute terms and relatively constant over all five periods (see Fig. 7.9). This is the only model that displays this pattern. As noted earlier, we do not believe that this assumption is very plausible.

All of the candidates-per-position ratios for the humanities and

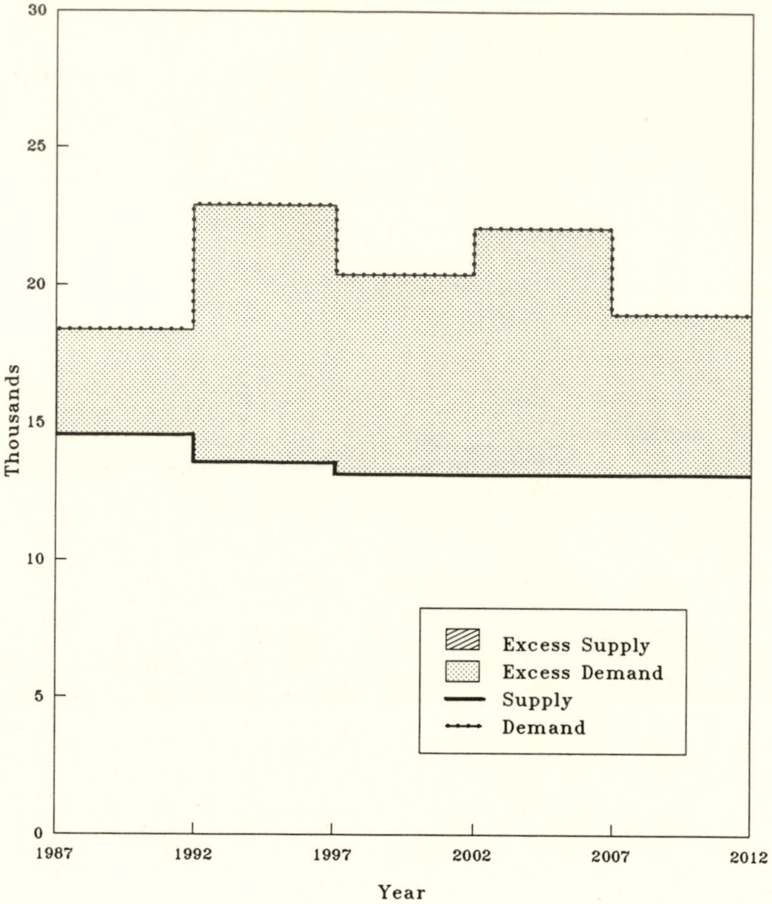

FIGURE 7.9
Supply and Demand Projections, Humanities and Social Sciences: Model IV
Source: See text.
Note: In Model IV, recovery in arts-and-sciences shares of enrollment is combined with increasing student/faculty ratios.

social sciences are collected and displayed in Figure 7.10. This figure shows vividly the low ratios of candidates per position projected from 1997 to 2012.

The humanities and social sciences cluster is by no means a monolithic aggregate. Between 1977 and 1987, the humanities grew less rapidly than the social sciences (16 percent versus 21 percent), and the more traditional fields within the humanities grew even less rapidly (14 percent) than the humanities as a whole. If these patterns

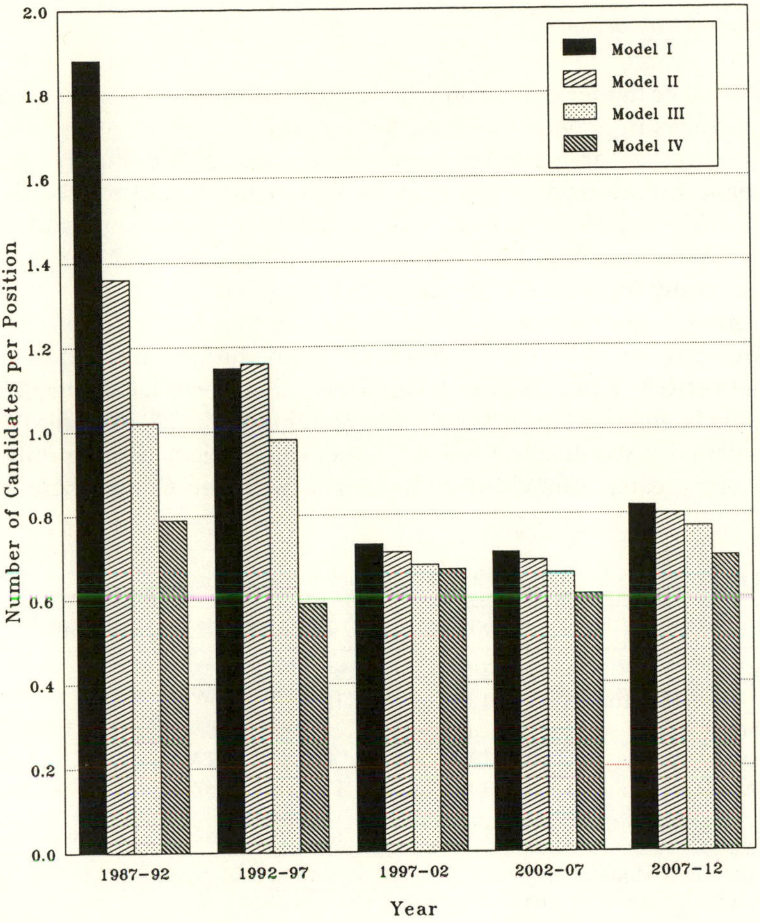

FIGURE 7.10
Projected Number of Candidates per Position, Humanities and Social Sciences: Comparison of Four Models
Source: See text.

hold in the future, only about 43 of every 100 projected new positions in the humanities and social sciences will be in the traditional areas of the humanities. These fields can also be expected to account for about half of the replacement demand, and thus for perhaps 45 percent of all positions that will become available.[9]

[9] These data on trends between 1977 and 1987 are from special SDR tabulations. In combining estimates of net new positions with estimates of replacement demand, we assumed that replacement demand will constitute roughly 90% of total demand (see discussion earlier in this chapter). We have defined "traditional" fields within the

Differences by Sector

While all of higher education will be affected in broadly similar ways by changes in general labor market conditions, there are significant differences in labor market prospects by sector. Specifically, while demand for arts-and-sciences faculty will increase markedly between 1987–92 and 1997–2002 in all five sectors, the *rates* of increase vary much more than might have been expected (see Table 7.7; we present results only for Model II to simplify the exposition).[10]

Perhaps the most noteworthy finding is that the situation of Research I universities differs markedly from the circumstances of all other sectors. Whereas demand for arts-and-sciences faculty in all five sectors is projected to be 82 percent greater in 1997–2002 than in 1987–92, demand within the Research I sector is projected to be only 57 percent greater. The clearest contrast is with the Comprehensive I

TABLE 7.7
Changes in Projected Demand, All Arts and Sciences, by Sector

Sector	*1987–92*	*1992–97*	*1997–2002*	*2002–07*	*2007–12*
Research I	1.00	0.99	1.57	1.61	1.41
Other Research/Doctorate	1.00	1.16	1.87	1.90	1.65
Comprehensive I	1.00	1.24	2.06	2.13	1.84
Liberal Arts I	1.00	1.30	2.17	2.22	1.95
Other Four-Year	1.00	1.15	1.67	1.67	1.47
All Five Sectors	1.00	1.13	1.82	1.86	1.62

Sources and Notes: Model II only. Index is based on setting total demand in 1987–92 equal to 1.00 in each sector. The underlying data are in Appendix Table F. 9.

humanities as history, English and American languages and literatures, foreign languages and literatures, and the following components of what is called "other humanities": comparative literature, classics, art history, and philosophy. As is explained in Appendix A, we excluded from the usual definition of "other humanities" music, theatre, and speech; including this latter group of fields would lead to significantly larger rates of increase, which can be misleading. Thus, "other humanities" as defined here is limited to American studies, letters, humanities-general, humanities-other, and religious studies. This category has been growing faster than the traditional fields within the humanities (68% between 1977 and 1987). Though demand in these fields may continue to increase relatively rapidly, this group still accounts for only 4% of all faculty positions in the cluster.

[10] These differences are particularly noteworthy because two basic assumptions used throughout this analysis (that enrollment shares by sector are constant and that the present pattern of student/faculty ratios does not change across sectors) minimize sectoral differences.

and Liberal Arts I sectors. In both of these sectors, demand is projected to more than double by 1997–2002.

These particularly divergent rates of increase are a direct consequence of the age distributions of faculties in 1987. Relatively large numbers of faculty in Research I universities are expected to exit from academia by 1992 because this sector starts out (in 1987) with relatively large numbers of faculty in both the youngest age groups (where quit rates are high) and the oldest age groups (where retirements occur). The Comprehensive I institutions, in contrast, had an unusually high fraction of their faculty in the 40–49 age group in 1987, and the exit rate for this sector is therefore lower in the initial period and higher later on. For these reasons, replacement demand in Research I universities is moderately *lower* in 1997–2002 than in 1987–92; in the Comprehensive I sector, replacement demand is 19 percent higher in 1997–2002 than in 1987–92.

The implications for faculty recruitment are clear. When all academic labor markets are projected to be the tightest (in 1997–2002 and 2002–07), the recruitment problems confronting the Research I universities, while still serious, will be relatively less difficult than those facing other sectors. By contrast, the Comprehensive I and Liberal Arts I institutions are likely to experience the greatest difficulties. Projected demand in these sectors peaks at the same time that the overall ratio of candidates per position is least favorable to institutions recruiting faculty.

The outlook for faculty recruitment in some sectors may be even more ominous if we consider the qualitative dimensions of the supply of new doctorates discussed at the end of Chapter Six. To the extent that some academic institutions prefer to hire faculty members with doctorates from certain universities, the supply/demand ratio that is relevant to them could be even more unfavorable than the overall supply/demand ratio. And if competition for faculty in general becomes acute, as may well happen in 1997–2002, the competition for faculty who hold doctorates from the most prestigious universities is sure to become even more intense. In such circumstances, many of the strongest Liberal Arts I institutions, for example, could find it very hard to continue to recruit faculty members from the universities that have educated a large number of their current staff.

Of course, the supply of new doctorates may increase, and we discuss this mode of adjustment in detail at the end of Chapter Eight. Projected imbalances between supply and demand would be altered significantly if prospective graduate students, current holders of doctorates, and academic institutions responded vigorously to changes in labor market conditions.

CHAPTER EIGHT

Adjustment Mechanisms

THIS COUNTRY'S SYSTEM of higher education is far more adaptable than people often assume. It is easy to draw wrong inferences from examples of rigidity on individual campuses or, for that matter, within sectors of higher education. Institutions, individuals, and markets all adjust, and that is a principal reason why the kinds of numbers projected in Chapter Seven will never be observed.

Though these projections are valuable, we believe, in providing advance warning of the labor market problems that will have to be confronted, they should not be thought to show more than the likely consequences of adopting specified assumptions and extrapolating defined trends. They make no allowance for adjustments that are likely to occur as markets seek to equilibrate, and they do not incorporate possible policy responses by private institutions, state governments, and, most important of all, the federal government.

In addition, higher education, as part of the larger society, will continue to be subject to unforeseen "shocks" that can affect academic labor markets drastically—as we have learned from historical experience with wars, economic dislocations, political currents (the effects of Mrs. Thatcher's program on British higher education come immediately to mind), and such events as the launching of Sputnik. Humility is plainly in order when even alluding to such large questions, and we will not burden this study with our own speculations on future economic, political, or scientific developments.

The dynamics of adjustment processes within higher education are themselves extraordinarily complex, and they deserve more careful analysis than they can be given here. We have developed what we hope are useful perspectives on ways in which academic institutions, faculty members, and graduate students may respond to shifts in labor market conditions (with particular emphasis on supply-side adjustments because these are, in our view, the most important). But we have not attempted to build new models or collect new data that would permit strong statements about the degree to which salaries can be expected to reflect altered supply/demand relationships, the elasticity of demand for faculty in various fields of study, or related questions. Full-scale studies of such topics, building on earlier work, are very much needed.[1]

In this chapter we comment on the role of salaries in the adjustment process and discuss other ways in which academic institutions may adapt to tightening labor markets. We then examine probable supply-side responses at greater length. Fluctuations in market conditions may cause individuals who are already employed to change their plans concerning retirement or to alter decisions to leave or reenter academia. Of even greater long-term significance are the responses that will be made by students in the process of deciding whether to seek Ph.D.'s as preparation for academic careers.

Faculty Salaries

In any labor market analysis, it is customary to look first to salaries as a principal nexus for reconciling supply and demand. Academic labor markets are no exception to this rule. The rapid expansion of higher education in the 1960s was accompanied by the only significant, sustained improvement in the real income of faculty members since World War II, and the substantial excess demand for faculty at that time was surely a major part of the explanation. Beginning in about 1969, slower growth in enrollments and in spending for research and development produced a slackening in demand; simultaneously, the pool of Ph.D.'s was enlarging rapidly. The condition of the academic labor market changed dramatically, moving from substantial excess demand to a surfeit of candidates for positions. Table 8.1 documents the dramatic changes in faculty salaries that accompanied these swings in labor market conditions.

The middle column in this table shows the decline in real salaries experienced by faculty members between 1970–71 and 1983–84. Faculty salaries fell 19 percent in real terms, while compensation in most other occupational categories more or less kept up with inflation. The decline was so great that it eliminated entirely the gains in real salaries that had been achieved in the 1960s: average real faculty salaries in 1983–84 were no higher than they had been in 1960–61.

[1] Freeman's 1971 study remains the most ambitious effort to apply traditional price theory and basic econometric techniques to this area. Freeman subsequently did other work, addressed principally to the markets for scientific and engineering personnel. Cartter (1976) and Radner and Miller (1975) comment on aspects of the adjustment process, but neither of those studies focuses primarily on the actual workings of markets. W. Lee Hansen (1986) has made the most comprehensive study of academic salaries in recent years. Breneman and Youn (1988) present both a review of the literature and many bibliographic references.

TABLE 8.1
Changes in Faculty Salaries Compared to Changes in Earnings of Other Groups, 1960–61 to 1983–84 (Percentage Changes in Real Dollars)

Occupational Group	*1960–61 to 1970–71*	*1970–71 to 1983–84*	*1960–61 to 1983–84*
1. All Faculty Members	+23.0	−18.7	0.0
2. Private Sector Employees in Jobs Equivalent to GS Grades 11–15 (Group C)	+18.0	+1.8	+20.2
3. Wage and Salary Income per FTE Worker, All Domestic Industries	+22.5	−2.0	+20.0
4. Manufacturing	+17.4	+3.3	+21.2
5. Government	+28.4	−1.3	+26.8
6. Disposable Personal Income per Employed Member of Civilian Labor Force	+26.4	+3.0	+30.1
7. Disposable Personal Income per Capita	+33.2	+15.5	+53.8

Sources and Notes: This table is reproduced from Hansen 1986, p. 89.

All salary and income figures are adjusted for price level changes. Data in line 2 use the Consumer Price Index converted to an academic year basis. Data in lines 3–7 are for calendar years 1970, 1976, and 1983.

Line 1: 1960–61 to 1970–71 increases are based on data for a selected group of 36 institutions drawn from AAUP data.

Line 2: Bureau of Labor Statistics, U.S. Department of Labor, *National Survey of Professional, Administrative, Technical and Clerical Personnel*, various issues. Based on March survey data (March 1971, 1976, and 1984). These private sector employees are mainly professionals such as attorneys, engineers, and accountants.

Lines 3–5: U.S. Department of Commerce, *Survey of Current Business*, July issues.

Line 6: Disposable personal income divided by employed members of the civilian labor force, *Economic Report of the President, 1985*, Appendix Tables B-24 and B-29.

Line 7: *Economic Report of the President, 1985*, Appendix Table B-24.

Most other occupational groups, in contrast, experienced increases in real earnings of at least 20 percent over this extended period.[2]

Given our interest in salary responses to the tightening academic labor markets projected in Chapter Seven, the data for 1960–61 to 1970–71 are especially revealing. Real salaries rose by 23 percent during this period, but it is important to note that the gain in academic

[2] For a general discussion of faculty salaries, see Hansen 1986. The reported figures may exaggerate to some extent the declines in real salaries and earnings between 1970–71 and 1983–84 because of problems with the CPI as a deflator—principally the treatment of housing costs during this period. *Relative* changes in salaries and earnings are not affected, however. For a careful analysis of salary behavior in both the 1960s and the subsequent period in the context of a formal supply-and-demand model, see Freeman 1980.

salaries relative to salaries elsewhere was hardly impressive. Wage and salary income in all domestic industries went up almost as much as faculty salaries (22.5 percent), and wages and salaries in government rose even faster.[3]

The 1960s were, as many have observed, a "golden era" for education in general, as well as for the academic profession. It is not just that the conventional balance between supply and demand was highly favorable then. These were also the years when federal support for higher education was rising more rapidly that ever before, and when academic institutions were enjoying exceptionally strong financial and political support from every quarter. Expenditures for higher education rose from 7.1 billion dollars in 1959 to 27.5 billion in 1970. Higher education's share of the GNP nearly *doubled*, rising from 1.4 percent in 1959 to 2.7 percent in 1970.[4]

Unless tightening labor markets in the future are accompanied by a corresponding resurgence of external support, it is far from obvious that similar salary increases should be anticipated. And it is sobering to be reminded that even in the exceptionally favorable setting of the 1960s, faculty salaries do not appear to have increased markedly relative to salaries in the economy at large.

The significant role played by general economic conditions, and especially the rate of inflation, is another aspect of salary behavior that deserves attention. Table 8.2 permits a comparison of average increases in salaries with increases in the Consumer Price Index (CPI). From 1972–73 through 1980–81, increases in salaries were outstripped each year by increases in the CPI, and real salaries fell accordingly. While inflation is of course a problem for the economy as a whole, it is a particularly serious problem for institutions of higher education—the double-digit inflation of the 1970s was a major contributor to the disproportionate decline in the real income of academics that occurred then. It seems equally clear that the sharp reduction in the rate of

[3] There is this qualification to be noted. The measure of faculty salaries being used here is an average for all ranks and is therefore affected by changes in the age distribution of faculties. The expansion of higher education that occurred in the 1960s surely lowered the average age. For this reason, average faculty salaries, as measured here, increased less rapidly than they would have had they been adjusted for changes in age distribution. Average salaries in the broadly defined occupational groups used in Table 8.1 were not affected as significantly by this factor, and the comparisons made in the table and in the text therefore presumably understate to some extent the relative gains in salary achieved by faculty members of a given age.

[4] See *Digest of Education Statistics* 1988, Table 23. Between 1970 and 1979, higher education's share of the GNP fell to 2.5%; it returned to 2.7% in 1986.

TABLE 8.2
Changes in Faculty Salaries and in the Consumer Price Index, 1971–72 to 1987–88

Year[a]	*Average Increase in Monetary Salary (%)*[b]	*Average Increase in CPI (%)*	*Average Increase in Real Salary (%)*[c]
1972–73	4.1	4.0	0.1
1973–74	5.1	9.0	−3.6
1974–75	5.8	11.1	−4.8
1975–76	6.0	7.1	−1.0
1976–77	4.7	5.8	−1.0
1977–78	5.3	6.7	−1.3
1978–79	5.8	9.4	−3.3
1979–80	7.1	13.3	−5.5
1980–81	8.7	11.6	−2.6
1981–82	9.0	8.7	0.3
1982–83	6.4	4.3	2.0
1983–84	4.7	3.7	1.0
1984–85	6.6	3.9	2.6
1985–86	6.1	3.0	3.0
1986–87	5.9	2.2	3.6
1987–88	4.9	4.0[d]	0.9

Source: AAUP, *Academe* March-April 1988: Table 1.

[a]We use "1972–73" as a simplified way of writing 1971–72 to 1972–73.

[b]Measured in current dollars. These figures are for all academic ranks in all institutions reporting comparable data for each of the periods since 1971–72.

[c]The average increase in real salaries is the percentage increase in monetary salary less the percentage increase in the Consumer Price Index.

[d]The change in the Consumer Price Index for March through June 1988 has been estimated.

inflation in the 1980s played a decisive role in permitting a significant recovery in real salaries.[5]

It would be surprising indeed if academic salaries were immune to swings in labor market conditions, and research indicates plainly that they are not. There has been less agreement, however, on just how responsive salaries are to market imbalances, as contrasted with how much they are affected by political and institutional forces that operate

[5] The higher education price index developed by D. Kent Halstead (1974) has tended to rise more rapidly than the CPI. And even this index understates the effects of inflation on colleges and universities in periods such as the 1970s, because it incorporates the depressed salary levels that were themselves partly a consequence of the harsh economic conditions. A more fundamental reason why inflation is so hard on higher education is that colleges and universities feel the ill effects of inflation right away, but they are much slower than organizations in most other parts of the economy to adjust their own income streams to compensate for the higher costs they must cover.

at least partially outside the market framework. After examining a variety of explanations for recent salary movements, Hansen concluded that "decisions of state legislators have been most critical in accounting for the deteriorating salary position of faculty members." Cartter had previously emphasized the dominance of the public colleges and universities, the relative inflexibility of salaries in these institutions, and the steady increase in their relative share of faculty positions over the years. The implication is that academic salaries in the future may be less responsive to changes in market conditions than they have been in the past.[6]

Recognizing the importance of general economic phenomena and institutional/political considerations certainly does not preclude recognizing that shifts in supply and demand schedules also will continue to influence salaries—and that changes in both salary levels and salary differentials will in turn moderate imbalances in academic labor markets. But we are reluctant to assign too dominant a role to salaries in the adjustment process. We suggest below that movements in salaries sometimes serve as proxies for other variables, and that other modes of adjustment may be more important.

Demand-side Responses by Academic Institutions

Responses by academic institutions to changing labor market conditions must be considered in the context of their characteristics as "firms" in a most unusual "industry." Colleges and universities are highly complex entities, with some of the attributes of a "consumer" as well as some of the attributes of a "producer." Any successful effort to understand these institutions better must begin with a sharper appreciation of their objectives and their modes of decision-making than has characterized a good deal of the recent discussion of the economics of education.

In certain respects, academic institutions should be expected to behave like ordinary firms in other industries. For instance, they have the same incentive to economize by substituting inputs that are becoming cheaper for inputs that are becoming more expensive whenever relative prices change and such substitutions are permitted by their production functions. Such "substitution effects" may well be

[6] See Hansen 1986, p. 98; and Cartter 1976, p. 151. Cartter's more general conclusion was that academic salaries are "not as flexible as . . . those in business and industry," and he did not expect them to "clear the market," at least in the short run (p. 157). Freeman has been the staunchest exponent of the power of the market mechanism, emphasizing the extent to which salaries are "determined, albeit with a lag, by supply and demand" (Freeman 1971, p. xxvi).

less important within higher education, however, than the kinds of "income effects" ordinarily associated with consumer behavior.

A college or university differs from the typical business firm in having central objectives that are qualitative, and that drive budget-making in ways that would not be predicted by thinking of it solely as a producer in the usual sense. In particular, "income" (or, more broadly, the flow of resources available to the academic institution) is a dominant determinant of the extent to which colleges and universities are able to realize such important objectives as raising the quality of the faculty.[7]

The financial circumstances of individual institutions will influence significantly how they respond to heightened competition for potential faculty members. Institutions facing severe budgetary problems will find it difficult even to consider significant salary adjustments. Also, as indicated above, private institutions may have more salary-setting flexibility than public institutions.

Budgetary constraints and limited salary flexibility are, however, only part of the explanation for the reluctance of many institutions to bid aggressively for new appointees when labor markets tighten. Colleges and universities have strong traditions of collegiality, and tenured faculty members and elected faculty committees often participate in the process of setting salaries. Because of both the relatively non-hierarchical nature of this process and the need for faculty of all ages and disciplines to feel that they are members of a single com-

[7] The significance of this general observation may be clearer if we consider another important objective of many academic institutions: providing the student aid required to enhance the quality and the diversity of their student populations. The confusion that can be caused by inappropriate application of ordinary theory-of-the-firm reasoning to issues in higher education is illustrated all too well by former Secretary of Education William Bennett's proposition that "federal student aid is . . . important in allowing colleges to raise their costs because it constitutes a major subsidy of higher education that insulates them from normal market forces of supply and demand" (quoted from a background paper circulated by Secretary Bennett to the governors of the states in 1987).

It can be demonstrated that the Secretary's implicit model of institutions of higher education seen as firms applies, if at all, only to the *profit-making proprietary sector* of higher education. When applied to other sectors, it leads to precisely the wrong conclusion about the impact on tuition of reduced federal support for student aid. The Secretary was led astray by implicitly assuming that institutions of higher education are (1) profit-maximizers; (2) with no excess demand for places in the entering class; and (3) no direct interest in the composition of their student populations. When the characteristics of most institutions of higher education are specified correctly, it is easily demonstrated that reduced federal support for student aid is likely to lead to higher tuition charges, not to lower ones, as institutions seek other sources of revenue to replace the student aid funds withdrawn by the government. (See Bowen 1987.)

munity, academic institutions are extremely conscious of the potentially harmful effects on morale of market-driven salary adjustments. Perceptions of internal equity matter—and they raise the institutional "cost" of salary responses. Such considerations are particularly relevant on small campuses, where everyone knows everyone else, and at institutions where salaries are a matter of public record.

Institutions are able to respond to changed labor market conditions in a variety of ways other than simply altering salaries. Changes in hiring standards are one of the most common forms of response. When labor markets tighten, academic institutions in general—and particularly those most reluctant to adjust salaries—may be forced to allow hiring standards to decline. Conversely, many colleges and universities will choose to raise hiring standards when there is a plentiful supply of talented young faculty.[8]

Increased competition for faculty members may also stimulate modifications in the perquisites and teaching obligations of faculty members. These can range from early promotion (often a disguised form of salary increase), to more generous research allowances, more frequent leaves of absence, and reduced teaching loads. While this last form of adjustment may help a particular institution recruit or retain a faculty member, it serves no larger, societal purpose, because it fails to close any part of the gap between demand and supply. On the contrary, such changes in faculty teaching schedules *reduce* student/faculty ratios at the very time that we might expect such ratios to rise—thus exacerbating the imbalance between supply and demand that increased the competition for faculty in the first place.[9]

[8] Studies of faculty appointments in the late 1960s and early 1970s show clearly what an important role changes in the quality of appointments can play in the adjustment process. During this downturn in the labor market, relatively less prestigious institutions were particularly successful in raising their hiring standards. The proportion of new doctorates obtaining positions in universities rated I or II by Cartter was halved. It was also found that new doctorates were increasingly likely to obtain positions in institutions with lower ratings that those from which they had obtained their own degrees. (See Niland 1973, cited in Freeman 1980, pp. 95–96.)

[9] We are indebted to Arjay Miller, former Dean of the School of Business at Stanford University, for calling our attention to the potential importance of this phenomenon. It has of course also been recognized by college and university administrators, who seem increasingly concerned about the consequences of lower teaching loads. Many recognize the potentially harmful effects of this response to increased competition for faculty, but it is hard for any one institution, or even any group of institutions, to resist such pressures. Other non-salary adjustments, such as early promotions, also can have adverse effects in the long run, especially if they force premature decisions about tenure. We believe that the welfare of the educational enterprise would often be served better if direct forms of salary adjustment were seen as more acceptable. (For an earlier

Other demand-side responses will lead to *rising* student/faculty ratios. For example, faculty positions may go unfilled, especially if institutions faced with tightening labor markets choose not to make significant adjustments in either salaries or hiring standards. In such circumstances, job searches are likely to fail, and an increase in vacancies will often be the more-or-less unconsciously chosen outcome. This may be a temporary form of adjustment, but we also know that vacancies can persist for some considerable time when labor market conditions are adverse and both salaries and hiring standards are relatively inflexible.

A more permanent (or at least longer-lasting) demand-side response to tightening labor markets is to reduce the number of authorized faculty positions. This is, of course, the most conventional economic response to an increase in the relative price of a particular "factor of production." One rigorous study of this mode of adjustment concluded that "demand for faculty responds to changes in academic salaries with a small but reasonably well-specified elasticity [about -0.3 to -0.4] and with some lag."[10]

When institutions have difficulty attracting faculty members at salary levels that they believe they can afford, some of them may also substitute faculty without doctorates for those with doctorates. Greater use of such faculty, perhaps combined with greater use of adjunct and part-time faculty, will be reflected in higher ratios of students to *full-time faculty with doctorates* (the group with which we are concerned in this study).

The overall effects of changing labor market conditions on student/faculty ratios are difficult to assess. Considered in isolation from other factors, we would expect tightening labor markets to lead to higher student/faculty ratios—as institutions are compelled to recruit from limited pools of able candidates and to economize on their utilization of an increasingly scarce resource. This is what happened during the early stages of the postwar expansion of higher education, when student/faculty ratios drifted upward.

Contrary to what we might have expected, however, student/faculty ratios actually fell somewhat during the years of even faster expansion (1963–67), before rising again in 1967–72 when enrollment increases were more modest. There are, we believe, two explanations for this seemingly perverse pattern of behavior. First, as indicated earlier, heightened competition for faculty can lead to lighter teaching

---

discussion of the effects of governmentally imposed salary rigidity in the British context, see Bowen 1963.)

[10] See Freeman 1980, pp. 124–25.

schedules and thus to lower student/faculty ratios. This may explain some of the decline in student/faculty ratios between 1963 and 1968, when competition for faculty was especially keen.[11]

The second explanation is more fundamental and relates to the emphasis at the start of this section on the importance of "income effects" in determining how academic institutions respond to changes in circumstances. The observed pattern of changes in student/faculty ratios between 1963 and 1967 (falling) and between 1967 and 1972 (rising) is entirely consistent with the simple proposition that institutions always *want* to have more faculty and will add faculty positions *when they can afford to do so*—just as they will cut back, however reluctantly, when economic circumstances force such actions. As noted earlier, 1963–67 was a period of rising affluence for higher education, just as 1967–72 was a difficult period for many reasons (including the effects of the war in Vietnam on support for higher education).

The fall in student/faculty ratios between 1977 and 1987 that we noted in Chapter Five can be explained similarly. Pressures to reduce faculty positions were intense through the 1970s, as institutions experienced what was popularly called a "new depression" in higher education. As a result, student/faculty ratios were in some sense abnormally high in 1977. When economic conditions gradually improved, largely because the inflation rate was brought under control, institutions were able to restore some positions eliminated earlier. It is not surprising, then, that student/faculty ratios were lower in 1987 than in 1977. (We suspect that this fall in student/faculty ratios was also due in part to an increasing emphasis on research during this period—with lighter teaching loads—and perhaps to greater use of graduate students as teaching assistants.)

Demand-side adjustments are likely to relieve somewhat the future imbalances between supply and demand projected in Chapter Seven, but they will vary from one type of institution to another as a consequence of differences in resources and objectives. A Research I university, for example, may increase its efforts to recruit outstanding faculty members from abroad while simultaneously raising salaries aggressively; another institution may not have such options (or wish to pursue them), and instead may cut out some low-enrollment courses and make greater use of adjunct faculty.

Institutions of all kinds are especially likely to make demand-side adjustments when faced with difficult economic constraints at the same time that labor markets tighten. There are also countervailing

[11] See Cartter 1976, pp. 102–07. Cartter's study is also the source of the overall data on changes in student/faculty ratios during the postwar expansion.

forces at work, however, and the *extent* of demand-side responses seems limited in any event. In part for these reasons, we continue to believe that the far more significant adjustments will occur on the supply side of the equation.

Supply-side Responses: Quit Rates and Retirement Rates

Changes in labor market conditions evoke two kinds of supply-side responses. They clearly affect the "flow" of *new* doctorates to academia—an important mode of adjustment that we consider in detail in the next section of this chapter. First, however, we want to examine likely responses by *current* holders of Ph.D.'s, who constitute the existing "stock" of potential academics.

Some of those who already have doctorates may make new decisions to move into or out of teaching, thus affecting what we have called quit rates for full-time faculty members. Similarly, others with doctorates may either accelerate or delay decisions to retire, thus affecting retirement rates.

The general conclusions of this part of our analysis, which are described in detail below, can be summarized succinctly. First, the long-term effects of both lower quit rates and lower retirement rates on replacement demand (and on supply) are significantly smaller than the short-term effects. This result follows from the dynamics of the process whereby changes in quit rates and retirement rates alter the age distribution of the faculty over time. A second, more far-reaching finding, is quantitative. Using the Model II projections of Chapter Seven as a reference point, we estimate that even a dramatic reduction in the quit rate would ultimately reduce replacement demand by a relatively modest amount. An equally dramatic reduction in the retirement rate would have an even smaller long-term effect.

Quit Rates

We would certainly expect tightening labor markets to reduce quit rates. Decisions by faculty members to leave teaching altogether are influenced not only by opportunities in non-academic fields, but also by those created—or closed off—by academic institutions themselves. If labor markets are tight and good replacements are hard to recruit, colleges and universities will naturally be somewhat more inclined to create incentives intended to retain individuals already on their staffs. And those faculty members who nonetheless fail to be reappointed or promoted at one institution will undoubtedly have a greater chance of finding a satisfactory position at another college or university when labor market conditions are favorable. A larger number of job opportunities, higher salaries, and more appealing employment conditions could also encourage doctorates employed in other sectors to seek academic appointments.[12]

While plausible, this discussion must remain abstract in the absence of empirical studies of the effects of changing labor market conditions on flows of doctorates between academic and non-academic employment. Without such studies, it is not possible to construct reliable behavioral relationships between quit rates and labor market conditions. Fortunately, however, there is another way to assess the potential significance of quit rates in the adjustment process. The mechanism for making projections that we developed for this study allows us to analyze the implications for supply/demand relationships of any number of alternative assumptions about quit rates. We can then see if believable changes in quit rates would imply radically different labor market conditions.

To bound the potential effects of changing quit rates on supply/demand ratios, it is useful to examine the consequences of making an extreme assumption—namely, that all of the age-specific five-year "quitting probabilities" decline to *half* the standard-quit assumptions used to generate the projections presented in Chapter Seven. This is roughly equivalent to assuming that only 0.25 percent of tenured faculty and only 2.5 percent of non-tenured faculty leave academia each year, as contrasted with the standard-quit assumptions of 0.5 percent and 5.0 percent, respectively. It should be emphasized that these new low-quit assumptions imply significantly less movement out of academic employment than has been observed in recent years or has been assumed by other authors.[13]

When we substitute these low-quit assumptions for the standard-quit assumptions, the number of faculty members projected to exit from academia in the 1987–92 period is reduced by about 4,500 (see Table 8.3). This is equivalent to reducing the projected replacement demand by 17.2 percent or (alternatively) to enlarging supply by 13.9 percent. Substituting the low-quit assumptions has the overall effect

[12] As explained in Chapter Two and Appendix B, the quit rates used in this study should be regarded as measuring net flows, which include not only exits from academia but also returns to academia from other sectors of the economy.

[13] The recently published longitudinal data for humanists holding doctorates suggest a quit rate that is almost exactly equal to the standard-quit assumptions used in this study and thus twice the new low-quit assumptions that we are now introducing. These same data imply that both gross quit rates (which measure only exits from academia) and net quit rates (which also take account of returns to academia from other employment sectors) have been quite stable over the last decade. See Appendix B for a detailed explanation of how quit rates were inferred from these SDR data.

TABLE 8.3
Comparison of Demand Projections Using Low-Quit Rates and Standard Assumptions

	1987–92	*1997–2002*	*2007–12*
Projected Supply of New Doctorates	32,538	30,934	30,934
Projected Replacement Demand:			
Standard Assumptions	20,378	37,091	32,993
Low-Quit Rates	15,854	33,875	29,610
Difference	4,524	3,216	3,383
Percentage of Standard-Quit Rates	17.2	11.3	10.4
Percentage of Supply of New Doctorates	13.9	10.4	10.9
Supply/Demand Ratio:			
Standard Assumptions	1.60	0.83	0.94
Low-Quit Rates	2.05	0.91	1.04

Sources and Notes: See Table 7.1, Appendix Table D.9, and text. Projections are for all arts and sciences; projected demand is based on Model II assumptions.

in this instance of increasing the projected ratio of candidates per position (the supply/demand ratio) from 1.60 to 2.05.[14]

In the 1997–2002 period, substituting the low-quit assumptions for the standard-quit assumptions increases the projected supply of academics by a significantly smaller number (3,216 or 11.3 percent of replacement demand) and causes the supply/demand ratio to rise from 0.83 to 0.91. In the last period, the introduction of the low-quit assumptions has a similar effect: the projected supply/demand ratio increases from 0.94 to just over unity (1.04).

Two major conclusions emerge from this analysis. First, even if quit rates were somehow to fall to these extremely low levels, there would be no radical change in the basic picture of prospective imbalances between supply and demand presented in Chapter Seven. This conclusion holds for each of the clusters of fields of study, as well as for all of the arts and sciences. For instance, substituting the low-quit assumptions for the standard-quit assumptions raises the supply/demand ratios for the humanities and social sciences from 1.36 to 1.72

[14] These results are for all faculty in the arts and sciences and for Model II only. Similar calculations have been made for the three clusters of fields of study and for the other models. While the numerical results of course vary, the pattern of findings is consistent across fields and models. We have also presented results for just three of the five periods because, again, the pattern is so consistent.

in 1987–92, from 0.71 to 0.78 in 1997–2002, and from 0.80 to 0.89 in 2007–12 (again using Model II assumptions).

The second major conclusion pertains to the time-path of the adjustment process. Substituting the low-quit rates for the standard-quit rates reduces replacement demand in the arts and sciences by about 17 percent initially, but then by only 10 to 11 percent when enough years have passed to allow the full effects of new quit rates to be experienced. More generally, any decrease in quit rates will have its greatest impact right away; over time, the impact will diminish but not disappear.

The dynamics of this adjustment process are fascinating. In the first period, the low-quit assumptions have their full effect on the number of faculty projected to leave—and there are as yet none of the offsetting effects felt later. Subsequently, the low-quit assumptions "age" the faculty by allowing larger numbers of faculty members to move through the age distribution. As a consequence, the new low-quit rates for the younger age groups (which is where these rates differ most from the standard-quit rates) have a less powerful effect after the initial period because they apply to the relatively smaller numbers of faculty now in these age groups.

There is another, even more important, way in which substituting low-quit rates affects the ageing of the faculty. As the years pass, those faculty members "saved" from quitting by the use of the low-quit assumptions move inexorably into the retirement-age categories and begin to retire in significant numbers. We find, then, that the contribution of lower quit rates to lower overall exit probabilities (which is the predominant effect in the early years) is offset in good part by a greater number of retirements in later years. It is for these reasons that the effects of the low-quit assumptions on replacement demand diminish over time and plateau at a steady-state level that is significantly below the initial level of impact.

To recapitulate: under the assumptions employed here, cutting the standard-quit rates in half ultimately reduces replacement demand (increases supply) by about 10 percent. And, as indicated above, it seems highly unlikely that quit rates would fall nearly this much, even if labor markets were to tighten markedly.

Retirement Rates

As we noted in Chapter Two, there is a good deal of research underway that will improve our knowledge of how retirement decisions in academia are affected by financial incentives and other variables. Many people are particularly concerned right now about the potential effects of "uncapping" (the elimination by law of mandatory retirement at any age). As part of the 1986 legislation, the National Academy of Sciences has been charged by Congress with assessing the consequences of allowing the present exemption of tenured faculty from the provisions of the Age Discrimination Act to expire in 1994.

We have concentrated on only one part of this complex terrain—namely, on the question of whether changes in retirement patterns that might be induced either by tighter labor markets or by the end of mandatory retirement would have an appreciable effect on labor markets in the arts and sciences over the next decades. Our answer to this question is an emphatic "No." While particular colleges and universities—and, even more so, particular fields and departments—could be affected significantly, the available evidence convinces us that the overall quantitative effect of an end to mandatory retirement would be negligible. In our judgment, it is the other consequences—for individuals, of course, but also for intellectual vitality, for leadership of departments and programs, for the productivity and cost of higher education, and for the capacity of fields to change direction—that deserve the most careful attention.

Two quite different sources of evidence lead us to such a strong conclusion about the likely (or, rather, the *un*likely) quantitative effects of retirement patterns on labor markets: (1) the same kind of analysis that was so helpful in clarifying the significance of hypothetical changes in quit rates for supply/demand projections; and (2) empirical evidence of observed similarities in retirement patterns between "capped" and "uncapped" institutions.

To sharpen our understanding of the sensitivity of our results to various retirement assumptions, we have tried out a new retirement assumption that is as extreme as the low-quit assumption used in the previous section. Specifically, we have cut in half the expected retirement rate of all faculty in the 65–69 age group, reducing the per annum retirement rate from 34 percent to 17 percent. The consequences of this drastic change in assumptions for projected supply/demand relationships in the arts and sciences (again using the Model II specifications) are summarized in Table 8.4.[15]

[15] Working out the full effects of introducing the low retirement-rate assumption is a complex process that will not be described here. It involves recalculating retirement life tables, among other things, and this in turn leads to new five-year survival probabilities for *both* the 60–64 and 65–69 age groups (which rise from 0.45 to 0.59 for the 60–64 group and from 0.08 to 0.29 for the 65–69 group), even though the *annual* retirement rate is changed only for the 65–69 group. The reason for this apparent anomaly is that these are *five*-year survival probabilities. Some faculty members who were age 60–64 at the start of a new five-year period will move into the 65–69 age range early

TABLE 8.4
Comparison of Demand Projections Using Low Retirement Rates and Standard Assumptions

	1987–92	*1997–2002*	*2007–12*
Projected Supply of New Doctorates	32,538	30,934	30,934
Projected Replacement Demand:			
Standard Assumptions	26,863	28,472	32,553
Low Retirement Rates	24,740	27,937	31,892
Difference	2,123	535	661
Percentage of Standard Replacement Demand	8.0	1.9	2.1
Percentage of Supply of New Doctorates	6.5	1.7	2.1
Supply/Demand Ratio:			
Standard Assumptions	1.60	0.83	0.94
Low Retirement Rates	1.78	0.85	0.96

Sources and Notes: See Table 7.1, Appendix Table D.9, and text. Projections are for all arts and sciences; projected demand is based on Model II assumptions.

If the sharply lower retirement rate were to take effect immediately (or, rather, if it had been in effect at the start of the 1987–92 period), approximately 2,100 fewer faculty would have left higher education by the start of the 1992–97 period. This number is 8 percent of the total replacement demand under standard assumptions and is equivalent to a 6.5 percent increase in supply. The overall supply/demand ratio would increase from 1.60 to 1.78. Thus, there is a clear first-period impact, even though it is not strong enough to alter drastically the general labor market outlook.

The change in replacement demand (and supply) caused by the lower retirement-rate assumptions is much smaller in later periods. *In 1997–2002, the low retirement-rate assumptions reduce replacement demand by just over 500 faculty positions in all of the arts and sciences.* The situation is similar in 2007–12. Once a new "steady state" has been reached, replacement demand under the low retirement assumptions is only about 2 percent lower than replacement demand under the standard retirement assumptions. This central finding is a principal reason why we do not believe that the debate over mandatory retirement should focus on the quantitative effects on faculty vacancies.

As in the case of quit rates, it is the age-specific character of our analysis that permits a clear appreciation of the difference between

in the new five-year period and therefore will be subject to the new retirement rate applicable to the 65–69 age group.

initial effects and ultimate effects. This difference is especially pronounced for retirements, because *eventually* everyone exits from academia by one route or another.

The dynamics of the adjustment process can be described as follows. In the first period, a lower retirement rate is translated directly into fewer exits from academia. In subsequent periods, the lower retirement rates produce a somewhat older age distribution, which in turn reduces quits by lowering the fraction of the total faculty who are in the youngest age groups and thus are most susceptible to quitting. In the 65–69 age group, there are now conflicting forces at work: the applicable retirement rate is lower, but there are more faculty in the age group (because the low retirement-rate assumption increased the probability of "surviving retirement" for five years for those in the 60–64 age group). Thus, the total number of retirements may actually be greater. And the low retirement assumptions then cause more people to be in the over-69 group, from which everyone still living is assumed to retire.

Before we move from this discussion of the effects of hypothetical changes in retirement rates to an examination of recent empirical studies of actual retirement patterns, we would like to compare these retirement-rate results with the comparable findings for quit rates. The two sets of results reinforce each other, as we see in Figure 8.1. The convergence over time of the supply/demand projections is evident, and we see that it takes about ten years for a new set of steady-state relationships to be established. By then, the supply/demand ratios are not very different using the low-quit and low-retirement assumptions rather than the standard assumptions. In 1997–2002, for example, the respective supply/demand ratios are 0.83 for the standard assumptions, 0.91 for the low-quit assumptions, and 0.85 for the low-retirement assumptions. Figure 8.1 also reminds us that halving the retirement rate has a much smaller long-term effect on supply/demand ratios than halving the quit rate.

We would not want to leave the impression (based on the extreme assumption that we made for the purposes of this analysis) that there is any real possibility that retirement rates will in fact be cut in half. Recent studies of the actual experience of a number of colleges and universities suggest that age-at-retirement has been surprisingly constant at most institutions for some years and that there is no significant difference in age-at-retirement between colleges with no mandatory retirement age and colleges with mandatory retirement. In most institutions, there are very few faculty members who serve until age 70 in the absence of mandatory retirement.[16]

[16] The primary source for these observations is preliminary data from the Project on Faculty Retirement, Industrial Relations Section, Princeton University, Princeton, N.J.

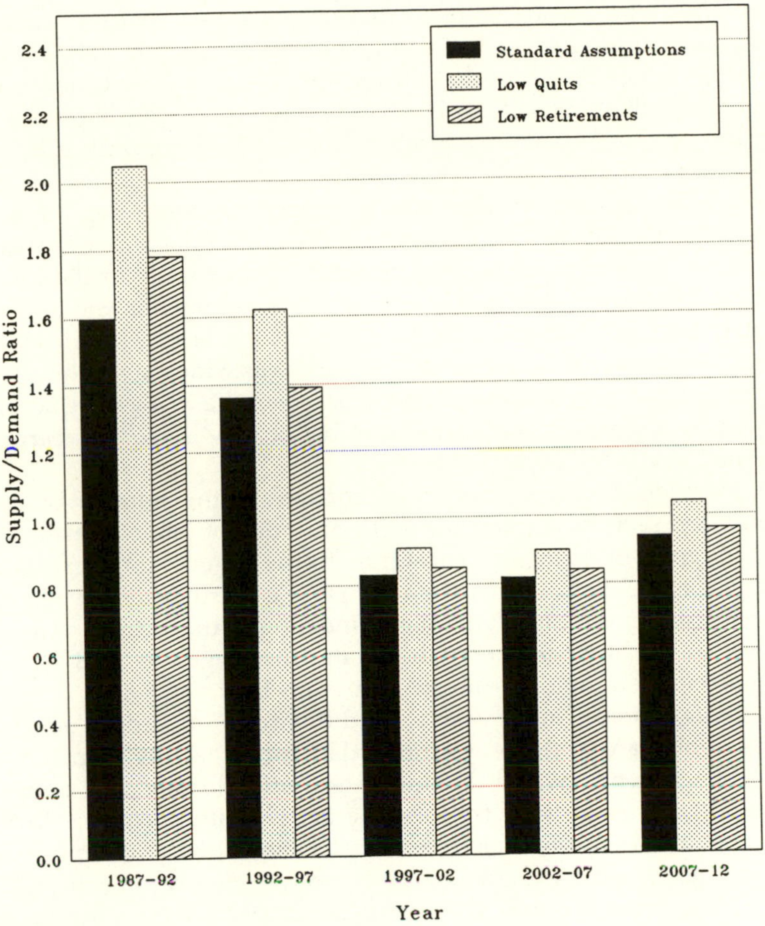

FIGURE 8.1
Comparison of Supply/Demand Ratios, Using Alternative Quit Rate and Retirement Rate Assumptions
Source: See text.

SUPPLY-SIDE RESPONSES: NEW DOCTORATES

The projected supply of new academics is affected most directly by the flow of new doctorates. Students who are beginning to plan careers are more flexible—and more susceptible to influences of many

---

The directors of this project (Albert Rees and Sharon Smith) point out, however, that the private Research I universities exhibit different patterns of retirement than other sectors, and that some of these universities may well experience significant increases in average age-at-retirement if uncapping occurs.

kinds, including improved labor market prospects—than those who have finished their schooling and embarked on careers. While many variables affect decisions to pursue graduate study, students are surely more likely to seek Ph.D.'s, and to think seriously about teaching and research vocations, when employment opportunities in academia are attractive.

The historical record offers strong support for this simple line of reasoning. We saw in Chapter Six that the number of newly awarded doctorates in almost every field increased dramatically in the 1960s. It is no coincidence that those were also the years when the number of academic appointments was growing rapidly, faculty salaries were rising, and financial aid for graduate study was widely available. Subsequently, the grim academic labor markets of the 1970s were accompanied by a sharp decline in the number of new doctorates earned, especially by U.S. residents.

A more detailed examination of changes in the number of new doctorates, seen in conjunction with an index of labor market conditions, gives even greater substance to these general observations (see Fig. 8.2). There is an extremely close congruence between the movements of the supply/demand index and the year-to-year increases in the number of new doctorates that began in 1958–62 and then accelerated rapidly from 1962 through 1970.[17]

Although there is no way to extend this series of supply/demand ratios (which are based on Cartter's data for all faculty members in all fields) beyond 1972 by linking these ratios to our own supply/demand ratios (which are for full-time faculty with doctorates in the arts and sciences), there are reasons to believe that any supply/demand ratio would have remained well above unity during the 1970s and 1980s. Impressionistic comments about labor market conditions certainly support such an interpretation. In addition, as we reported in Chapter Seven, our retrospective analysis of the 1977–87 period resulted in a supply/demand ratio of 1.60 for full-time faculty with doctorates in the arts and sciences. This characterization of labor market conditions in the post-1972 period (as marked by significant excess supply) is consistent with the sharp decline in the number of new doctorates—and particularly new doctorates awarded to U.S. residents—that occurred after the 1972 peak.

[17] The index of supply/demand relationships for the years 1958 to 1972 was derived from data in Cartter's 1976 study. In brief, we calculated a crude supply/demand ratio by dividing Cartter's figures for numbers of new doctorates awarded each year in all fields (not just the arts and sciences) by his estimates of the corresponding numbers of junior faculty openings in all fields. We then smoothed the data by calculating a three-year moving average of these ratios.

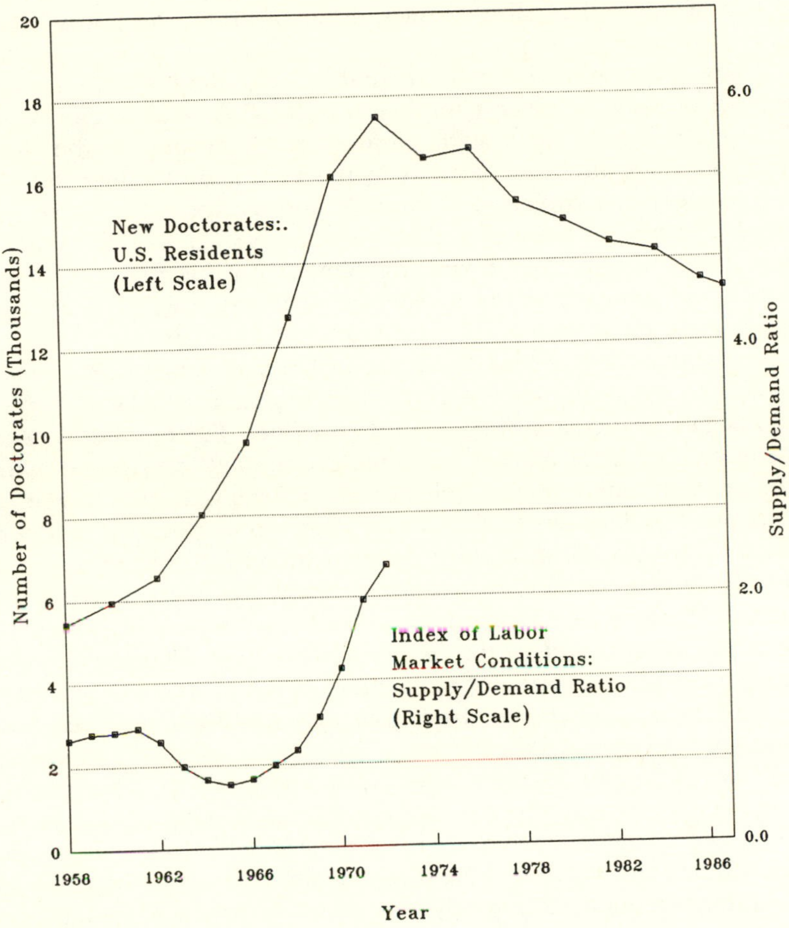

FIGURE 8.2
New Doctorates in the Arts and Sciences in Relation to Labor Market Conditions
Source: SED tabulations and text.

Response Lags and Time-to-Degree

There is also clear evidence of sizeable time lags in the response of the output of new doctorates to changes in labor market conditions. The supply/demand ratio reached its lowest point in 1965, when excess demand for academics was at its peak; the annual output of new doctorates peaked about seven years later, in 1972. While this response lag is the product of many forces, it is related most directly to one of the indisputable characteristics of Ph.D. programs—their long duration.

It should be stressed, however, that "time-to-degree" (the median number of years between completion of the B.A. and receipt of the Ph.D.) is by no means a static parameter. At the time of the sharp expansion of graduate education in the 1960s, the median time-to-degree between completion of the B.A. and receipt of the Ph.D. was about 7.7 years for the arts and sciences. In 1987, it was 9.5 years. A close inspection of year-to-year movements in this measure of the duration of graduate study suggests that time-to-degree is affected significantly by labor market conditions (see Fig. 8.3).

We see that median time-to-degree began to decline in 1962 (when it was 8.3 years)—the same year in which the number of faculty openings began to increase sharply and to exceed the number of new doctorates. As labor market conditions continued to improve markedly, median time-to-degree fell steadily, reaching its own low of 7.2 years in 1970. Between 1970 and 1972, the supply/demand ratio was above unity and rising rapidly; median time-to-degree rose just as steadily, but less rapidly. Although (for reasons explained above) this particular supply/demand index cannot be calculated beyond 1972, we can be quite confident that the number of new doctorates consistently exceeded the number of faculty openings; and we see from Figure 8.3 that median time-to-degree increased each year, reaching a high of 9.5 years in 1986.

Although time-to-degree is affected by many factors, labor market conditions are plainly one relevant consideration. Graduate students have a natural tendency to make more determined efforts to complete their studies and move into full-time faculty positions when job opportunities are good. Conversely, when jobs are harder to find, graduate students have less incentive to finish their Ph.D.'s. They are more inclined to keep working in the hope that an ever-better dissertation, combined with teaching experience, will improve their competitive position in the job market.

This analysis explains what otherwise would be a puzzling empirical relationship. We saw from Figure 8.2 that, in the 1960s and early 1970s, the output of Ph.D.'s responded to changing labor market conditions with a lag of about 7 years. This response lag was *shorter* than median time-to-degree, whereas we might have expected the response lag to have been somewhat *longer*. After all, it surely takes students some time to assimilate new information about labor market conditions, to apply to graduate schools, and to make other arrangements that pre-date the beginning of graduate study. The explanation for this apparent anomaly lies in the responsiveness of time-to-degree

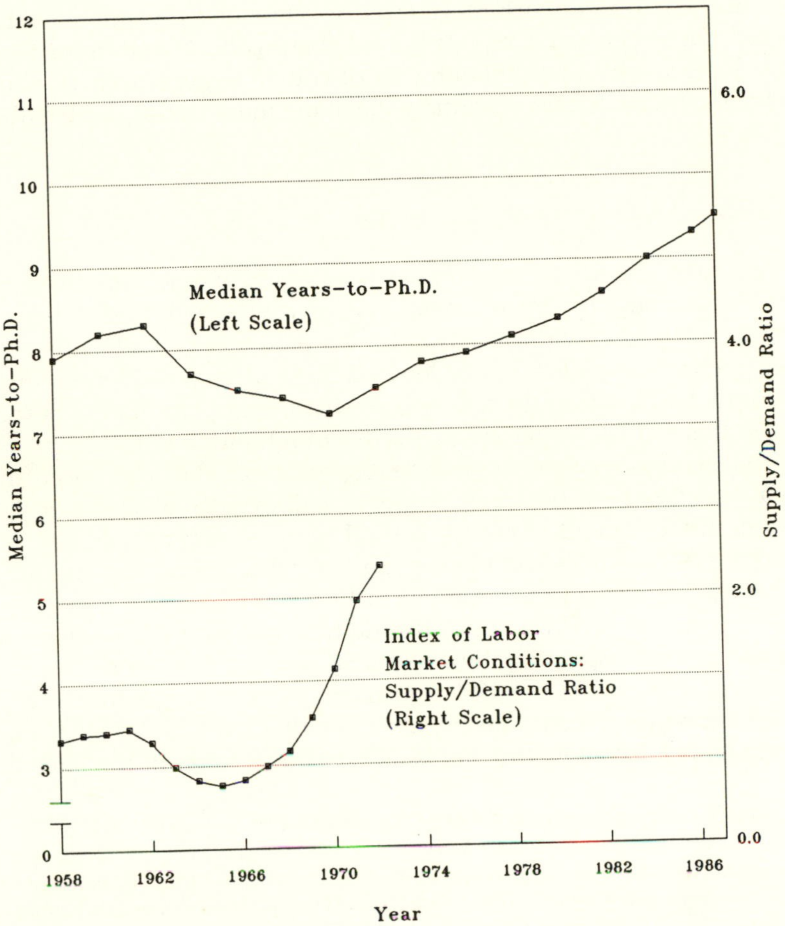

FIGURE 8.3
Median Years-to-Ph.D. in Relation to Labor Market Conditions
Source: See text.

to labor market conditions. When students already in graduate school are encouraged to finish their degrees sooner, the measured response lag is shorter than it would be if it were a function only of the length of time that it takes new students to begin and then to complete their Ph.D.'s.

From the standpoint of adjustment mechanisms, the implication of this analysis is that when labor markets tighten, colleges and universities seeking to fill positions may find some short-term relief in the tendency of graduate students "already in the pipeline" to complete their degree work more rapidly. Thus, supply-side responses need not be delayed completely until a new cohort of students begins graduate work—even though it is of course larger numbers of new Ph.D. candidates that eventually make the more lasting contribution.

Estimating Numbers of New Doctorates

We return now to the question of how much of a quantitative effect changes in supply/demand relationships can be expected to have on the number of new doctorates. There are no recent studies that provide reliable evidence of the likely degree of responsiveness in the various fields within the arts and sciences, and perhaps the best approach is to make what are avowedly rough judgments.[18]

In considering what supply-side response we believe is conceivable, one benchmark is the peak number of doctorates awarded to U.S. residents at the end of the last period of expansion of graduate education (1972). For the humanities and social sciences, the number of Ph.D.'s awarded to U.S. residents in 1972 was 67 percent greater than the number awarded in 1987; for mathematics and the physical sciences, the corresponding figure was 58 percent; and for the arts and sciences as a whole, the 1972 figure was 32 percent greater than the 1987 figure. (It is important to remember that the total for all arts and sciences is affected by the number of new doctorates in the biological

[18] The most rigorous examination of the relationship between labor market conditions and the output of doctorates (in science) was made by Freeman (1975). Unlike almost everyone else who projected changes in the number of new doctorates between 1970 and 1980 (including Cartter, whose "variable coefficients" model projected continuing growth in Ph.D.'s in all fields from 35,000 in 1972–73 to 45,000 in 1983), Freeman foresaw a sharp drop. Moreover, his forecast of the number of physics Ph.D.'s in 1980 turned out to be remarkably accurate.

Nonetheless, we are reluctant to use Freeman's equations to generate quantitative forecasts for the periods ahead. First, our interest is by no means limited to physics, and it is difficult to know whether markets for humanists and social scientists respond at all similarly to the variables emphasized by Freeman (which include spending on research and development). Also, Freeman's parameters are based heavily on experience in physics during the 1950s and 1960s, which was a most unusual time; all of the factors at work then—including generally positive attitudes toward science and very generous support for graduate students—may not reappear the next time that labor markets tighten. Finally, Freeman's forecast was for approximately six years ahead of the year in which he was writing, and the lagged dependent variable in his equation has a great deal of influence on his results. In all likelihood, the same equation would not have forecast the leveling-off of Ph.D. output that occurred immediately after 1980. In general, the kind of model developed by Freeman is better suited to forecasting supply a few years ahead than it is to making longer-term projections.

sciences and psychology, which were 8 percent *lower* in 1972 than in 1987.)

We can be reasonably confident that many universities have the latent capacity to expand the supply of Ph.D.'s. There has been little, if any, contraction in the number of Ph.D. programs, and faculty members generally are eager (sometimes too eager) to expand such programs whenever there seems to be any justification for doing so. Some institutions may be able to increase graduate enrollments substantially without having to make major new investments in faculty positions. However, other universities, including some of those with the strongest graduate programs, may find it harder to expand their programs. Faculty members may already be heavily committed, and additional staff may be required if more graduate students are to be supervised adequately. In short, while we do not believe that the overall capacity of doctoral programs is constrained in any rigid way, it would be a mistake to assume that large-scale expansion can occur easily or without cost.[19]

Other barriers to expanding the supply of new doctorates also need to be considered. It is far from clear that incentives for students with B.A.'s to pursue Ph.D. programs will be powerful enough to stimulate a strong recovery in the number of new doctorates awarded to U.S. residents. The appeal of Ph.D. programs will depend principally on factors such as: the general perception by potential Ph.D. candidates of the job outlook in higher education; the resources available to improve faculty salaries and other conditions of academic employment; the appeal of alternative career prospects; and financial aid available to graduate students in the arts and sciences.

Response lags must also be taken into account. It is difficult to know how rapidly Ph.D. output could increase, even under highly favorable conditions. Some modest increase in new doctorates could occur as early as the 1992–97 period, especially if students, universities, and the government were to plan ahead in anticipation of shortages. However, it is probably unrealistic to expect major changes in the number of new doctorates until at least the 1997–2002 period, when labor

[19] A different kind of potential constraint on capacity should be mentioned. The debate over the quality of elementary and secondary education raises questions concerning the size and depth of the pool of students who could eventually become reasonable candidates for Ph.D. programs. It has been suggested that this may be a particularly serious problem in mathematics and the sciences. (See National Research Council 1988b.) It is at least modestly reassuring, however, to see that the number of B.A. degrees conferred in mathematics has been rising in recent years. In 1985–86, 16,306 B.A.'s in mathematics were conferred; the low was 11,078 in 1980–81. (See *Digest of Education Statistics* 1987, Table 174.)

markets are projected to be significantly tighter and when students have had more opportunity to respond to earlier signals of improving job prospects.

Response lags could delay the major part of the increase in new doctorates until an even later period. If we were to use only the most recent data on median time-to-degree as the relevant measure of lags, full responses would not occur for approximately 7 years in mathematics and the physical sciences, 11 years in the social sciences, and over 12 years in the humanities. There are ways to reduce these lags, however, and we will concentrate on the 1997–2002 period and assume (perhaps too optimistically) that the full impact of an increasing number of new doctorates will be felt by then.

If there are strong incentives and sufficient resources, it is conceivable that the number of Ph.D. candidates might increase by as much as two-thirds of the amount by which Ph.D. output fell between 1972 and 1987. A recovery of Ph.D. output on this scale would translate into a 45 percent increase in doctorates in the humanities and social sciences, a 40 percent increase in mathematics and the physical sciences, and a 29 percent increase in the arts and sciences overall (holding the biological sciences and psychology constant).

These are clearly very large increases, and they would have a significant impact on projected supply/demand ratios if they were to occur. Specifically, the supply/demand ratio for the humanities and social sciences in 1997–2002 would increase from 0.71 to 1.00; the corresponding ratio for mathematics and the physical sciences would increase from 0.80 to 1.05; and the ratio for all of the arts and sciences would increase from 0.83 to 1.04. (All of these calculations, and others described below, are based on Model II projections. The results obviously would change if other models were employed.)

To avoid any possible misinterpretation, we should stress that it is pure accident that these supply/demand ratios—produced by assuming that the supply of new doctorates recovers to two-thirds of the 1972 peak values—are so close to 1.0. These results are convenient, however, in that they tell us that this is the general scale of recovery in the output of Ph.D.'s that would be required (accepting the other assumptions underlying the projections) to produce approximately one candidate per position in 1997–2002.

But there is certainly nothing special about this particular relationship between supply and demand, and it is not the relationship that has prevailed generally. A supply/demand ratio of 1.0 means that labor market conditions would be considerably tighter in 1997–2002 than they have been for almost all of the last two decades, and also tighter than they are projected to be in 1987–92 and 1992–97. (For the humanities and social sciences, the projected supply/demand ratios for 1987–92 and 1992–97 are 1.36 and 1.16, respectively; for mathematics and the physical sciences, these ratios are 1.51 and 1.30. See Tables 7.5 and 7.6.)

In light of both historical experience and the results of these projections, a supply/demand ratio of approximately 1.3 seems nearer to the norm than does a ratio of 1.0. Moreover, even a ratio of 1.3 would imply tighter labor market conditions than we have known recently—the supply/demand ratio for all of the arts and sciences calculated retrospectively for the 1977–87 period was 1.60. Therefore, it is useful to know how large a percentage increase in supply would be required to reach a ratio of 1.3 candidates per position. This information is provided in the bottom panel of Table 8.5. The top panel of this table reproduces the supply/demand ratios described above (based on the assumption that new doctorates increase by two-thirds of the amount by which they declined between 1972 and 1987) so that comparisons can be made readily.

The principal conclusion to be drawn from the first of the new calculations is that using a ratio of 1.3 candidates per position as a criterion, while leaving all other assumptions unchanged, would require a vast expansion of graduate education: an increase of 92 percent in the number of new doctorates in the humanities and social sciences, for instance. The output of new doctorates would have to rise well beyond the 1972 peak, and it is hard to believe that such an expansion could occur under any plausible set of conditions.

Other assumptions incorporated in these projections can also be modified, however, and changes in them make a considerable difference. For example, all of the supply projections used in Chapter Seven assume that the share of doctorates employed in academic institutions continues to decline at least modestly. Tightening academic labor markets could halt this trend, and we show in Table 8.5 the implications of assuming that the share of new doctorates seeking academic positions remains constant at its 1987 level. Under this assumption, the increase in new doctorates needed to reach a supply/demand ratio of 1.3 falls from 92 percent to 75 percent in the humanities and social sciences, and from 82 percent to 67 percent in mathematics and the physical sciences.

We have also assumed that there will be no major change in the relative number of non-resident holders of doctorates employed by academic institutions in this country. It is possible that tightening academic labor markets will lead to even more active recruitment of academics from overseas, but there is no easy way to quantify this mode of adjustment. Much will depend on government policy con-

Table 8.5
Alternative Projections of Supply of New Doctorates, by Field of Study, 1997–2002

	Percentage Change in the Number of New Doctorates[a]		
	Hum./Soc. Sci.	*Math/Phys. Sci.*	*All Arts/Sci.*
Assuming Two-Thirds Recovery of 1972 Levels of Ph.D. Output[b]	45	40	29
[Supply/Demand[c]]	[1.00]	[1.05]	[1.04]
New Doctorates Needed to Reach Supply/Demand Ratio of 1.3:[d]			
Model II Demand and Declining-Share Supply Projections	92	82	64
Model II Demand and Constant-Share Supply Projections	75	67	51
5% Reduction in Model II Demand and Declining-Share Supply Projections[e]	82	71	55
5% Reduction in Model II Demand and Constant-Share Supply Projections[e]	66	57	43

[a]Calculated as percentages of the base projections of supply for 1997–2002 in Table 7.6.

[b]The assumptions concerning recovery of output of new doctorates are explained in the text. The percentage increases in the humanities/social sciences and in mathematics/physical sciences are approximately two-thirds of the declines in output experienced between 1972 and 1987. This is equivalent to assuming that output of doctorates in the humanities and social sciences increases 45% over the previously projected level for 1997–2002; and in mathematics and the physical sciences 40%. The percentage increase for all arts and sciences (29%) was calculated after we first found the absolute increase in new doctorates for all arts and sciences by summing the increases for humanities/social sciences and mathematics/physical sciences. This procedure was followed because doctorates in biological sciences/psychology did not decline between 1972 and 1987 (and therefore could not be assumed to "recover"); in effect, we held the output of doctorates in biological sciences/psychology constant at its 1987 level in calculating percentage increases in new doctorates for all arts and sciences.

[c]The supply/demand ratio shown here was calculated by dividing the new total supply projection by the previous projection of demand, using Model II assumptions.

[d]All of these increases in the supply of new doctorates were calculated after specifying (for reasons given in the text) a supply/demand ratio of 1.3. The increase in supply needed to achieve this ratio was then calculated for each set of assumptions about supply and demand listed on the table. Throughout, we assumed that the number of non-resident Ph.D.'s included in the supply of doctorates to academia was constant at the previously projected level. Thus, the increases in new doctorates are U.S. residents only, and the percentage increases are percentages of the number of U.S. residents in the previously projected supply figures.

[e]The assumed 5% reduction in demand is intended to represent the possible contribution to the adjustment process of a combination of some decrease in quit rates and retirement rates (each of which reduces replacement demand) and some demand-side response to tightening labor markets.

cerning immigration, as well as the overall degree of mobility of highly educated individuals across national boundaries.

We have made some very rough calculations to determine what difference it would make if tightening labor markets reduced quit rates and retirement rates, and simultaneously induced institutions of higher education to reduce their demand for academics at least modestly. For reasons given earlier in this chapter, we do not believe that any of these modes of adjustment would have large effects; taken together, however, they might reduce demand by, say, 5 percent, and that is the assumption used here.

Particularly interesting calculations are shown in the last line of Table 8.5. There it is assumed that tightening labor markets both arrest the decline in the share of doctorates seeking academic employment and induce a 5 percent reduction in demand. Under these assumptions, the increases in new doctorates required to move the supply/demand ratio to 1.3 are 66 percent in the humanities and social sciences and 57 percent in mathematics and the physical sciences.[20] If such increases were to occur, the Ph.D. output in both of these clusters would be almost precisely equal to the levels reached in 1972. (As noted earlier, the exact percentage increases needed to regain the 1972 peaks are 67 percent and 58 percent, respectively.)

Too much should not be made of what is basically an interesting coincidence. But perhaps we can conclude that the combination of adjustment mechanisms discussed in this chapter have the potential to restore the supply/demand ratios in 1997–2002 and later periods to the range of 1.0 to 1.3—*provided* that the necessary resources and incentives are in place to permit the significant increase in the number of new doctorates, which is the truly critical factor.

[20] These same assumptions can of course be combined with the projections of increased output of Ph.D.'s shown in the top panel of Table 8.5. If that were done, the supply/demand ratios shown there would rise somewhat.

CHAPTER NINE

Questions of Policy

When we first outlined this study, we intended to make little, if any, reference to questions of policy. Our emphasis was—and is—on understanding as fully as possible the outlook for academic employment and the forces shaping it. Subsequently, we decided that the substance of our analysis, and especially the extent of the shortages projected in 1997–2002, compelled us to comment more fully on at least some policy issues. This chapter is not, however, a comprehensive analysis of actions that might be taken. That would require a study all its own.

For reasons stated in earlier chapters, we believe that the most important questions of policy pertain to graduate education. This study has direct relevance for prospective graduate students, academic administrators whose decisions may affect the character and duration of graduate study, and private and governmental entities able to influence the future supply of Ph.D.'s through financial aid programs. The pronounced changes in academic labor markets projected in Chapter Seven give special urgency to this range of issues.

There is a particularly strong *national* stake in graduate education. Talented and highly motivated graduate students—both as students and later as faculty members—contribute to our collective capacity to generate new ideas as well as to educate new generations of students. In these ways, they add immeasurably to the intellectual capital of the country. Graduate education benefits the society as a whole, not just individual students; it is essential to our ability as a nation to achieve political, social, and moral objectives, as well as economic and technological progress. In important respects, it is the foundation of the higher learning on which so much else depends.

In the last part of this chapter, we discuss what we believe to be the federal government's responsibilities for graduate education. First, however, we examine the role of colleges and universities.

The Role of Academic Institutions

One responsibility of academic institutions is to provide advice and counselling about careers and professional opportunities. Teachers unavoidably influence their students' perceptions of the academic world, and it is obviously desirable to impart as realistic a picture as possible of what academic life is like, and what it may be like in the future.

In the 1960s, many faculty members, administrators, and others unwittingly created false expectations, thereby contributing to later frustrations when many who had worked hard to obtain Ph.D.'s had difficulty finding good jobs.[1] Subsequently, faculty members and other advisors became sensitized to the risks of overpromising, and in some cases vigorously discouraged students from pursuing what may have been empty hopes of academic careers.

The danger today is that faculty advisors will remain too pessimistic for too long. If the analysis presented here is even approximately on target, students with the ability and inclination to consider academic careers should be encouraged to do so. Faculty members are in a unique position to help students anticipate future opportunities, thereby reducing the response lags that are such a formidable problem.

Although teachers can encourage promising students to seek Ph.D.'s, the availability of attractive graduate programs depends on decisions made—and resources provided—by doctorate-granting institutions. While such decisions will be influenced significantly by funding made available through government programs and other sources of support, academic institutions must in the end determine their own priorities.

Of first importance is a willingness to commit the resources needed to increase graduate enrollments in the arts and sciences. But this should not be done mechanically, or across the board. Qualitative considerations deserve to be emphasized. We believe that universities with the strongest graduate programs should make—at the very least—a proportionate contribution to the increased supply of doctorates that is needed. It is not desirable, in our view, for the percentage of all doctorates awarded by Research I universities to continue to decline as it has over the last thirty years. All institutions contemplating expansion, including those within the Research I sec-

[1] Cartter (1976, p. 241) observed: "Those who worked closely with graduate students between 1968 and 1971 well remember the angry sense of betrayal that many students felt when it first became evident that desirable post-Ph.D. placement opportunities were becoming scarce. Science students, in particular, felt that they had been induced into graduate school by attractive federal fellowship programs and encouraged by their faculty advisers only to find that their services were superfluous. . . . Current and future students need to be much better informed about job prospects. . . ."

tor, should give strong consideration to concentrating resources on those Ph.D. programs that are of the highest quality.

A related problem is time-to-degree. We noted in Chapter Eight that it currently takes the typical graduate student in the humanities more than 12 years (from time of receipt of B.A. degree) to receive a Ph.D., a student in the social sciences more than 11 years, and a student in mathematics or the physical sciences about 7 years. The average duration of graduate study has increased by about 1.5 years since 1970, and the prospect of such a long period of preparation is undoubtedly discouraging for potential doctoral students—and especially for some of the ablest students, who have many options.

The primary source of this problem is not that students take time off between completing their B.A. degrees and entering graduate school; indeed, it is often desirable for students to gain experience before making a commitment to the rigors of advanced study, and students should not be pressured to begin graduate work before they are ready to do so. However, once graduate students have matriculated, they should be encouraged to complete their work as expeditiously as they can, consistent with high quality performance.

The grim job prospects of recent years and the ever-increasing complexity of many fields of knowledge have no doubt contributed to the upward movement in time-to-degree. Another consideration—which we wish to emphasize—is that graduate students are now expected to spend more time teaching undergraduates. There is an important difference between asking graduate students to do some teaching and, in effect, requiring them to do too much teaching. It is generally desirable for graduate students to gain teaching experience, particularly if they are helped to learn to teach well; however, the main purposes of graduate education can be subverted if students are asked to teach too many hours per year or for too many years.

Reliable data on the amount of teaching done by students do not seem to be available at an aggregate level, but it is clear that teaching assistantships have become more important as sources of financial assistance. Of all students receiving doctorates in the arts and humanities in 1967, 56 percent had held teaching assistantships; by 1977, the corresponding figure was 65 percent; and by 1987, it was 70 percent. In the social sciences, the comparable increase was from 43 percent in 1967 to 55 percent in 1987.[2] The provost of one university

[2] Data are based on tabulations prepared for this study by Arthur M. Hauptman, following the same methodology used in his *Students in Graduate and Professional Education: What We Know and Need to Know* (1986), ch. 2. Other data presented later in this chapter showing changes in the composition of financial aid are also from this source. These figures are based on SED tabulations and reflect the experiences of Ph.D. recipi-

echoed the sentiments of many when he observed: "Students teach too much, don't finish their degrees, feel underpaid, and become resentful."

The decrease in the number of fellowships provided by the government and other benefactors has surely contributed to the increasing reliance by graduate students on teaching assistantships for financial support. We suspect, however, that other factors have also been at work. For instance, changes in undergraduate curricula have been accompanied by increases in the number of course offerings, which in turn have led to greater demand for teaching assistants. A related factor is the continuing growth of interest in research by faculty in all fields. More research, with corresponding reductions in teaching loads for faculty, leads inexorably to calls for more teaching assistants.

In our opinion, this is an appropriate time to reexamine this entire panoply of factors, looking at their combined effects on the attractiveness of graduate study, the quality of education at all levels, and educational costs. We are encouraged by the interest of a number of presidents, provosts, and graduate deans in this kind of comprehensive review. This process could usefully include a reassessment of the educational content of many graduate programs. Much has been said about rigidity and overspecialization at the graduate level, and some reshaping of curricula (particularly in the humanities and social sciences), combined with increased attention to the training of potential teachers, could be beneficial.[3]

Resource constraints are very real for universities, and they must be taken into account when considering how academic institutions can be expected to respond to the need for more holders of doctorates. Graduate education is expensive, it competes directly with other priorities, and it often has less appeal than other programs to legislators and generous alumni. For all of these reasons, there is clearly a limit to the investment that individual universities can be expected to make in graduate education. Many of the leading universities deserve credit for having made vigorous efforts to increase the number of fellowships awarded from their own funds during recent years,

---

ents in all of their post-B.A. years. Thus, they are a "moving average" of experiences of individuals over a number of years—which tends to dampen differences between any two points in time.

[3] These are not new concerns. In an entertaining essay on graduate education written in 1950, Professor Jacob Viner warned against excessive specialization. He referred to the "professional blinders" that a graduate student acquires, as "we [in the graduate schools] endeavor—often successfully—to make out of him a trufflehound, or, if you prefer, a race-horse, finely trained for a single small purpose and not much good for any other. We then let him loose on the undergraduates" (1958, pp. 378–79).

when fellowship support was critically needed and yet far from easy to provide.[4] In our judgment, it would be unrealistic to expect continued large increases in the number of fellowships that these universities award.

It may be more realistic, however, to expect universities to find the resources required to meet other needs associated with increased graduate enrollments. As noted in Chapter Eight, additional investments may have to be made in faculty positions. Some of the graduate programs of highest quality may experience particularly serious staffing problems because they operate within departments where rising undergraduate enrollments have already absorbed any excess teaching capacity.

Expanding graduate programs may also require expenditures for other purposes, ranging from provision of more academic space and facilities (including equipment and computing time) to graduate student housing. While it is easy for graduate students and faculty members to assume that such needs are obvious and can be met readily, priorities must be set, and hard choices must be made. Primary responsibility for coping has to rest with the individual doctorate-granting institutions, assisted by their own donors and traditional providers of support.

The Role of the Federal Government

In our view, the case is compelling for a renewed commitment by the federal government to graduate education in the arts and sciences. It rests not only on the national interest in doctoral education, but also on the magnitude of the projected imbalance between supply and demand. No other source of support can be expected to provide the resources that are required if there is to be a significant expansion in the number of doctorates conferred.

State governments can and should help, but graduate education by its nature transcends state boundaries. Students should seek out the best Ph.D. programs available, whether they are "in-state" or not. Moreover, states cannot expect recipients of doctorates—who are (properly) among the most mobile members of our population—to remain in the localities where they received their Ph.D.'s.

Private benefactors (foundations, corporations, and individuals) also have important roles to play. At the most general level, it would be helpful if they were to accord graduate education in the arts and

[4] In 1967, 18% of all recipients of doctorates in the arts and sciences had received institutional fellowships; by 1987, this figure had risen to 24%.

sciences a higher priority than it has received in recent years. Private patrons can make certain kinds of contributions that the federal government should not be expected to make. For example, they can provide the institutional support that will be essential if universities are to strengthen their graduate programs without simultaneously sacrificing other important goals. It may also be easier for some private benefactors than for the government to discriminate qualitatively among graduate programs. In addition, such benefactors may be able to encourage universities to undertake the kind of critical review of their graduate programs (including time-to-degree) that seems to us to be desirable.

By providing institutional support and by filling special niches, donors can sustain the idea of a public/private partnership in higher education. Many would agree that the distinctively American blend of private and public support has been instrumental in sustaining the excellence of graduate education in this country. The involvement of a variety of decision-makers may also offer some protection against serious misjudgments, although we saw in the 1960s and 1970s that "bandwagon" effects can diminish this advantage of multiple sources of funding.

Historical Patterns of Federal Support

To assign an important share of responsibility for support of graduate education to the federal government is hardly a radical idea. The expansion in graduate education between the mid-1950s and 1970 was fueled by research assistantships and government fellowship and traineeship programs such as those sponsored by the National Science Foundation (NSF), the National Institutes of Health (NIH), NASA, and other mission agencies. Equally important were the Title IV National Defense Education Act (NDEA) fellowships and the Title VI foreign language and area studies fellowships.

Between 1954 and 1969, federal fellowships and traineeships increased from 1,600 to 60,000, and research assistantships increased from 5,900 to 20,000. In short, 80,000 graduate students received federal support in 1969, as contrasted with just 7,500 in the mid-1950s. Although this support was directed primarily to the sciences and engineering, the humanities and the social sciences also benefited, particularly under the NDEA fellowship program.[5]

[5] See *Signs of Trouble and Erosion* 1983. The report was prepared by the National Commission on Student Financial Assistance's Graduate Education Subcommittee, which was chaired by John Brademas, president of New York University. Robert Snyder (1981) shows that between 1954 and 1969, the percentage of science students in doctoral

It is clear that the increase in the number and average value of stipends had a significant impact on the number of Ph.D.'s awarded. This is suggested by the crudest correlations with increased enrollments and degrees conferred. More precise relationships have been estimated through an analysis of the behavioral effects on students of reductions in the net cost of graduate education resulting from more generous stipends.[6]

The period of dramatic increases in stipends and in other forms of federal support was followed by a period of sudden retrenchment. Funding of fellowships and traineeships fell from $430 million in 1970 to $201 million in 1975 (measured in constant dollars)—a decline of more than 50 percent over just five years. Some programs (such as the NDEA fellowships) were terminated; others were reduced sharply in scale.[7]

The sources and forms of financial aid received by doctoral candidates in the arts and sciences changed considerably over this period. The percentage of all aid contributed by federally funded fellowships and traineeships was only half as large in 1987 as in 1967 (9 percent versus 19 percent). Institutional fellowships, provided mainly by the universities themselves, compensated for part of this drop. In 1973, the federal government contributed 2.5 dollars in fellowships and traineeships for every dollar contributed by academic institutions; by 1987, the relationships were reversed, and academic institutions contributed 1.4 dollars for every federal dollar.

All fields of study have been affected. In the physical sciences, NSF fellowships alone supported 18 percent of all doctoral candidates in 1967, as compared with 3 percent in 1987 (see Table 9.1). The NDEA fellowships, which in 1967 supported 6 percent of all doctoral candidates in the social sciences and 10 percent in the humanities, were discontinued in 1973. The Javits fellowships, first awarded in 1985, have been important symbolically but have supported only about 100 to 200 new students per year in all of the arts, humanities, and social sciences.

The last budget of President Reagan's administration (for FY 1990) included a proposal to phase out all support for the Javits Fellowship

---

programs who received federal fellowships or traineeships increased from 14% to 56%. For data on the distribution of NDEA fellowships by field, see Harmon 1977.

[6] The correlation between the number of stipends in science and engineering and the annual number of Ph.D.'s awarded in the same fields is shown in a recent study by the Office of Technology Assessment (*Educating Scientists and Engineers* 1988, Fig. 3–13). See Freeman 1971, ch. 6, for the results of labor-supply regressions using stipends as one explanatory variable.

[7] See *Signs of Trouble and Erosion* 1983, p. 67.

TABLE 9.1
Major Forms of Financial Aid for Doctorate Recipients, by Field of Study, 1967 and 1987

Form of Aid	*Physical Sciences*		*Social Sciences*		*Arts/ Humanities*		*All Arts/ Sciences*	
	1967	*1987*	*1967*	*1987*	*1967*	*1987*	*1967*	*1987*
NSF Fellowship	18	3	5	2	0	1	10	2
NDEA Fellowship	5	0	6	0	10	0	6	0
Institutional Fellowship	14	19	22	23	31	40	18	24
Teaching Assistantship	64	73	43	55	56	70	50	57
Research Assistantship	59	71	38	39	8	16	40	48
Loan(s)	5	16	11	45	14	35	8	30

Source: Tabulations prepared by Arthur M. Hauptman based on SED data.
[a]Data include support received during any year of graduate study. Students often receive more than one of these forms of support as well as forms of support not shown on this table.

program over a three-year period. The reason given was: "Funding for the Javits Fellowships program duplicates a wide variety of Federal and non-Federal sources of financial support currently available for graduate and professional study in the arts, humanities and social sciences."[8] It is difficult to understand this statement in light of available data. Given the cutbacks since 1970, and fresh proposals for even further reductions, it is not surprising that graduate students continue to be pessimistic about the future.

The only form of federal support (other than loans) that did not decline between 1967 and 1987 was research assistantships. The percentage of all recipients of doctorates in the arts and sciences holding research assistantships (funded mainly from government research contracts awarded primarily in the sciences) was constant at about 40 percent from 1967 through 1981; by 1987, nearly half of all students receiving degrees had held research assistantships.

The substitution of loans for grants has been one of the most noteworthy—and controversial—aspects of federal financial aid policies in recent years. The first report on graduate students from the U.S. Department of Education's 1987 National Postsecondary Student Aid Study showed that, in 1986, loans were made to 15.6 percent of all doctoral candidates in the physical sciences; 17.8 percent of all candidates in the arts and humanities; and 21.1 percent in the social sciences.[9]

A more comprehensive picture of the debt incurred by 1987 doc-

[8] "The Fiscal Year 1990 Budget" (1989).
[9] "Student Financing of Graduate and Professional Education" (1988), p. 44.

torate recipients (at both undergraduate and graduate levels over all years of study) is provided by the most recent Survey of Earned Doctorates. Approximately 41 percent of all recipients of Ph.D.'s in the physical sciences and approximately half of all Ph.D.'s in the humanities and the life sciences had borrowed; in the social sciences, the corresponding figure was 61 percent. As can be seen from Figure 9.1, the median level of debt among those who had borrowed was also highest in the social sciences (nearly $9,500).

These data must be interpreted with great care. Because of the length of time spent obtaining doctorates, many of these graduate students were undergraduates in the mid- to late-1970s, when borrowing was much less extensive. At the graduate level also, borrowing was less pervasive ten to fifteen years ago. Today the Guaranteed Student Loan Program permits students studying for advanced de-

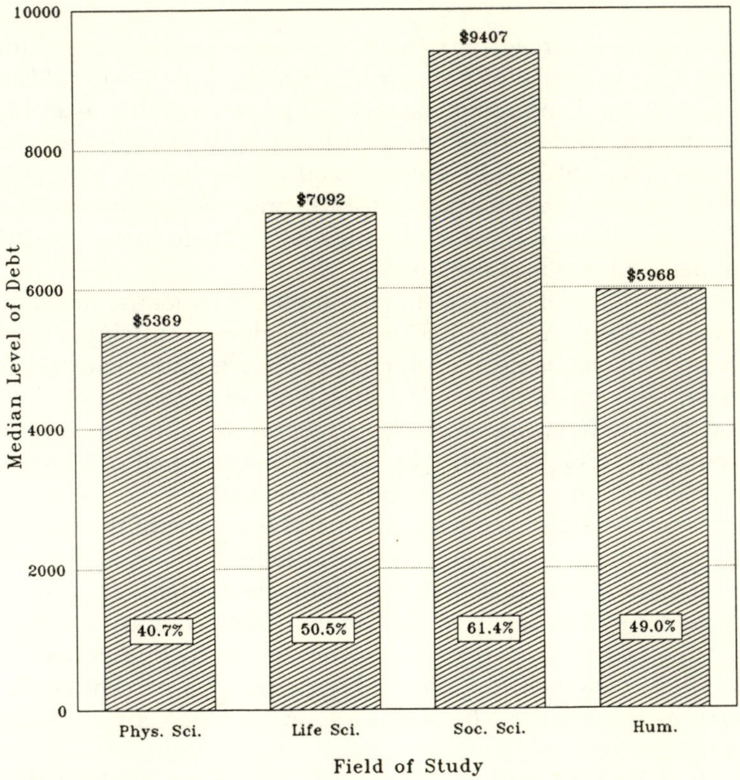

FIGURE 9.1
Doctorate Recipients with Debt, by Field of Study, 1987
Source: SED, *Summary Report 1987*, p. 22.

grees to borrow up to $7,500 per year (to a potential cumulative total of nearly $55,000). Thus, students currently in the early or middle stages of graduate study are likely to have assumed far larger loan burdens than their predecessors by the time they receive their doctorates. This could well discourage some students from choosing academic careers, particularly if faculty salaries lag behind salaries in other fields.[10]

Possible Federal Initiatives

This is the right time, we believe, for the federal government once again to assume a leadership role in graduate education. We do not pretend to be in a position to develop specific legislative proposals, but we would like to suggest certain general propositions that could be reflected in legislation.

1. *Emphasize Stipends.* If graduate education in the arts and sciences is to be made more appealing to prospective students, the "returns" must be made more attractive. In principle, this can be done in two ways. One approach is to enhance general conditions of employment in academia (especially salaries), thereby augmenting the anticipated benefits associated with an individual's own investment of time and resources in graduate education. Alternatively, it is possible to focus more directly on student aid, thereby reducing the cost to the prospective student of obtaining a doctorate.

These approaches are not mutually exclusive, and progress needs to be made on both fronts. At least some improvement in salaries and other conditions of employment is likely to occur through regular market mechanisms when demand increases relative to supply. From the standpoint of policy determination, however, we believe that primary emphasis should be placed on the direct support of graduate students. This is the most cost-effective way of increasing the number of doctorates in the arts and sciences because it allows available resources to be concentrated on new entrants. Otherwise, resources have to be found to raise the return on graduate education for all academics (including those already employed) sufficiently to accomplish the same purpose.[11]

Since one objective is to reduce the financial burdens associated with pursuit of Ph.D. programs, it is important to provide more fel-

[10] Much too little is known about the behavioral effects of loan finance, and this is an area in which additional research would be welcome.

[11] The latter approach will cost considerably more because it will entail paying economic "rent" to some individuals already committed to the academic profession.

lowship stipends to students and not to rely primarily on loans as a substitute for stipends. Additional fellowship support obviously increases the returns to graduate education more than comparable amounts of loan finance (even when loans are subsidized). Fellowship programs also convey a far clearer message as to the importance attached to graduate education by the government; for this reason, as well as for more straightforward economic reasons, they are likely to have a greater impact on the supply of potential graduate students.

2. *Provide Support for All of the Arts and Sciences.* It would be a serious error, in our judgment, for the government to limit its role in graduate education to science and engineering—an especially strong temptation today because of widespread worries about lack of "competitiveness." At present, approximately 75 to 80 percent of all funding for fellowships and traineeships goes to science and engineering, and this pattern would be even more pronounced if we took account of the distribution of research assistantships. Yet one of the clearest conclusions of this study is that serious labor-market imbalances should be anticipated in the humanities and social sciences, as well as in mathematics and the physical sciences. Outstanding faculty members must be recruited in all of the major fields of study if this country's educational system is to be strong.

At the same time, fellowship funds within the arts and sciences should not be targeted too narrowly. Changes in the intellectual appeal of various fields and in market conditions make it exceedingly difficult to forecast field-specific supply and demand relationships with great precision, even if it were thought wise to do so. Also, targeted fellowship programs may distort choices by enticing students to enter a currently "hot" field when they might have made greater long-term contributions elsewhere.

3. *Emphasize Portable Merit Fellowships.* This approach has been tested through the existing NSF and Javits fellowship programs (as well as through national fellowship competitions administered by foundations), and the arguments for it are well known and persuasive. It serves qualitative objectives that are especially important now. Prospective graduate students who are chosen on merit may take their fellowships to the graduate programs that they believe will best serve their needs. This approach provides an especially effective mechanism for making judgments about quality. All universities, and all departments within universities, have distinct pockets of strength, and these

are more likely to be identified by prospective graduate students than through any other process that would be acceptable politically.[12]

Of course, there are also other important goals to be served by federal fellowship programs, including increasing the number of minority students enrolled in Ph.D. programs and the number of women scholars attracted to science. Complementary programs can be, and have been, designed for such purposes. Similarly, programs intended to promote graduate education in particular regions or types of institutions could supplement the kind of overall national merit fellowship program proposed here.

4. *Provide Sufficient Fellowships on a Sustained Basis.* While any addition to the number of federally funded fellowships would be most welcome at this juncture, it is highly desirable that a new federal initiative be large enough to convey both a symbolic and a substantive message. The government should be seen to care about the health of graduate education and to be prepared to make significant investments in the arts and sciences. "Announcement" effects can be very important, and our government needs to say again—as it did in the late 1950s and 1960s—that academics make essential contributions to the national welfare. This theme can be communicated effectively only through commitments of resources that are large enough to matter.

At the same time, care should be taken to avoid crash programs that cannot be sustained. One of the lessons of the last three decades is that an on-again, off-again pattern of support is harmful to doctoral education, to individual candidates for Ph.D.'s, and to those institutions (academic and non-academic) dependent on more or less predictable flows of new doctorates. The country will be better off, in our view, if efforts are made to restore—and then to sustain—support for graduate education at some reasonable steady-state level.

Overdramatic responses and abrupt changes in patterns of support can lead to misallocation of resources. It would not be wise to encourage again the extraordinary increase in the number of new doctoral programs in universities that occurred in the 1960s and early 1970s. What is needed is not a large number of new programs, but

[12] An economist with considerable experience administering educational programs commented as follows on the number of Ph.D. programs and the advantages of portable fellowships: "In 1980, there were 93 doctoral programs in economics. I would advise any college senior who could not be admitted to one of the best 40 of these to think about some other line of work. . . . It is one of the merits of [a] portable fellowship [program] that it automatically works against mindless proliferation." One of the unfortunate features of the earlier NDEA fellowship program is that it stimulated some of the proliferation of Ph.D. programs to which this commentator refers.

more effective utilization of existing programs. It also would be unwise to attempt to anticipate and to correct for all labor-market fluctuations—a goal sure to prove elusive in any case. Rather, the objective should be to provide a reasonably steady flow of well-prepared Ph.D.'s that will prevent damaging shortages but not create the levels of excess supply that have been so discouraging to prospective academics.[13]

An illustrative set of calculations may help to suggest the number of fellowships and the resources required to provide an appropriate level of support. Suppose that the number of new fellowship awards were to be increased by 1,000 per year in mathematics and the physical sciences and by 2,000 per year in the humanities and social sciences. While such increases would be significant, they would not come close to restoring the overall number of federal fellowships to the levels of the 1960s.[14]

If each of these new awards were for three years (as is the case with the current NSF program), and if stipends and cost-of-education grants to institutions were kept at about the current NSF levels ($12,300 and $6,000, respectively), we could assume a three-year cost

[13] The relevance of the general points made in these paragraphs is illustrated by Cartter's vivid description of what happened in the 1960s and early 1970s (1976, pp. 20–23). The experiences of those years also demonstrate the need to be guided by at least a rough sense of what lies ahead. Cartter observed: "Right up until 1969, when the first signs of a weakening job market for college teachers began to emerge . . . , it was difficult to get either educators or federal government officials to take seriously the likelihood of an oversupply of Ph.D.'s. . . . " Cartter then documented the pressures for continued expansion of Ph.D. programs, including the creation of a number of new programs, well into the 1970s. He concluded: "Looking backward, it seems evident that this emerging problem [of oversupply] could (and should) have been recognized by public-policy makers a decade ago. . . . We can ill afford the mistaken judgments and optimism of the 1960's—nor is today's pessimism a compensating antidote. Perhaps some parts of this research effort will lay the foundation of much improved analyses and policy guidance for the future." While we would not claim to have produced "much improved analyses and policy guidance," we are glad to acknowledge our debt to Cartter for having done so much to point all of us who are concerned about these issues in sensible directions.

[14] In 1988, the NSF made 685 new awards under its regular fellowship program and 75 under its minority program; the Javits program made 204 new awards in that year. In contrast, over 7,000 new awards were made under the NDEA program alone in 1967, and the NSF made over 1,300 new awards under its regular fellowship program in its peak year (1966). The impact on the arts and sciences is even more pronounced when we take account of the increased emphasis that has been given to engineering relative to the arts and sciences within the NSF fellowship program. Between 1972 and 1981, approximately 13.5% of all new NSF regular fellowships went to students in engineering; between 1987 and 1989, the comparable percentage was 21.7. (Data provided by John Vaughn of the Association of American Universities.)

per award of about $60,000—or $180 million for 3,000 three-year awards when the program is at steady-state. If an allowance were made for attrition (see below), the steady-state cost in constant dollars, with no allowance for inflation, might be more like $150 million. While this would almost double the current federal investment in all fellowship and traineeship programs, the resulting level of federal expenditure would still amount to less than 10 percent of what the government spends annually for its principal undergraduate grant program, the Pell Grants.[15]

In order to estimate the contribution that such a program would make to the supply of new doctorates likely to seek academic employment, we first assume that 75 percent of those awarded fellowships complete their Ph.D.'s. In addition, of those who do earn doctorates, we assume that 50 percent in mathematics and the physical sciences and 70 percent in the humanities and social sciences enter academia.[16] Of course, some of the awards made under any new program will go to students who would have entered graduate school anyway. Still, the institutional aid and other forms of support that would have been allocated to such students could now go to other students, who might not have been able to attend graduate school without aid. For present purposes, we make the simplifying assumption that the net effect of the new fellowships would be to increase the number of graduate students by 75 percent of the number of new awards.

Under these assumptions, there would be annual increases in the supply of Ph.D.'s seeking academic employment of 281 in mathematics and the physical sciences and 788 in the humanities and social sciences. Graduate programs would have to expand by 12 percent in mathematics and the physical sciences and by 20 percent in the humanities and social sciences to absorb such numbers, and we believe this is a realistic possibility. (These percentage increases have been calculated using the numbers of new doctorates in 1987 as the base numbers; see Table 6.2.) The implications for projected supply/demand ratios are considerable. Using Model II assumptions (see Table 7.6), the supply/demand ratio in the humanities and social sciences

[15] Robert K. Durkee of Princeton University assisted with these calculations.

[16] The 25% attrition rate is roughly comparable to the experience of the first cohort of Andrew W. Mellon Foundation Fellows in the Humanities. The percentages of doctorates projected to seek academic employment are based on the data in Appendix Table D.5. Of course, individuals who receive doctorates under a program such as this and who then choose non-academic employment also make valuable contributions; investments in their graduate studies are not wasted.

for 1997–2002 increases from 0.71 to 0.92; in mathematics and the physical sciences, the supply/demand ratio rises from 0.80 to 0.95.

We wish to reemphasize the purely illustrative nature of these very crude calculations. The actual results achieved by any new program would depend on how the specific design of the program affects key parameters such as attrition, career choices, and commitments of other resources to graduate programs. This is an important subject in its own right. Conventional assumptions—such as the desirability of assured multi-year support for students—should be evaluated carefully. Consideration could also be given to the possibility of conditioning fellowship support on institutional commitments concerning funding, the extent of teaching obligations expected of students, and success in reducing time-to-degree. In addition, financial aid programs could include incentives for students to pursue academic careers.

Still, these illustrative calculations do indicate, at least in general terms, what might be accomplished by a new federal initiative in graduate education. While a new program on this scale would not eliminate the projected shortages in the academic labor market, it would make a substantial contribution to alleviating them; at the same time, it also would have a highly positive impact on the quality of the pool of candidates for academic appointments. Moreover, a program of this kind could be modified in the light of changing circumstances without returning to a "start-and-stop" approach to the funding of graduate education.

Efforts to anticipate future problems, of the kind represented by the analysis presented in this book, should be subject to constant review. There is too much we do not know, and there is no substitute for persistent monitoring of experience. But there is also no substitute for acting on the implications of what we do know and adopting those policies most likely to achieve beneficial long-term results.

APPENDIX A

Principal Sources of Data and Definitions of Fields of Study and Sectors

SOURCES

This study relies heavily on three primary sources of data: the Survey of Doctorate Recipients (SDR), the Survey of Earned Doctorates (SED), and the Higher Education General Information Surveys (HEGIS).

The Survey of Doctorate Recipients

The SDR is a longitudinal survey that reports demographic and employment characteristics of Ph.D. recipients who have resided in this country during the last 42 years. It has been conducted every other year since 1973 for doctoral scientists and engineers, and since 1977 for humanities doctorates. The SDR provides us with information about the present faculty in the arts and sciences. It is our main data source for Chapter Two.

The National Research Council (NRC) has assembled summaries of the data since 1977, which have been published in the form of biennial reports: *Science, Engineering, and Humanities Doctorates in the United States*. Special issues are also produced periodically using the SDR data. Recent publications include: *The Effects on Quality of Adjustments in Engineering Labor Markets* (1988a), *Humanists on the Move: Employment Patterns for Humanities Ph.D.s* (1985), *Departing the Ivy Halls: Changing Employment Situations for Recent Ph.D.s* (1983), and *Employment of Minority Ph.D.s: Changes over Time* (1981).

Respondents provide information about field of degree, year of degree, type of institution attended, employment status, primary work activity, and salary, as well as gender, race, and citizenship. When respondents indicate that they are faculty members, the SDR also collects academic rank and tenure status.

For the scientific fields of study, the survey sample includes doctorates of employable age living in this country who either by education or by current employment could be classified as doctoral-level scientists or engineers; for the humanities, it includes individuals of similar age who have earned doctorates in the humanities.

To ensure adequate representation of small groups within the population, different sampling rates are used. Since not all characteristics measured by the SDR are equally represented in the sample, each is assigned a differential weight so that the statistics represent, as nearly as possible, the results that would have been obtained if the entire population had been surveyed. For more detailed information about sampling procedures and sampling errors, see the methodological report for the survey year in question.

Most of the SDR data used in this study are from special tabulations that were prepared to conform to our universe of faculty and institutions, as described in Chapter One. Separate tabulations were provided by field and sector.

The Survey of Earned Doctorates

The SED has been conducted annually since 1958 by the National Research Council. It surveys graduate students who have just completed their doctorates and thus complements the SDR data, which describe the characteristics of those who received doctoral degrees in earlier years. Questionnaire forms are distributed with the help of the graduate deans of universities, and they are filled out by graduates as they complete the academic requirements for their Ph.D.'s. If the students fail to fill out the questionnaire, abbreviated records are completed using information from commencement bulletins. Professional-degree recipients are not included in this survey.

It is possible to obtain a considerable amount of basic information about the students from the SED, including year of Ph.D., elapsed time between receipt of the B.A. and receipt of the Ph.D., primary source of financial support, gender, race, citizenship status, field of study, and type of graduate institution attended. Postgraduate plans, as well as anticipated employer, are also reported.

Again, we made intensive use of special tabulations prepared for this study. The SED is our main data source for Chapter Six.

Summaries of the survey results have been published by the National Research Council annually since 1967 in a series of reports titled *Doctorate Recipients from United States Universities.* Trends from earlier periods can be found in NRC, *A Century of Doctorates: Data Analyses of Growth and Change* (1978).

Higher Education General Information Survey

The third primary data source was HEGIS, now called the Integrated Postsecondary Education Data System (IPEDS). It is administered by the National Center for Education Statistics at the U.S. Department of Education. HEGIS covered a base of 3,500 accredited institutions granting two-year or higher degrees. IPEDS, which covers a much broader base, is sent to all institutions accepted as accredited by any federal agency, including one-year vocational and technical schools.

HEGIS/IPEDS includes a group of surveys that gather detailed information on institutional characteristics, enrollment numbers, finances, tenured and part-time faculty, and salary levels, as well as race and gender. Summaries using these data have been published annually since 1962 in the *Digest of Education Statistics*.

We use the "Degrees and Other Formal Awards Conferred" surveys and "Earned Degrees Conferred" surveys for our analysis of fall enrollments and degrees. These surveys contain detailed information about bachelors', masters', and doctors' degrees conferred by field of study. Published data are available from 1970. We also arranged for special tabulations in order to focus on trends in the number of degrees conferred between 1977 and 1987 within the arts and sciences, classified by sector. We chose 1977 as our base year since that was the first year of the survey that contained a sufficiently expanded sample of humanists. These surveys are an important data source in Chapters Three and Four.

The HEGIS and SED data sources refer to the academic year differently. In the SED, a student who earns a doctoral degree between July 1, 1984 and June 30, 1985 is placed in the 1985 period. In the HEGIS, however, that period is cited as 1984–1985.

Definitions

In order to examine trends and make projections in finer detail, we have analyzed the data whenever possible by field of study and by sector of higher education.

Fields of Study

Within the arts and sciences, we have concentrated on eight broad fields: (1) mathematics; (2) physics and astronomy; (3) chemistry; (4) earth, environmental, and marine sciences (hereafter referred to as "earth sciences"); (5) biological sciences; (6) psychology; (7) social sciences; and (8) humanities. Some of the subsequent analysis includes a breakdown of the humanities into four components: (a) history; (b) English and American languages and literatures; (c) foreign languages and literatures; and (d) other humanities. These definitions apply consistently to the SDR data in 1977 and 1987.

There are some differences in the SED and HEGIS definitions. History is treated as one of the social sciences in the HEGIS/IPEDS data, rather than as one of the humanities. In the SED, the field of English and American languages and literatures is combined with other fields such as classics and comparative literature and presented as "letters." In HEGIS, the humanities consists of letters, foreign languages, and philosophy/religion.

The "other humanities" component is defined slightly differently over time within each data source; definitions also vary somewhat among the different sources. In the SED, "other humanities" includes such fields as American studies, archeology, art history and criticism, philosophy, religion, humanities-general, and humanities-other. The SDR data are nearly identical, except that archeology is considered to be a social science.

At various points in time, "other humanities" in the SED has also included art-applied, classics, comparative literature, library and archival sciences, linguistics, letters-general, and letters-other. The SDR has included art—fine and applied, and religion/theology. Classics, comparative literature, and linguistics were included in the field of "letters."

Music was not included as a field in the special tabulations compiled using the SDR and SED data sources. There are numerous faculty and doctorate recipients in music, and if we had included them in these tabulations, we would not have been able to achieve consistency when we related these data to the degrees-conferred data (which exclude all performing and visual arts). A significant portion of the doctorates granted in music are non-research degrees, and it is unclear how many of these doctorates are awarded to individuals planning careers in teaching and research within the arts and sciences.

We also exclude the fields of speech/debate and theatre criticism from all the SDR data and from the projections made using the SED data. It was not practical, however, to remove these fields from the SED data going back to 1958, given the changes in classifications that have been made. These fields are relatively small in any event.

We have chosen at many points in the text to recombine fields of study into three larger groups, which we have referred to as "clusters": humanities and social sciences; biological sciences and psychology; and mathematics and physical sciences. The use of clusters enables us to accommodate various changes that took place in classification systems (e.g., history is considered a social science by one source and a part of the humanities by another). The particular definitions of clusters that we have used reflect some similar characteristics, particularly patterns of doctorates granted (see Chapter Six).

Sectors of Higher Education

In defining sectors, we use the institutional classification system of the Carnegie Foundation for the Advancement of Teaching. This system assigns both private and public academic institutions to the categories of Research I; Research II; Doctorate I; Doctorate II; Comprehensive I; Comprehensive II; Liberal Arts I; Liberal Arts II; Other; Specialized; and Two-Year institutions.

As with fields of study, it was not always possible or necessary to define sectors in such fine detail. We worked with five principal sectors: Research I universities; Other Research and Doctorate universities, which consists of Research II as well as Doctorate I and II universities; Comprehensive I institutions; Liberal Arts I institutions; and Other Four-Year institutions, which consists of Comprehensive II institutions and Liberal Arts II institutions.

Some institutions were reclassified in 1987, and whenever possible we use the 1987 classification. When that is impossible, we use the 1976 classification. We developed a method of comparing data based on the two classifications, and this method is discussed in Appendix C.

Research I universities offer a full range of baccalaureate programs and provide graduate education through the doctorate degree. They also give a high priority to research. Each of these universities annually receives at least $33.5 million in federal support and annually awards at least 50 Ph.D.'s. This sector includes such institutions as Harvard University, Michigan State University, and the University of Washington.

Research II institutions differ from the Research I institutions by the amount of support they receive from the federal government. Research II institutions annually receive between $12.5 million and $33.5 million. This category includes Brandeis University, Florida State University, and Temple University.

Doctorate I and II institutions also offer a full range of baccalaureate programs. Doctorate I institutions annually award at least 40 Ph.D.'s in five or more academic disciplines, and Doctorate II institutions annually award 20 or more Ph.D.'s in at least one discipline, or 10 or more Ph.D. degrees in three or more disciplines. Examples of Doctorate I institutions are the College of William and Mary, Lehigh University, and the University of Notre Dame. Doctorate II institutions include Cleveland State University, Pepperdine University, and the University of South Dakota.

The Comprehensive I and II institutions offer baccaluareate programs and, with few exceptions, graduate education through the master's degree. More than half of the baccalaureates are awarded in such occupational or professional disciplines as business and engineering. Comprehensive I institutions enroll at least 2,500 students, and they include institutions such as Arkansas Tech University, Hawaii Pacific College, and Providence College. Comprehensive II institutions enroll between 1,500 and 2,500 students, and they include institutions such as Elmira College, Southern Utah State College, and the University of Tampa.

Liberal Arts I and II institutions are primarily undergraduate colleges that award more than half of their degrees in the arts-and-sciences fields. Those classified as Liberal Arts I are more selective than Liberal Arts II institutions, and they are primarily private institutions, such as Amherst College, Carleton College, and Reed College. Some of the Liberal Arts II institutions may award less than half of their degrees in liberal arts, but they are too small to be considered comprehensive. Selma University, Mesa College, and Oklahoma Baptist University are all Liberal Arts II institutions.

The Other and Specialized institutions offer degrees ranging from the baccalaureate to the doctorate, and they award at least 50 percent of their degrees in a single specialized field. These institutions include schools of business and management, schools of medicine, schools of law, and teachers colleges, as well as schools that offer religious instruction or train members of the clergy. The Art Institute of Seattle, SUNY Health Science Centers, and New York Law School are examples.

The Two-Year institutions offer certificate or degree programs and generally do not award baccalaureate degrees. Anchorage Community College, Bowling Green Junior College of Business, and Tulsa Junior College are included in this sector.

For a more detailed description of the Carnegie classification system, see Carnegie Foundation for the Advancement of Teaching, *A Classification of Institutions of Higher Education* (1987).

APPENDIX B

Derivation of Exit Probabilities

THE OBJECTIVE of this part of our work has been to derive age-group exit probabilities.[1] As explained in Chapter Two, these probabilities represent "net" flows out of academia, reflecting the balance between faculty members leaving higher education and faculty members returning to higher education from other employment sectors or from outside the labor force. These exit probabilities must be interpreted in this way and not simply as one-way movements ("gross" flows) out of higher education.

The exit probabilities can then be combined with age distributions to estimate the number of faculty members in each five-year age group who will *not* be present in the next five-year age group in five years' time. Multiplying the overall exit probability for a five-year age group by the number of faculty members in the age group at the start of the period yields an estimate of the number that will be gone by the start of the next five-year period. Subtracting the number expected to be gone from the number of faculty who started the period yields an estimate of the number expected to continue into the next period. Some fraction of these continuing faculty members will, in their turn, exit, yielding further estimates of numbers gone, numbers continuing into the next five-year period, and so on.

In principle, it is of course possible to estimate separate exit probabilities for each field of study and each sector of higher education. In practice, we lack the data needed to make reasonable estimates of this kind. Therefore, in this appendix we concentrate on explaining the derivation of the overall exit probabilities that are used with field-specific and sector-specific age distributions to project vacancies by field and sector in sequential five-year periods.

Overall exit probabilities for faculty members in each five-year age group were built up from separate estimates of the probabilities of *not* being present in the next age group in five years' time as a result

[1] Our colleague at The Andrew W. Mellon Foundation, Dr. Carolyn Makinson, Program Associate in Population and Public Affairs, provided invaluable technical assistance in deriving these exit probabilities and in drafting parts of this appendix. Charles Westoff, director of the Office of Population Research at Princeton University, also assisted with this part of our work.

of: (1) voluntary and involuntary decisions to leave academia altogether in order to pursue options elsewhere—which we call "quits"; (2) voluntary or involuntary decisions to retire; and (3) deaths.

Quit Rates

As explained in the text, quit rates are the most difficult of the three exit probabilities to estimate. Since it is quits from all sectors of academia that constitute quits for the purposes of this analysis, institutional case studies are of limited use. Many individuals who resign from one institution are likely to accept a position in another institution, and such individuals are not quitting academia—they are simply moving from one institution to another.

Because of the uncertainties, we chose to use two sets of assumptions: a "high-quit" set based on the simple assumptions of a 1.0% per annum quit rate for all tenured faculty and a 10.0% per annum quit rate for all non-tenured faculty; and a "standard-quit" set obtained (essentially) by dividing in half the five-year quit probabilities generated by the high-quit assumptions. In this part of the appendix, we will first explain in detail the derivation of the exit probabilities generated by the high-quit assumptions and then explain the adjustments used to produce the corresponding probabilities generated by the standard-quit assumptions.

The quit rates implicit in both sets of assumptions are within the range of previous estimates (see Chapter Two for references to the literature). At the same time, working with two sets of quit rates, and starting with round numbers such as 1% and 10%, should protect against any sense of specious precision.

Having adopted these assumptions, the next step was to translate them into age-specific rates. These were calculated by combining the tenured quit rate (1%) and the non-tenured quit rate (10%), using the proportions of tenured and non-tenured faculty in each age group as weights. The calculations for all age groups are shown below in Table B.1.

The age-specific quit rates were used to construct a "quitting life table." Age-group survival ratios were then calculated from the life table, and these ratios were used to project the population forward by five-year age groups for five-year periods—i.e., to estimate the probability that the members of each five-year age group would "survive quitting" and be present in the subsequent five-year age group five years later. Calculations were made as shown below, in life table notation.

TABLE B.1
Tenure Ratios and Quit Rates, by Age Group, 1987

Age Group	*Proportion Tenured*	*Proportion Non-Tenured*	*Per Annum Age-Specific Quit Rates*[a]
30–34	0.12	0.88	0.0897
35–39	0.40	0.60	0.0640
40–44	0.71	0.29	0.0361
45–49	0.82	0.18	0.0262
50–54	0.88	0.12	0.0208
55–59	0.89	0.11	0.0199
60–64	0.89	0.11	0.0199
65–69	0.89	0.11	0.0199
70+	0.89	0.11	0.0199

Source: The tenured and non-tenured proportions were derived from SDR tabulations for our universe of faculty members.
[a]Based on high-quit assumptions.

1. Construction of the Life Table

Probability of quitting between the beginning and end of each five-year *age* interval x to $x + 5$, where ${}_5m_x$ is the per annum age-specific quit rate:

$$ {}_5q_x = \frac{5\,({}_5m_x)}{1 + \frac{5}{2}({}_5m_x)} . $$

Probability of *not* quitting between the beginning and end of each five-year *age* interval x to $x + 5$:

$$ {}_5p_x = 1 - {}_5q_x . $$

Number of survivors (of quitting) at the beginning of each five-year age interval, given the age-specific quit rates used in the life table calculation:

$$ l_{x+5} = (l_x)\,({}_5p_x) . $$

Person-years lived between age x and age $x + 5$:

$$ {}_5L_x = \frac{5\,(l_x + l_{x+5})}{2} . $$

2. Projection of the Population

The probability that members of each five-year age group would survive quitting and be present in the subsequent five-year age group five years later was then calculated by:

$$_5\Pi_x = \frac{_5L_{x+5}}{_5L_x}.$$

The five-year-period survival probabilities with regard to quitting—using the high-quit assumptions—are given below:

Age Group	*Five-Year-Period Survival Probabilities with Regard to Quitting (High-Quit Assumptions)*
30–34	0.6687
35–39	0.7705
40–44	0.8539
45–49	0.8881
50–54	0.9032
55–59	0.9053
60–64	0.9050
65–69	0.9052
70+	0.9052 (assumed equal to 65–69)

As indicated in Chapter Two, we concluded that these high-quit survival probabilities were best thought of as a bound on the problem of estimating quits, in the sense that they generate a rate of exodus from higher education that we believe to be an upper limit—especially in the younger age groups. For instance, in the 30–34 and 35–39 age groups, where non-tenured faculty predominate, these rates imply that only two-thirds to three-quarters of all faculty will survive the hazard of quitting during these first five-year intervals. Given the fact that we are concerned only with full-time faculty members who possess doctorates in the arts and sciences, these rates seem high and could lead to exaggerated estimates of the number of vacancies caused by quitting.

To obtain what we regard as more realistic probabilities (the standard-quit assumptions), we reduced the assumed quit rates for both tenured and non-tenured faculty by approximately one-half—from 1% and 10%, respectively, in the high-quit assumptions, to approximately 0.5% and 5%, respectively, in the standard-quit assumptions. We say "approximately" because, for computational convenience, we divided the quit probability for each age group by two and then estimated a new survival probability by subtracting this new (lower) quit probability from 1.0. (The differences introduced by this simpler procedure, as compared with the more precise approach of recalculating the life table, are so small as to be negligible.)

The five-year-period survival probabilities with regard to quitting obtained by using the standard-quit assumptions are shown below:

Age Group	*Five-Year-Period Survival Probabilities with Regard to Quitting (Standard-Quit Assumptions)*
30–34	0.8344
35–39	0.8853
40–44	0.9270
45–49	0.9441
50–54	0.9516
55–59	0.9527
60–64	0.9525
65–69	0.9525
70+	0.9525 (assumed equal to 65–69)

When we compare these two sets of ratios, we see the extent of the differences that result from substituting the standard-quit assumptions for the high-quit assumptions. In the two younger age groups, in particular, these differences are considerable. For instance, in the 35–39 age group, we see that the probability of surviving the hazard of quitting increases from 77% (using the high-quit assumptions) to 89% (using the standard-quit assumptions). The differences are much smaller in the middle age ranges—with the survival ratio rising from 89% to 94% in the 45–49 age group, for example. In the upper age ranges, the difference is consistently four percentage points—91% using the high-quit assumptions as contrasted with 95% using the standard-quit assumptions.

The standard-quit assumptions are consistent with the available longitudinal data for the humanities published by the National Research Council in the spring of 1989 (*Humanities Doctorates in the United States, 1987 Profile*). Through an excruciating process, we converted these longitudinal data into net quit rates expressed on an annual basis. We also converted our own age-specific standard-quit assumptions into average annual rates for all age groups, using the 1987 age distribution. The resulting rates are 1.8% (derived from our standard-quit assumptions) and 1.85% (derived from the NRC data).[2]

[2] We derived the 1.85% annual net quit rate from the NRC data as follows. First we calculated a gross exit rate by subtracting the percentage of all those who remained in four-year colleges and universities over a two-year period from 100% and then averaging these percentages over the three two-year sub-periods of 1977–79, 1981–83, and

Retirement Rates

The average age of retirement is assumed to be 65. This assumption is consistent with the findings of the Lozier-Dooris survey of 20 AAU universities (all but two are public universities), reported in November 1987. This is the most recent survey that yields data in a form consistent with our requirements. This survey found that the average retirement age for the 12 universities (of the sample of 20) supplying these particular data was 65.1 years of age over the five-year interval from 1981–82 through 1985–86, with no discernible trend.

Using the data from Tables 3 and 4 of the Lozier-Dooris survey, it is possible to develop age-group retirement probabilities. From Table 4, we obtained the total number of faculty members in each age group at the 14 universities supplying such data (as of 1985–86). However, since only 12 of these universities supplied data on the age distribution of retirements, we had to reduce the overall faculty numbers by the factor 12/14 (assuming no systematic differences in size of faculty for the two universities that provided one set of data but not the other, as contrasted with the 12 universities that provided both sets of data). We then expressed the numbers of retirements in the 12 universities in 1985–86 for each age group as a percentage of these (calculated) faculty numbers in each age group to obtain annual retirement rates by age group. These calculations are summarized below in Table B.2.

1985–87. The result was an average two-year gross exit rate of 7.6%.

Next we took account of the fact that the NRC gross exit rates do not distinguish between those faculty who exit for other employment and those faculty who retire. It was also necessary to adjust for the inclusion of part-time faculty in the NRC retirement data.

An average retirement rate for full-time faculty (1.6%) was calculated for the three two-year sub-periods. An average two-year retirement rate for part-time faculty (8.23%) was also calculated. A "blended" retirement rate (2.2%) was then calculated by averaging these rates, using the ratio of full-time to part-time faculty as the weighting factor—91.2% of all faculty were full-time.

The blended retirement rate of 2.2% was next deducted from the average gross *exit* rate of 7.6% over a two-year period. Thus, we obtained an average gross *quit* rate of 5.4% for a two-year period.

The next step was to determine flows of faculty back to academia so that we could move from gross to net quit rates. The NRC has published data showing the fractions of all doctorates in other employment sectors (e.g., business/industry and elementary/secondary school) who moved back to four-year colleges and universities over the same two-year periods. We adjusted the bases of these percentages by using other NRC data showing the number of doctorates in each of these sectors as a percentage of doctorates in four-year colleges and universities. This resulted in an estimated return flow from all other employment sectors of 1.7% over a two-year period.

Subtracting the return flow of 1.7% from the gross quit rate of 5.4% produced a net quit rate of 3.7% for a two-year period, or roughly 1.85% on an annual basis.

TABLE B.2
Age-Specific Retirement Rates

(1) Age Group	(2) Faculty in 14 Universities (N)	(3) 12/14 × Col. (2)	(4) Retirements in 12 Universities (N)	(5) Per Annum Retirement Rate (Col. [4] ÷ Col. [3]) (%)
Under 50	13,584	11,641	—	0
50–54	2,902	2,487	8	0
55–59	2,508	2,149	33	2
60–64	1,873	1,605	105	7
65–69	719	616	208	34
70+	207	177	52	34[a]

Source: See text.

[a]The retirement rate for the 70+ group was set at the rate applicable to the 65–69 age group rather than at the (slightly) lower rate implied by actual numbers (29%) so that we could use a single rate for all faculty over 64. (This is a small point because the 70+ group does not contain a significant number of faculty members within the actual age distributions against which this rate is applied.)

The age-specific retirement rates were then used to construct a "retirement life table," from which five-year-period survival ratios (${}_5\Pi_x$) were derived, in the manner already described above with regard to the estimation of the probability of surviving quitting. (The age group "under 50" was treated as age group 45–49, and age group "70+" as 70–74. All faculty aged 70+ were assumed to have retired by the beginning of the next five-year period; in calculating ${}_5\Pi_{65}$, ${}_5L_{70}$ was assumed to be $5\left(\frac{l_{70}}{2}\right)$.)

The five-year-period survival probabilities with regard to retirement are given below:

Age Group	*Five-Year-Period Survival Probabilities with Regard to Retiring*	
45–49	0.9921	
50–54	0.9552	
55–59	0.8264	
60–64	0.4537	
65–69	0.0780	
70+	0	(assumed)

There is every reason to believe that these estimates are reliable for public universities as of 1985–86, since they are built up from detailed data drawn from the recent experiences of the public universities in the Lozier-Dooris survey. There is also another set of data that is quite consistent and, therefore, reassuring. The COFHE survey of 36 institutions conducted in November 1987 included data for eight public universities. This survey found an average age at retirement of 64.8, which compares with an average age at retirement of 65.1 for the public universities in the Lozier-Dooris survey. We are unable to check the reliability of these estimates against the experiences of other kinds of institutions, but we know of no reason for there to be any systematic differences.

The 1987 COFHE survey referred to above found an average age at retirement of 66.3 years for the 28 private colleges and universities included in the survey as of academic year 1985–86. Thus, faculty members in these private institutions seemed to retire, on average, about 1.3 years later than their counterparts in the public universities. Nonetheless, we did not calculate separate retirement probabilities for the private institutions (in part because we do not have detailed distributions of retirements by age group); rather, we used the retirement probabilities listed above for all institutions of higher education included in this study. This simplifying assumption introduces some (modest) bias into the estimates—particularly, we suspect, for the Liberal Arts I sector, which is the only one of our five principal sectors that contains more private than public institutions.

More recent data obtained by Sharon Smith (of the Project on Faculty Retirement, Industrial Relations Section, Princeton University) provide a further check on our retirement-rate assumptions. Using data from 20 colleges and universities, Smith calculated an average annual retirement rate of 2.2% for tenured faculty. This is equivalent to an average annual retirement rate of 1.6% for all faculty, assuming that the retirement rate for non-tenured faculty is zero and using the ratio of tenured to non-tenured faculty in our universe (71%) as the weighting factor.

To provide a basis for comparison, we converted our retirement-rate assumptions to an equivalent annual rate—2.2%. It is reassuring to find that our rate is higher than the rate calculated from Smith's data. The average age at retirement at private universities is slightly higher than the average age at retirement at public universities, and the private universities are much more heavily represented in Smith's survey than in ours. Also, the assumption that no non-tenured faculty retire, which was used with Smith's data for tenured faculty, understates the true retirement rate.

Mortality Rates

Information on mortality of TIAA policyholders was supplied by Dr. Peggy Heim at TIAA-CREF. Though we believe that the mortality of TIAA policyholders will be similar to that of current faculty members, there are two important differences between the groups: (1) TIAA policyholders include professional, clerical, and service staff, whose mortality may differ from that of faculty members—about 40% of TIAA policyholders are faculty members; (2) current faculty members in the older age groups may well be healthier, and have lower mortality, than all TIAA policyholders of the same age, since policyholders with health problems are likely to retire earlier.

We obtained separate age-specific survival probabilities for males and females (i.e., a set of $_5p_x$), which we then combined into overall age-specific survival probabilities by weighting the age-specific male and female rates by the relative numbers of men and women within each age group in our universe of faculty members. The calculations are summarized in Table B.3

The age-specific survival probabilities were then used to construct a life table, from which five-year-period survival ratios ($_5\Pi_x$) were

TABLE B.3
Age-Specific Survival Probabilities with Respect to Mortality

(1)	(2) Probability of Surviving from Age x to x + 5	(3)	(4) Proportion of All Faculty	(5)	(6)
Age x	Male	Female	Male	Female	Combined Survival Probability[a]
30	.9959	.9976	70.7	29.3	0.996
35	.9948	.9969	72.7	27.3	0.995
40	.9915	.9956	78.7	21.3	0.992
45	.9850	.9932	83.8	16.2	0.986
50	.9761	.9889	86.3	13.7	0.978
55	.9662	.9828	85.1	14.9	0.969
60	.9516	.9729	85.0	15.0	0.955
65	.9230	.9561	87.0	13.0	0.927
70	.8750	.9293	87.9	12.1	0.882

Source: See text.

[a]This is the male and female combined probability of surviving from age x to age $x+5$ ($_5p_x$), calculated by taking the average of Columns (2) and (3), weighted respectively by Columns (4) and (5).

derived, in the manner already described above with regard to the estimation of the probability of surviving quitting.

The five-year-period survival probabilities with regard to mortality are given below:

Age Group	*Five-Year-Period Survival Probability with Regard to Mortality*
30–34	0.9955
35–39	0.9936
40–44	0.9890
45–49	0.9821
50–54	0.9735
55–59	0.9622
60–64	0.9413
65–69	0.9054

The Overall Exit Probabilities

The five-year-period survival probabilities (ratios) for quitting, retirement, and mortality were multiplied together to obtain overall survival probabilities—i.e., the probability that each five-year age group of faculty would survive all three hazards over a five-year period. These overall survival probabilities were then used to project the population of faculty over a series of five-year periods beginning with 1987–92 and ending with 2007–12. Table B.4 summarizes the age-group survival ratios *using the high-quit assumption for the quitting variable.*

TABLE B.4
Age-Specific Survival Ratios: High-Quit Assumptions

(1)	*(2)*	*(3)*	*(4)*	*(5)*
	Five-Year-Period Survival Ratio with Respect to:			
Age Group	*Quitting*	*Retiring*	*Dying*	*Combined Survival Ratio*
30–34	0.6687	1.0000	0.9955	0.6657
35–39	0.7705	1.0000	0.9936	0.7656
40–44	0.8539	1.0000	0.9890	0.8445
45–49	0.8881	0.9921	0.9821	0.8653
50–54	0.9032	0.9552	0.9735	0.8399
55–59	0.9053	0.8264	0.9622	0.7199
60–64	0.9050	0.4537	0.9413	0.3865
65–69	0.9052	0.0780	0.9054	0.0639
70+		0.0000		0.0000

Source: See text.

TABLE B.5
Age-Specific Survival Ratios: Standard-Quit Assumptions

(1)	(2)	(3)	(4)	(5)
	Five-Year-Period Survival Ratio with Respect to:			*Combined*
Age Group	*Quitting*	*Retiring*	*Dying*	*Survival Ratio*
30–34	**0.8344**	1.0000	0.9955	**0.8306**
35–39	**0.8853**	1.0000	0.9936	**0.8796**
40–44	**0.9270**	1.0000	0.9890	**0.9168**
45–49	**0.9441**	0.9921	0.9821	**0.9198**
50–54	**0.9516**	0.9552	0.9735	**0.8849**
55–59	**0.9527**	0.8264	0.9622	**0.7575**
60–64	**0.9525**	0.4537	0.9413	**0.4068**
65–69	**0.9525**	0.0780	0.9054	**0.0673**
70+		0.0000		**0.0000**

Source: See text.

If we now substitute the standard-quit assumptions for the high-quit assumptions, we replace Columns (2) and (5) in the above table with new columns (see discussion under "Quit Rates"); the other columns remain the same. The two new columns are shown in Table B.5 in bold type.

This format also facilitates the analysis of hypothetical changes in any of the other exit parameters. For instance, changes in the law governing retirement, or changes in pension plans, could affect the five-year survival ratios pertaining to retirement. New ratios can be substituted in these tables, and the results traced through the projections of vacancies and replacement demand. Similarly, it is possible to test out the effects of different five-year quit ratios. Work of this kind is reported in Chapter Eight.

APPENDIX C

Correcting for Shifts in the Carnegie Classification of Institutions

As INDICATED in Chapter Five, we wanted to compare student/faculty ratios by sector between 1977 and 1987. This proved to be exceedingly difficult. The 1987 ratios could be calculated in a straightforward way, using the enrollment and faculty data by sector for 1987 without adjustments. The 1977 faculty data, however, had to be adjusted significantly if any meaningful comparisons were to be made.

The need to adjust the 1977 data arises from the fact that the Carnegie Classification (which is used to assign academic institutions to one sector or another) is not static. Particular academic institutions are moved from one classification to another over time. For instance, between 1977 and 1987, 19 universities were "promoted" to Research I; of these, 16 came from the Research II category, 2 came from Doctorate I, and 1 came from Specialized (see Appendix A). If we were to ignore such reclassifications, attempts to make comparisons by sector between 1977 and 1987 would yield nonsensical results—as we learned painfully, by failing initially to understand the seriousness of this problem.

The enrollment data that we have used for 1977 and 1987 are not affected by these reclassifications, since we were able to impose the 1987 Carnegie Classification on enrollment data for both years. That is, if a university was classified as Research I in 1987, that university's enrollment was credited to Research I in both 1977 and 1987. Unfortunately, it turned out to be impossible to impose a similar procedure on the faculty data. (The National Research Council could not recode the faculty data for 1977 to associate each faculty member's institution in 1977 with its 1987 Carnegie Classification.)

Thus, the number of faculty shown to be in Research I universities in 1987 is sharply higher than the corresponding number in 1977 simply because of the increase in the number of universities classified as Research I between the two years. If we ignored this problem, the student-faculty ratio for Research I universities would have appeared to have plummeted between 1977 and 1987 because the student numerator is based on enrollments in a constant number of universities, whereas the faculty denominator would have been based on the number of faculty in an increasing number of universities. The effects of such reclassifications are even more complex in the case of other sectors, where we find both institutions added and institutions subtracted—i.e., where reclassifications moved institutions both into and out of the sector. For instance, the Comprehensive I sector gained 100 new institutions between 1977 and 1987 and simultaneously lost 60 of its former members.

It proved possible to identify each of the more than 400 institutional reclassifications that occurred, to map the movements of individual institutions into and out of various sectors, and to associate each of these movements with a corresponding shift of enrollments. Thus, we were able to calibrate, at least roughly, the sizes (as measured by enrollments) of the flows into and out of each sector.

We then assumed that an institution moving between sectors had a student/faculty ratio equal to the mean of the ratios of its "new" and "old" sectors. This process allowed us to adjust the faculty numbers in 1977 so that they would correspond at least roughly to the institutional size of the sector in 1987. That is, we sought to create adjusted faculty numbers by sector in 1977 that would match the faculty numbers in the same sectors in 1987 by, in effect, imposing the 1987 Carnegie Classification on the 1977 faculty data. It is these adjusted faculty numbers for 1977 that were then used to calculate the student/faculty ratios for 1977 shown on Figure 5.1.

Overall, this aggravatingly laborious process of adjustment produced results that look believable. We were helped by the fact that we could constrain the adjustments to fit within a known faculty total for 1977. Every increase in the number of faculty assigned to one sector had to be matched by an equal decrease in another sector.

We have described this problem and our approach to it in some detail not only because the reader deserves to know the extent to which the raw data were manipulated, but also because others should be aware of the pitfalls involved in making comparisons between the unadjusted 1977 and 1987 faculty data classified by sector.

APPENDIX D

Additional Tables for Chapters Four, Six, and Seven

TABLE D.1
Percentage Shares of FTE Enrollment, by Sector, 1976–86

Sector	*1976 (%)*	*1980 (%)*	*1982 (%)*	*1986 (%)*
Research I	15.8	15.3	14.9	15.7
Other Research/Doctorate[a]	17.2	17.0	16.5	16.9
Comprehensive I	24.2	24.1	24.0	24.9
Liberal Arts I	2.4	2.3	2.2	2.3
Other Four-Year[b]	6.6	6.6	6.3	6.6
Five-Sector Total	66.2	65.3	63.9	66.4
Two-Year	27.9	29.9	31.1	28.5
Other, Specialized, and Not Classified	5.9	4.8	5.0	5.1

Sources and Notes: Percentage shares were calculated from computer tapes based on the HEGIS Earned Degrees Conferred surveys. Detail will not add to total because of rounding.

[a]Other Research/Doctorate is the sum of Research II, Doctorate I, and Doctorate II. (See Appendix A for definitions of all sectors.) In 1986, the individual enrollment percentages for these three sectors were (respectively) 5.9%, 6.3%, and 4.7%. They changed very little between 1976 and 1986.

[b]Other Four-Year is the sum of Comprehensive II and Liberal Arts II. In 1986, the individual enrollment percentages for these two sectors were (respectively) 3.0% and 3.6%. They, too, were very stable between 1976 and 1986.

TABLE D.2
Projected FTE Enrollments in the Arts and Sciences, by Field of Study and Sector, Option A: Continuing Decline

	Projected Arts/Sci. Shares			*Projected FTE Enrollment (Thousands)*					
Sector and Field	*1987*	*1992*	*1997 and Thereafter*	*1987*	*1992*	*1997*	*2002*	*2007*	*2012*
Research I:									
Hum./Soc. Sci.	0.157	0.157	0.157	210.6	200.8	195.3	208.3	217.1	217.8
Math/Phys. Sci.	0.053	0.053	0.053	71.1	67.8	65.9	70.3	73.3	73.5
Biol. Sci./Psych.	0.085	0.079	0.077	114.0	101.6	96.1	102.5	106.9	107.2
All Arts/Sci.	0.296	0.290	0.287	397.0	370.2	357.3	381.2	397.3	398.5
Other Res./Doct.:									
Hum./Soc. Sci.	0.125	0.125	0.125	180.5	172.1	167.4	178.5	186.1	186.6
Math/Phys. Sci.	0.039	0.039	0.039	56.3	53.7	52.2	55.7	58.1	58.2
Biol. Sci./Psych.	0.072	0.067	0.065	104.0	92.7	87.6	93.5	97.4	97.7
All Arts/Sci.	0.235	0.231	0.229	339.3	318.5	307.2	327.8	341.6	342.6
Comprehensive I:									
Hum./Soc. Sci.	0.098	0.075	0.071	208.5	152.4	140.2	149.5	155.8	156.3
Math/Phys. Sci.	0.031	0.031	0.031	65.9	62.9	61.2	65.2	68.0	68.2
Biol. Sci./Psych.	0.066	0.062	0.060	140.4	125.2	118.4	126.3	131.6	132.0
All Arts/Sci.	0.196	0.168	0.162	416.9	340.4	319.7	341.1	355.4	356.5
Liberal Arts I:									
Hum./Soc. Sci.	0.410	0.410	0.410	80.6	76.7	74.7	79.7	83.1	83.3
Math/Phys. Sci.	0.083	0.083	0.083	16.3	15.5	15.1	16.1	16.8	16.9
Biol. Sci./Psych.	0.155	0.145	0.141	30.5	27.2	25.7	27.4	28.5	28.6
All Arts/Sci.	0.651	0.637	0.634	127.9	119.4	115.5	123.2	128.4	128.8
Other Four-Year:									
Hum./Soc. Sci.	0.114	0.087	0.083	64.3	47.0	43.2	46.1	48.1	48.2
Math/Phys. Sci.	0.033	0.033	0.033	18.6	17.7	17.3	18.4	19.2	19.2
Biol. Sci./Psych.	0.085	0.079	0.077	47.9	42.7	40.4	43.1	44.9	45.1
All Arts/Sci.	0.233	0.200	0.193	131.4	107.5	100.9	107.6	112.2	112.5
Total (Five Sectors):									
Hum./Soc. Sci.	0.131	0.120	0.118	743.1	649.0	620.8	662.2	690.1	692.2
Math/Phys. Sci.	0.040	0.040	0.040	226.9	216.3	210.4	224.5	233.9	234.7
Biol. Sci./Psych.	0.077	0.072	0.070	436.8	389.4	368.3	392.8	409.4	410.7
All Arts/Sci.	0.249	0.232	0.228	1412.5	1254.7	1199.5	1279.6	1333.5	1337.5

Sources and Notes: See text, pp. 57ff., for sources and general explanation of projections. See Table 4.5 for percentage shares. Detail may not add to total because of rounding.

In Option A, the declines in the projected enrollments in the humanities and social sciences between 1987–92 and 1992–97 are allocated to the Comprehensive I and Other Four-Year sectors. This was done by making the projections for all the other sectors first, using the 1987 shares, then making the projection for all five sectors using the shares given in Table 4.5, and finally calculating the figures for the Comprehensive I and Other Four-Year sectors as residuals. (The declines in biological sciences and psychology are proportionate by sector, using the 1987 enrollment figures as the factors of proportionality.)

TABLE D.3
Projected FTE Enrollments in the Arts and Sciences, by Field of Study and Sector, Option B: Steady State

Sector and Field	Projected Arts/Sci. Shares for All Years	Projected FTE Enrollment (Thousands)					
		1987	1992	1997	2002	2007	2012
Research I:							
Hum./Soc. Sci.	0.157	210.6	200.8	195.3	208.3	217.1	217.8
Math/Phys. Sci.	0.053	71.1	67.8	65.9	70.3	73.3	73.5
Biol. Sci./Psych.	0.085	114.0	108.7	105.7	112.8	117.5	117.9
All Arts/Sci.	0.296	397.0	378.5	368.2	392.8	409.3	410.6
Other Res./Doct.:							
Hum./Soc. Sci.	0.125	180.5	172.1	167.4	178.5	186.1	186.6
Math/Phys. Sci.	0.039	56.3	53.7	52.2	55.7	58.1	58.2
Biol. Sci./Psych.	0.072	104.0	99.1	96.4	102.8	107.2	107.5
All Arts/Sci.	0.235	339.3	323.5	314.7	335.7	349.8	350.9
Comprehensive I:							
Hum./Soc. Sci.	0.098	208.5	198.8	193.3	206.2	214.9	215.6
Math/Phys. Sci.	0.031	65.9	62.9	61.2	65.2	68.0	68.2
Biol. Sci./Psych.	0.066	140.4	133.9	130.2	138.9	144.8	145.2
All Arts/Sci.	0.196	416.9	397.5	386.7	412.5	429.9	431.2
Liberal Arts I:							
Hum./Soc. Sci.	0.410	80.6	76.8	74.7	79.7	83.1	83.3
Math/Phys. Sci.	0.083	16.3	15.5	15.1	16.1	16.8	16.9
Biol. Sci./Psych.	0.155	30.5	29.0	28.2	30.1	31.4	31.5
All Arts/Sci.	0.651	127.9	122.0	118.6	126.6	131.9	132.3
Other Four-Year:							
Hum./Soc. Sci.	0.114	64.3	61.3	59.6	63.6	66.3	66.5
Math/Phys. Sci.	0.033	18.6	17.7	17.3	18.4	19.2	19.2
Biol. Sci./Psych.	0.085	47.9	45.7	44.4	47.4	49.4	49.6
All Arts/Sci.	0.233	131.4	125.3	121.8	130.0	135.4	135.9
Total (Five Sectors):							
Hum./Soc. Sci.	0.131	743.1	708.5	689.2	735.2	766.2	768.5
Math/Phys. Sci.	0.040	226.9	216.3	210.4	224.5	233.9	234.7
Biol. Sci./Psych.	0.077	436.8	416.4	405.1	432.1	450.3	451.7
All Arts/Sci.	0.249	1412.5	1346.7	1310.0	1397.4	1456.3	1460.7

Sources and Notes: See text, pp. 57ff., for sources and general explanation of projections. See Table 4.5 for percentage shares. Detail may not add to total because of rounding.

In Option B, the percentage shares in 1987 (by field and sector) are assumed to remain constant for all future years.

TABLE D.4
Projected FTE Enrollments in the Arts and Sciences, by Field of Study and Sector, Option C: Recovery

	Projected Arts/Sci. Shares			*Projected FTE Enrollment (Thousands)*					
Sector and Field	*1987*	*1992*	*1997 and Thereafter*	*1987*	*1992*	*1997*	*2002*	*2007*	*2012*
Research I:									
Hum./Soc. Sci.	0.157	0.158	0.178	210.6	202.0	221.4	236.2	246.1	246.9
Math/Phys. Sci.	0.053	0.048	0.051	71.1	61.4	63.4	67.7	70.5	70.7
Biol. Sci./Psych.	0.085	0.090	0.107	114.0	115.1	133.1	142.0	148.0	148.4
All Arts/Sci.	0.296	0.296	0.336	397.0	378.5	418.0	445.9	464.6	466.1
Other Res./Doct.:									
Hum./Soc. Sci.	0.125	0.131	0.156	180.5	180.3	208.9	222.8	232.2	232.9
Math/Phys. Sci.	0.039	0.036	0.038	56.3	49.6	50.9	54.3	56.6	56.7
Biol. Sci./Psych.	0.072	0.078	0.093	104.0	107.4	124.5	132.8	138.4	138.9
All Arts/Sci.	0.235	0.246	0.287	339.3	338.6	384.3	409.9	427.2	428.5
Comprehensive I:									
Hum./Soc. Sci.	0.098	0.122	0.155	208.5	247.4	305.8	326.2	339.9	341.0
Math/Phys. Sci.	0.031	0.027	0.031	65.9	54.8	61.2	65.2	68.0	68.2
Biol. Sci./Psych.	0.066	0.074	0.086	140.4	150.1	169.7	181.0	188.6	189.2
All Arts/Sci.	0.196	0.223	0.272	416.9	452.3	536.6	572.4	596.5	598.4
Liberal Arts I:									
Hum./Soc. Sci.	0.410	0.412	0.411	80.6	77.2	74.9	79.9	83.3	83.5
Math/Phys. Sci.	0.083	0.081	0.082	16.3	15.2	14.9	15.9	16.6	16.7
Biol. Sci./Psych.	0.155	0.168	0.181	30.5	31.5	33.0	35.2	36.7	36.8
All Arts/Sci.	0.651	0.656	0.673	127.9	122.9	122.6	130.8	136.3	136.8
Other Four-Year:									
Hum./Soc. Sci.	0.114	0.147	0.192	64.3	79.0	100.4	107.1	111.6	112.0
Math/Phys. Sci.	0.033	0.032	0.034	18.6	17.2	17.8	19.0	19.8	19.8
Biol. Sci./Psych.	0.085	0.099	0.107	47.9	53.2	56.0	59.7	62.2	62.4
All Arts/Sci.	0.233	0.280	0.333	131.4	150.5	174.1	185.8	193.6	194.2
Total (Five Sectors):									
Hum./Soc. Sci.	0.131	0.146	0.174	743.1	789.6	915.4	976.5	1017.6	1020.8
Math/Phys. Sci.	0.040	0.037	0.040	226.9	200.1	210.4	224.5	233.9	234.7
Biol. Sci./Psych.	0.077	0.085	0.098	436.8	459.7	515.6	550.0	573.2	574.9
All Arts/Sci.	0.249	0.267	0.312	1412.5	1444.0	1641.4	1751.0	1824.7	1830.3

Sources and Notes: See text, pp. 57ff., for sources and general explanation of projection. See Table 4.5 for percentage shares. Detail may not add to total because of rounding.

In Option C, the increases in projected enrollments between 1987–92 and 1992–97 are distributed among sectors by using the shares of degrees in the arts and sciences that were observed in 1984 and 1980 as the shares applicable to 1992 and 1997, respectively. This has the effect of concentrating a disproportionate share of the recovery in arts-and-sciences enrollments in the Comprehensive I and Other Four-Year sectors, since these were the sectors that experienced the greatest declines in shares between 1980 and 1986. A consequence of following this procedure is that the enrollment share in mathematics and the physical sciences *declines* between 1987 and 1992 in spite of the fact that this is, in general, a "recovery" option. The explanation is that the share of enrollments in mathematics and the physical sciences dipped in 1980 and then recovered in 1984.

TABLE D.5
Academic Shares of Doctorates, by Field of Study, 1977–97

Field of Study	*1977 (%)*	*1987 (%)*	*Projected* 1992 (%)	*Projected* 1997 (%)
Humanities	81.6	74.1	72.1	71.1
Social Sciences	79.0	62.5	57.5	54.5
Mathematics	82.4	73.4	70.4	67.4
Physics	55.9	46.7	43.7	41.7
Chemistry	36.1	30.7	28.7	27.7
Earth Sciences	45.1	52.2	52.2	52.2
Biological Sciences	70.5	61.7	58.7	56.7
Psychology	46.1	33.9	30.9	30.9

Sources and Notes: SDR tabulations. These are holders of doctorates employed in academia expressed as a percentage of all holders of doctorates.

TABLE D.6
Projections of New Doctorates Seeking Academic Appointment, by Field of Study, Assuming Constant Academic Shares

Field of Study	Percentage in Five Sectors[a]	1987 to 1992 All Sectors (N)[b]	1987 to 1992 Five Sectors (N)[c]	1992 to 1997 and Thereafter All Sectors (N)	1992 to 1997 and Thereafter Five Sectors (N)
Humanities	91.58	9,465	8,668	9,465	8,668
Social Sciences	93.70	6,377	5,975	6,145	5,758
Hum./Soc. Sci.		15,842	14,643	15,610	14,426
Mathematics	94.14	1,827	1,720	1,875	1,765
Physics/Astronomy	89.52	2,400	2,149	2,460	2,202
Chemistry	86.46	2,807	2,427	2,885	2,494
Earth Sciences	95.26	1,525	1,453	1,570	1,496
Math/Phys. Sci.		8,559	7,749	8,790	7,957
Biological Sciences	65.01	10,387	6,753	10,250	6,664
Psychology	82.25	5,060	4,162	5,060	4,162
Biol. Sci./Psych.		15,447	10,915	15,310	10,826
All Arts/Sciences		39,848	33,307	39,710	33,209

Sources: Table 6.6 and SDR tabulations.

[a]Obtained by dividing the number of faculty in *all* institutions of higher education in 1987 within each field by the number of faculty in the same field in our five sectors. Excluded are faculty in Specialized, Other, and Two-Year institutions. An inspection of similar data for 1977 indicates that these five-sector percentages have been quite stable (differing, for instance, for all faculty in the arts and sciences by about one percentage point). Rather than try to read too much into such tiny fluctuations, we simply used the 1987 percentages whenever it was necessary to adjust faculty data for all institutions of higher education to obtain estimates that could be used for the five sectors.

[b]These projections were obtained by converting the annual estimates of new doctorates in Table 6.6 to five-year flows. This was done by summing the estimates for the two endpoints of each period (e.g., 1987 and 1992), dividing by two to obtain an estimate of the average annual output during the period, and then multiplying by five.

[c]Obtained by multiplying the projections for each field for all sectors by the percentages in the five sectors in 1987—that is, by the percentages in the first column of this table. The subtotals for clusters of fields and the total for all arts and sciences were obtained by adding the figures for relevant fields and clusters. The implicit "Percentage in Five Sectors" for all arts and sciences is approximately 84%.

TABLE D.7
Projections of New Doctorates Seeking Academic Appointment, by Field of Study, Assuming Declining Academic Shares

	1987 to 1992		1992 to 1997		1997 to 2002 and Thereafter	
Field of Study	*All Sectors*[a]	*Five Sectors*[b]	*All Sectors*	*Five Sectors*	*All Sectors*	*Five Sectors*
Humanities	9,345	8,558	9,165	8,393	9,105	8,339
Social Sciences	6,165	5,777	5,592	5,240	5,465	5,121
Hum./Soc. Sci.	15,510	14,335	14,757	13,633	14,570	13,460
Mathematics	1,798	1,693	1,785	1,680	1,755	1,652
Physics/Astronomy	2,342	2,097	2,307	2,065	2,270	2,032
Chemistry	2,730	2,360	2,690	2,326	2,650	2,291
Earth Sciences	1,525	1,453	1,570	1,496	1,570	1,496
Math/Phys. Sci.	8,395	7,603	8,352	7,567	8,245	7,471
Biological Sciences	10,162	6,607	9,652	6,275	9,505	6,179
Psychology	4,855	3,993	4,650	3,824	4,650	3,824
Biol. Sci./Psych.	15,017	10,600	14,302	10,099	14,155	10,003
All Arts/Sciences	38,922	32,538	37,411	31,299	36,970	30,934

Sources: Table 6.6 and SDR tabulations.

[a]Obtained by converting the annual estimates of new doctorates in Table 6.6 to five-year flows. This was done by summing the estimates for the two endpoints of each period (e.g., 1987 and 1992), dividing by two to obtain the estimate of the average annual output during the interval, and then multiplying by five.

[b]Obtained by multiplying the projections for each field for all sectors by the percentages in the five sectors in 1987—that is, by the percentages in the first column of Appendix Table D.6. The subtotals for clusters of fields and the total for all arts and sciences were obtained by adding the figures for relevant fields and clusters. The implicit "Percentage in Five Sectors" for all arts and sciences is approximately 84%.

TABLE D.8
Projections of Demand for Faculty, by Field of Study and Sector: Model I

Sector and Field	Net New Positions 1987 to 1992	1992 to 1997	1997 to 2002	2002 to 2007	2007 to 2012	Replacement Demand 1987 to 1992	1992 to 1997	1997 to 2002	2002 to 2007	2007 to 2012	Total Demand 1987 to 1992	1992 to 1997	1997 to 2002	2002 to 2007	2007 to 2012
Research I:															
Hum./Soc. Sci.	74	−49	1316	885	67	4118	3737	4043	4620	4730	4192	3688	5359	5505	4797
Math/Phys. Sci.	41	−26	754	508	39	2464	2253	2321	2587	2616	2505	2227	3075	3095	2655
Biol. Sci./Psych.	−682	−312	673	453	34	2265	2087	2138	2364	2516	1583	1775	2811	2817	2550
All Arts/Sci.	−567	−387	2743	1845	140	8847	8077	8502	9571	9862	8280	7690	11245	11416	10002
Other Res./Doct.:															
Hum./Soc. Sci.	70	−47	1183	796	60	3424	3476	3840	4360	4341	3494	3429	5023	5156	4401
Math/Phys. Sci.	33	−21	607	409	31	1724	1937	2020	2148	2142	1757	1916	2627	2557	2173
Biol. Sci./Psych.	−593	−271	585	394	30	1761	1763	1834	2086	2272	1168	1492	2419	2480	2302
All Arts/Sci.	−490	−339	2375	1598	121	6909	7176	7694	8594	8755	6419	6837	10069	10192	8876
Comprehensive I:															
Hum./Soc. Sci.	−4902	−927	1031	694	53	3952	3612	4091	4721	4542	−950	2685	5122	5415	4595
Math/Phys. Sci.	34	−22	630	424	32	1633	1860	2145	2417	2320	1667	1838	2775	2841	2352
Biol. Sci./Psych.	−576	−264	569	383	29	1633	1736	1901	2134	2267	1057	1472	2470	2517	2296
All Arts/Sci.	−5445	−1213	2230	1501	114	7218	7208	8137	9272	9129	1773	5995	10367	10773	9243
Liberal Arts I:															
Hum./Soc. Sci.	10	−3	374	252	19	950	1103	1164	1270	1343	960	1100	1538	1522	1362
Math/Phys. Sci.	8	−5	149	101	8	402	426	478	533	498	410	421	627	634	506
Biol. Sci./Psych.	−123	−56	122	82	6	283	306	370	469	497	160	250	492	551	503
All Arts/Sci.	−105	−65	645	434	33	1635	1835	2012	2272	2338	1530	1770	2657	2706	2371
Other Four-Year:															
Hum./Soc. Sci.	−1452	−275	305	206	16	1379	1263	1174	1242	1233	−73	988	1479	1448	1249
Math/Phys. Sci.	8	−5	152	102	8	398	452	529	580	590	406	447	681	682	598
Biol. Sci./Psych.	−142	−65	140	94	7	477	425	405	495	543	335	360	545	589	550
All Arts/Sci.	−1586	−345	597	402	31	2254	2140	2108	2317	2366	668	1795	2705	2719	2397
Total (5 Sectors):															
Hum./Soc. Sci.	−6200	−1301	4209	2833	215	13823	13191	14312	16213	16189	7623	11890	18521	19046	16404
Math/Phys. Sci.	123	−80	2292	1543	117	6621	6928	7493	8265	8166	6744	6848	9785	9808	8283
Biol. Sci./Psych.	−2116	−968	2088	1405	107	6419	6317	6648	7548	8095	4303	5349	8736	8953	8202
All Arts/Sci.	−8193	−2349	8590	5781	439	26863	26436	28453	32026	32450	18670	24087	37043	37807	32889

Sources and Notes: The derivation of these projections is explained in Chapter Seven. Model I is defined in detail in Chapter Five. In brief, Model I assumes continuing decline in arts-and-sciences shares of enrollment and decreasing student/faculty ratios. Detail may not add to total because of rounding.

TABLE D.9
Projections of Demand for Faculty, by Field of Study and Sector: Model II

Sector and Field	Net New Positions 1987 to 1992	1992 to 1997	1997 to 2002	2002 to 2007	2007 to 2012	Replacement Demand 1987 to 1992	1992 to 1997	1997 to 2002	2002 to 2007	2007 to 2012	Total Demand 1987 to 1992	1992 to 1997	1997 to 2002	2002 to 2007	2007 to 2012
Research I:															
Hum./Soc. Sci.	−917	−511	1219	820	62	4118	3601	3869	4441	4516	3201	3090	5088	5261	4578
Math/Phys. Sci.	−526	−293	699	470	36	2464	2176	2221	2484	2494	1938	1883	2920	2954	2530
Biol. Sci./Psych.	−516	−288	685	461	35	2265	2110	2160	2388	2545	1749	1822	2845	2849	2580
All Arts/Sci.	−1958	−1092	2603	1751	133	8847	7887	8250	9313	9555	6889	6795	10853	11064	9688
Other Res./Doct.:															
Hum./Soc. Sci.	−824	−460	1096	737	56	3424	3354	3683	4199	4149	2600	2894	4779	4936	4205
Math/Phys. Sci.	−423	−236	562	378	29	1724	1874	1939	2065	2044	1301	1638	2501	2443	2073
Biol. Sci./Psych.	−448	−250	596	401	30	1761	1782	1853	2106	2297	1313	1532	2449	2507	2327
All Arts/Sci.	−1696	−946	2254	1517	115	6909	7010	7475	8370	8490	5213	6064	9729	9887	8605
Comprehensive I:															
Hum./Soc. Sci.	−991	−553	1317	886	67	3952	4148	4582	5254	5197	2961	3595	5899	6140	5264
Math/Phys. Sci.	−439	−245	583	393	30	1633	1795	2062	2331	2218	1194	1550	2645	2724	2248
Biol. Sci./Psych.	−436	−243	580	390	30	1633	1755	1920	2154	2292	1197	1512	2500	2544	2322
All Arts/Sci.	−1866	−1041	2480	1669	126	7218	7698	8564	9739	9707	5352	6657	11044	11408	9833
Liberal Arts I:															
Hum./Soc. Sci.	−261	−145	346	233	18	950	1066	1114	1219	1283	689	921	1460	1452	1301
Math/Phys. Sci.	−104	−58	138	93	7	402	410	459	512	474	298	352	597	605	481
Biol. Sci./Psych.	−93	−52	124	83	6	283	311	373	474	503	190	259	497	557	509
All Arts/Sci.	−458	−255	608	410	31	1635	1787	1946	2205	2260	1177	1532	2554	2615	2291
Other Four-Year:															
Hum./Soc. Sci.	−294	−164	390	263	20	1379	1422	1319	1400	1427	1085	1258	1709	1663	1447
Math/Phys. Sci.	−106	−59	141	95	7	398	436	508	559	565	292	377	649	654	572
Biol. Sci./Psych.	−107	−60	143	96	7	477	430	410	500	549	370	370	553	596	556
All Arts/Sci.	−507	−283	673	454	34	2254	2288	2237	2459	2541	1747	2005	2910	2913	2575
Total (5 Sectors):															
Hum./Soc. Sci.	−3287	−1833	4368	2939	223	13823	13591	14567	16513	16572	10536	11758	18935	19452	16795
Math/Phys. Sci.	−1597	−891	2123	1429	108	6621	6691	7189	7951	7795	5024	5800	9312	9380	7903
Biol. Sci./Psych.	−1601	−893	2128	1432	109	6419	6388	6716	7622	8186	4818	5495	8844	9054	8295
All Arts/Sci.	−6485	−3617	8619	5800	440	26863	26671	28472	32086	32553	20378	23054	37091	37886	32993

Sources and Notes: The derivation of these projections is explained in Chapter Seven. Model II is defined in detail in Chapter Five. In brief, Model II assumes steady-state arts-and-sciences shares of enrollment and constant student/faculty ratios. Detail may not add to total because of rounding.

TABLE D.10
Projections of Demand for Faculty, by Field of Study and Sector: Model III

Sector and Field	Net New Positions					Replacement Demand					Total Demand				
	1987 to 1992	1992 to 1997	1997 to 2002	2002 to 2007	2007 to 2012	1987 to 1992	1992 to 1997	1997 to 2002	2002 to 2007	2007 to 2012	1987 to 1992	1992 to 1997	1997 to 2002	2002 to 2007	2007 to 2012
Research I:															
Hum./Soc. Sci.	71	−46	1316	885	67	4118	3736	4043	4620	4730	4189	3691	5359	5506	4797
Math/Phys. Sci.	41	−26	754	508	39	2464	2253	2321	2587	2616	2505	2227	3075	3095	2655
Biol. Sci./Psych.	40	−26	740	498	38	2265	2186	2258	2489	2665	2305	2160	2998	2987	2703
All Arts/Sci.	151	−98	2810	1891	143	8847	8175	8622	9696	10011	8998	8077	11432	11587	10154
Other Res./Doct.:															
Hum./Soc. Sci.	64	−41	1183	796	60	3424	3476	3840	4360	4340	3488	3435	5023	5156	4400
Math/Phys. Sci.	33	−21	607	409	31	1724	1937	2020	2148	2142	1757	1916	2627	2557	2173
Biol. Sci./Psych.	35	−22	643	433	33	1761	1849	1939	2194	2401	1796	1827	2582	2627	2434
All Arts/Sci.	131	−84	2434	1638	124	6909	7262	7799	8702	8883	7040	7178	10233	10340	9007
Comprehensive I:															
Hum./Soc. Sci.	76	−49	1422	957	73	3952	4295	4770	5448	5428	4028	4246	6192	6405	5501
Math/Phys. Sci.	34	−22	630	424	32	1633	1860	2145	2417	2320	1667	1838	2775	2841	2352
Biol. Sci./Psych.	34	−22	626	421	32	1633	1819	2003	2239	2393	1667	1797	2629	2660	2425
All Arts/Sci.	143	−93	2678	1802	137	7218	7974	8918	10104	10141	7361	7881	11596	11906	10278
Liberal Arts I:															
Hum./Soc. Sci.	20	−13	374	252	19	950	1105	1164	1270	1343	970	1092	1538	1522	1362
Math/Phys. Sci.	8	−5	149	101	8	402	426	478	533	498	410	421	627	634	506
Biol. Sci./Psych.	7	−5	134	90	7	283	324	391	492	524	290	319	525	582	531
All Arts/Sci.	35	−23	657	443	33	1635	1855	2033	2295	2365	1670	1832	2690	2738	2398
Other Four-Year:															
Hum./Soc. Sci.	23	−15	421	284	22	1379	1466	1375	1457	1495	1402	1451	1796	1741	1517
Math/Phys. Sci.	8	−5	152	102	8	398	452	529	580	590	406	447	681	682	598
Biol. Sci./Psych.	8	−5	154	104	8	477	446	430	521	574	485	441	584	625	582
All Arts/Sci.	39	−26	727	490	38	2254	2364	2334	2558	2659	2293	2338	3061	3048	2697
Total (5 Sectors):															
Hum./Soc. Sci.	254	−164	4716	3174	241	13823	14078	15192	17155	17336	14077	13914	19908	20329	17577
Math/Phys. Sci.	123	−80	2292	1543	117	6621	6928	7493	8265	8166	6744	6848	9785	9808	8283
Biol. Sci./Psych.	123	−80	2297	1546	117	6419	6624	7021	7935	8557	6542	6544	9318	9481	8674
All Arts/Sci.	501	−323	9305	6263	475	26863	27630	29706	33355	34059	27364	27307	39011	39618	34534

Sources and Notes: The derivation of these projections is explained in Chapter Seven. Model III is defined in Chapter Five. In brief, Model III assumes steady-state arts-and-sciences shares of enrollment and decreasing student/faculty ratios. Detail may not add to total because of rounding.

TABLE D.11
Projections of Demand for Faculty, by Field of Study and Sector: Model IV

	Net New Positions					*Replacement Demand*					*Total Demand*				
Sector and Field	*1987 to 1992*	*1992 to 1997*	*1997 to 2002*	*2002 to 2007*	*2007 to 2012*	*1987 to 1992*	*1992 to 1997*	*1997 to 2002*	*2002 to 2007*	*2007 to 2012*	*1987 to 1992*	*1992 to 1997*	*1997 to 2002*	*2002 to 2007*	*2007 to 2012*
Research I:															
Hum./Soc. Sci.	−797	825	803	864	66	4118	3617	4065	4548	4647	3321	4442	4868	5412	4713
Math/Phys. Sci.	−1541	−153	391	420	32	2464	2037	2126	2340	2325	923	1884	2517	2760	2357
Biol. Sci./Psych.	105	1133	501	539	41	2265	2195	2425	2594	2787	2370	3328	2926	3133	2828
All Arts/Sci.	−2232	1805	1695	1824	139	8847	7849	8616	9482	9759	6615	9654	10311	11306	9898
Other Res./Doct.:															
Hum./Soc. Sci.	−15	1825	795	855	65	3424	3465	4088	4508	4509	3409	5290	4883	5363	4574
Math/Phys. Sci.	−1089	−177	318	343	26	1724	1783	1872	1961	1924	635	1606	2190	2304	1950
Biol. Sci./Psych.	316	1040	447	481	37	1761	1887	2116	2319	2548	2077	2927	2563	2800	2585
All Arts/Sci.	−788	2688	1561	1679	127	6909	7135	8076	8788	8981	6121	9823	9637	10467	9108
Comprehensive I:															
Hum./Soc. Sci.	3976	4469	1211	1303	99	3952	4830	5828	6376	6524	7928	9299	7039	7679	6623
Math/Phys. Sci.	−1598	498	339	365	28	1633	1636	2033	2247	2109	35	2134	2372	2612	2137
Biol. Sci./Psych.	646	767	439	472	36	1633	1903	2180	2373	2557	2279	2670	2619	2845	2593
All Arts/Sci.	3024	5734	1989	2140	162	7218	8369	10041	10996	11190	10242	14103	12030	13136	11352
Liberal Arts I:															
Hum./Soc. Sci.	−235	−406	202	217	16	950	1070	1081	1173	1238	715	664	1283	1390	1254
Math/Phys. Sci.	−155	−129	79	85	6	402	403	443	490	451	247	274	522	575	457
Biol. Sci./Psych.	67	−4	84	91	7	283	333	398	492	527	350	329	482	583	534
All Arts/Sci.	−324	−539	366	393	29	1635	1806	1922	2155	2216	1311	1267	2288	2548	2245
Other Four-Year:															
Hum./Soc. Sci.	1446	1627	382	411	31	1379	1661	1760	1801	1899	2825	3288	2142	2212	1930
Math/Phys. Sci.	−171	−33	84	91	7	398	427	505	547	552	227	394	589	638	559
Biol. Sci./Psych.	254	3	104	112	9	477	480	459	544	605	731	483	563	656	614
All Arts/Sci.	1529	1597	571	614	46	2254	2568	2724	2892	3056	3783	4165	3295	3506	3102
Total (5 Sectors):															
Hum./Soc. Sci.	4375	8340	3393	3650	277	13823	14643	16822	18406	18817	18198	22983	20215	22056	19094
Math/Phys. Sci.	−4554	7	1212	1304	99	6621	6286	6979	7585	7361	2067	6293	8191	8889	7460
Biol. Sci./Psych.	1388	2939	1577	1696	129	6419	6798	7578	8322	9024	7807	9737	9155	10018	9153
All Arts/Sci.	1209	11286	6181	6650	505	26863	27727	31379	34313	35202	28072	39013	37560	40963	35707

Sources and Notes: The derivation of these projections is explained in Chapter Seven. Model IV is defined in detail in Chapter Five. In brief, Model IV assumes recovery of arts-and-sciences shares of enrollment and increasing student/faculty ratios. Detail may not add to total because of rounding.

TABLE D.12
Supply and Demand Projections, Humanities and Social Sciences: Comparison of Four Models

	1987–92	*1992–97*	*1997–2002*	*2002–07*	*2007–12*
Projected Supply[a]	14,335	13,633	13,460	13,460	13,460
Model I:					
Projected Demand	7,623	11,890	18,521	19,046	16,404
Supply – Demand	6,712	1,743	−5,061	−5,586	−2,944
Supply/Demand[b]	1.88	1.15	0.73	0.71	0.82
Model II:					
Projected Demand	10,536	11,758	18,935	19,452	16,795
Supply – Demand	3,799	1,875	−5,475	−5,992	−3,335
Supply/Demand	1.36	1.16	0.71	0.69	0.80
Model III:					
Projected Demand	14,077	13,914	19,908	20,329	17,577
Supply – Demand	258	−281	−6,448	−6,869	−4,117
Supply/Demand	1.02	0.98	0.68	0.66	0.77
Model IV:					
Projected Demand	18,198	22,983	20,215	22,056	19,094
Supply – Demand	−3,863	−9,350	−6,755	−8,596	−5,634
Supply/Demand	0.79	0.59	0.67	−0.61	0.70

Sources and Notes: All data are for five sectors only. The demand projections are taken from Appendix Tables D.8–D.11. The supply projections are from Table 7.1 and Appendix Table D.7.

[a]We use the same supply projections with every model. These are the supply projections that assume continuing decline in the shares of doctorates seeking academic employment.

[b]The supply projection divided by the demand projection is the number of candidates per position.

TABLE D.13
Supply and Demand Projections, Mathematics and Physical Sciences: Comparison of Four Models

	1987–92	1992–97	1997–2002	2002–07	2007–12
Projected Supply[a]	7,603	7,567	7,471	7,471	7,471
Model I:					
Projected Demand	6,744	6,848	9,785	9,808	8,283
Supply – Demand	859	719	–2,314	–2,337	–812
Supply/Demand[b]	1.13	1.10	0.76	0.76	0.90
Model II:					
Projected Demand	5,024	5,800	9,312	9,380	7,903
Supply – Demand	2,579	1,767	–1,841	–1,909	–432
Supply/Demand	1.51	1.30	0.80	0.80	0.95
Model III:					
Projected Demand	6,744	6,848	9,785	9,808	8,283
Supply – Demand	859	719	–2,314	–2,337	–812
Supply/Demand	1.13	1.10	0.76	0.76	0.90
Model IV:					
Projected Demand	2,067	6,293	8,191	8,889	7,460
Supply – Demand	5,536	1,274	–720	–1,418	11
Supply/Demand	3.68	1.20	0.91	0.84	1.00

Sources and Notes: All data are for five sectors only. The demand projections are taken from Appendix Tables D.8–D.11. The supply projections are from Table 7.1 and Appendix Table D.7.

[a]We use the same supply projection with every model. These are the supply projections that assume continuing decline in the shares of doctorates seeking academic employment.

[b]The supply projection divided by the demand projection is the number of candidates per position.

TABLE D.14
Supply and Demand Projections, Biological Sciences and Psychology: Comparison of Four Models

	1987–92	*1992–97*	*1997–2002*	*2002–07*	*2007–12*
Projected Supply[a]	10,600	10,099	10,003	10,003	10,003
Model I:					
Projected Demand	4,303	5,349	8,736	8,953	8,202
Supply – Demand	6,297	4,750	1,267	1,050	1,801
Supply/Demand[b]	2.46	1.89	1.15	1.12	1.22
Model II:					
Projected Demand	4,818	5,495	8,844	9,054	8,295
Supply – Demand	5,782	4,604	1,159	949	1,708
Supply/Demand	2.20	1.84	1.13	1.10	1.21
Model III:					
Projected Demand	6,542	6,544	9,318	9,481	8,674
Supply – Demand	4,058	3,555	685	522	1,329
Supply/Demand	1.62	1.54	1.07	1.06	1.15
Model IV:					
Projected Demand	7,807	9,737	9,155	10,018	9,153
Supply – Demand	2,793	362	848	–15	850
Supply/Demand	1.36	1.04	1.09	1.00	1.09

Sources and Notes: All data are for five sectors only. The demand projections are taken from Appendix Tables D.8–D.11. The supply projections are from Table 7.1 and Appendix Table D.7.

[a]We use the same supply projections with every model. These are the supply projections that assume continuing decline in the shares of new doctorates seeking academic employment.

[b]The supply projection divided by the demand projection is the number of candidates per position.

Publications Cited

American Association of University Professors. 1988. "The Annual Report on the Economic Status of the Profession, 1987–1988." *Academe* 74, no. 2 (March-April).

Astin, Alexander W., Kenneth C. Green, William S. Korn, Marilynn Schalit, and Ellyne R. Berz. 1988. *The American Freshman: National Norms for Fall 1988.* University of California, Los Angeles, ACE-UCLA Cooperative Institutional Research Program. Los Angeles: American Council on Education [ACE].

Barber, Elinor G., ed. 1985. *Foreign Student Flows: Their Significance for American Higher Education.* Institute of International Education, Research Report no. 7. Report on the Conference held at The Spring Hill Center, Wayzata, Minnesota, April 13–15, 1984.

Berlin, Isaiah. 1978. *Russian Thinkers.* New York: Viking.

Bowen, Howard R., and Jack H. Schuster. 1986. *American Professors: A National Resource Imperiled.* New York: Oxford University Press.

Bowen, William G. 1963. "University Salaries: Faculty Differentials." *Economica* (November): 341–59.

———. 1981. *Report of the President, April 1981: Graduate Education in the Arts and Sciences: Prospects for the Future.* Princeton University.

———. 1987. "The Student Aid/Tuition Nexus." In *Ever The Teacher,* pp. 538–43. Princeton: Princeton University Press.

Breneman, David W., and Ted I.K. Youn. 1988. *Academic Labor Markets and Careers.* New York: The Falmer Press.

Brown, Prudence. 1987. "Part-time Employment among Humanities Doctorates." Office of Scientific and Engineering Personnel. Washington, D.C.: National Research Council.

Bureau of the Census. 1988. *School Enrollment—Social and Economic Characteristics of Students: October 1986.* Current Population Reports, Series P-20, No. 429. Washington, D.C.: U.S. Government Printing Office.

Carnegie Foundation for the Advancement of Teaching. 1987. *A Classification of Institutions of Higher Education.* Princeton: A Carnegie Foundation Technical Report.

Cartter, Allan M. 1974. "The Academic Labor Market." In *Higher Education and the Labor Market,* ed. Margaret S. Gordon, pp. 281–307. New York: McGraw-Hill.

———. 1976. *Ph.D.'s and the Academic Labor Market.* The Carnegie Commission on Higher Education. New York: McGraw-Hill.

Consortium on Financing Higher Education [COFHE]. 1982. *Graduate Admission Trends in Selected Departments of COFHE Graduate Research Project Institutions, 1970–1980.* [March.] Cambridge, Mass.: COFHE.

———. 1985. *The Highest Achievers: Post-Baccalaureate Enrollment of Four Classes between 1956 and 1981.* [January.] Cambridge, Mass.: COFHE.

———. 1987. "Early Retirement Programs for Faculty: A Survey of Thirty-six Institutions, 1987." [November.] Cambridge, Mass.: COFHE.

Davis, Cary, Carl Haub, and JoAnne Willette. 1983. "U.S. Hispanics: Changing the Face of America." *Population Bulletin* 38, no. 3 (June).

Digest of Education Statistics. 1987. National Center for Education Statistics. Washington, D.C.: U.S. Government Printing Office.

Digest of Education Statistics. 1988. National Center for Education Statistics. Washington, D.C.: U.S. Government Printing Office.

Educating Scientists and Engineers: Grade School to Grad School. 1988. Office of Technology Assessment. Washington, D.C.: U.S. Government Printing Office.

"The Fiscal Year 1990 Budget: Summary and Background Information." 1989. U.S. Department of Education.

Freeman, Richard B. 1971. *The Market for College-Trained Manpower: A Study in the Economics of Career Choice.* Cambridge, Mass.: Harvard University Press.

———. 1975. "Supply and Salary Adjustments to the Changing Science Manpower Market: Physics, 1948–1973." *American Economic Review* 65, no. 1 (March): 27–39.

———. 1980. "The Job Market for College Faculty." In *The Demand for New Faculty in Science and Engineering,* ed. Michael S. McPherson, pp. 85–134. Washington, D.C.: National Academy of Sciences.

Freeman, Richard B., and David W. Breneman. 1974. *Forecasting the Ph.D. Labor Market: Pitfalls for Policy.* NBGE Technical Report no. 2. Washington, D.C.: National Board on Graduate Education [NBGE].

Gappa, Judith M. 1984. "Part-time Faculty: Higher Education at a Crossroads." ASHE-ERIC Higher Education Research Report no. 3. Washington, D.C.: Association for the Study of Higher Education [ASHE].

Gordon, Margaret S., ed. 1974. *Higher Education and the Labor Market.* New York: McGraw-Hill.

Halstead, D. Kent. 1974. *Statewide Planning in Higher Education.* Department of Health, Education, and Welfare. Washington, D.C.: U.S. Government Printing Office.

Hansen, W. Lee. 1986. "Changes in Faculty Salaries." In Bowen and Schuster, *American Professors: A National Resource Imperiled,* pp. 80–112. New York: Oxford University Press.

Harmon, Lindsey R. 1977. *Career Achievements of The National Defense Education Act (Title IV) Fellows of 1959–1973.* National Research Council. A Report to the United States Office of Education by the Commission on Human Resources.

Hauptman, Arthur M. 1986. *Students in Graduate and Professional Education: What We Know and Need to Know.* Washington, D.C.: Association of American Universities.

Herring, Carol P., and Allen R. Sanderson. 1981. Technical Appendix. In

William G. Bowen, *Report of the President, April 1981: Graduate Education in the Arts and Sciences: Prospects for the Future*. Princeton University.

Involvement in Learning: Realizing the Potential of American Higher Education. 1984. Final Report of the Study Group on the Conditions of Excellence in American Higher Education, U.S. Department of Education, October. Washington, D.C.: National Institute of Education.

Jones, Lyle, Gardner Lindzey, and Porter Coggeshall, eds. 1982. *An Assessment of Research-Doctorate Programs in the United States*. Washington, D.C.: National Academy Press.

Kaufman, Philip. 1986. "Growth in Higher Education Enrollment: 1978 to 1985." In NCES, *The Condition of Education*, pp. 175–85. Washington, D.C.: U.S. Government Printing Office.

Levine, George, Peter Brooks, Jonathan Culler, Marjorie Gerber, E. Ann Kaplan, and Catharine R. Stimpson. 1989. *Speaking for the Humanities*. ACLS Occasional Paper no. 7. New York: American Council of Learned Societies [ACLS].

Lozier, G. Gregory, and Michael Dooris. 1987. "Is Higher Education Confronting Faculty Shortages?" A paper presented at the Annual Meeting of the Association for the Study of Higher Education, Baltimore, November 21–24, 1987. Office of Planning and Analysis, Pennsylvania State University.

McPherson, Michael S., and Gordon C. Winston. 1988. "The Economics of Academic Tenure: A Relational Perspective." In Breneman and Youn, *Academic Labor Markets*, pp. 174–99. New York: The Falmer Press.

"Medical Education in the United States, 1987–88." 1988. *Journal of the American Medical Association* 260, no. 8 (August 26).

Mooney, Carolyn J. 1989. "Uncertainty Is Rampant as Colleges Begin to Brace for Faculty Shortage Expected to Begin in 1990's." *The Chronicle of Higher Education*, January 25, A-14ff.

National Center for Education Statistics [NCES]. 1982. *Projections of Education Statistics to 1990–91*. Vol. 1. Washington, D.C.: NCES.

———. 1986. *The Condition of Education*. Washington, D.C.: U.S. Government Printing Office.

———. 1988. *Projections of Education Statistics to 1997–98*. Washington, D.C.: U.S. Government Printing Office.

National Research Council [NRC]. 1978. *A Century of Doctorates: Data Analyses of Growth and Change*. Washington, D.C.: National Academy of Sciences.

———. 1981. *Employment of Minority Ph.D.s: Changes over Time*. Washington, D.C.: National Academy of Sciences.

———. 1983. *Departing the Ivy Halls: Changing Employment Situations for Recent Ph.D.s*. Washington, D.C.: National Academy Press.

———. 1985. *Humanists on the Move: Employment Patterns for Humanities Ph.D.s*. Washington, D.C.: National Academy Press.

———. 1988a. *The Effects on Quality of Adjustments in Engineering Labor Markets*. Washington, D.C.: National Academy Press.

———. 1988b. *Everybody Counts: A Report to the Nation on the Future of Mathematics Education.* Washington, D.C.: National Academy Press.

———. 1988c. *Foreign and Foreign-Born Engineers in the United States: Infusing Talent, Raising Issues.* Washington, D.C.: National Academy Press.

———. 1989. *Humanities Doctorates in the United States: 1987 Profile.* Washington, D.C.: National Academy Press.

———. Various dates. *Science, Engineering, and Humanities Doctorates in the United States.* Washington, D.C.: National Academy Press. [Based on the Survey of Doctorate Recipients (SDR).]

———. Various dates. *Doctorate Recipients from United States Universities.* Washington, D.C.: National Academy Press. [Based on the Survey of Earned Doctorates (SED).]

Niland, J. 1973. "Where Have All the Ph.D.'s Been Going?" Ithaca, N.Y.: Cornell University. [Cited in Freeman 1980.]

1986–1987 Fact Book on Higher Education. 1987. American Council on Education/Macmillan Series on Higher Education. New York: Macmillan.

Radner, Roy, and Charlotte V. Kuh. 1978. *Preserving a Lost Generation: Policies to Assure a Steady Flow of Young Scholars until the Year 2000. A Report and Recommendations.* Berkeley, Calif.: Carnegie Commission on Higher Education.

Radner, Roy, and Leonard Miller. 1975. *Demand and Supply in U.S. Higher Education.* New York: McGraw-Hill.

Rosse, James N. 1987. "How Serious Is the Coming Shortage of Faculty and When Will It Come?" Remarks prepared for the annual meeting of the Western College Association, April 11, 1987.

Science and Engineering Indicators—1987. 1987. National Science Board. Washington, D.C.: U.S. Government Printing Office.

Signs of Trouble and Erosion: A Report on Graduate Education in America. 1983. National Commission on Student Financial Assistance. [December. Report prepared by the Commission's Graduate Education Subcommittee.]

Snyder, Robert. 1981. "Federal Support of Graduate Education in the Natural Sciences: An Inquiry into the Social Impact of Public Policy." Ph.D. Dissertation, Syracuse University.

Sovern, Michael. 1989. "Higher Education: The Real Crisis." *The New York Times Magazine* (January 22): 24ff.

"Student Financing of Graduate and Professional Education: A Report of the 1987 National Postsecondary Student Aid Study." 1988. NCES, U.S. Department of Education.

Survey of Doctorate Recipients [SDR]. See National Research Council, various dates, *Science, Engineering, and Humanities Doctorates in the United States.*

Survey of Earned Doctorates [SED]. See National Research Council, various dates, *Doctorate Recipients from United States Universities.*

Three Thousand Futures: The Next Twenty Years for Higher Education. 1980. Final Report of the Carnegie Council on Policy Studies in Higher Education. San Francisco: Jossey Bass.

Tuckman, Howard P. and Karen L. Pickerill. 1988. "Part-time Faculty and

Part-time Academic Careers." In Breneman and Youn, *Academic Labor Markets*, pp. 98–113. New York: The Falmer Press.

Viner, Jacob. 1958. "A Modest Proposal for Some Stress on Scholarship in Graduate Training." In *The Long View and the Short; Studies in Economic Theory and Policy*, pp. 369–81. Glencoe, Ill.: Free Press.